To Joy

DIVISIONS

Phyllis Spencer

Copyright © 2012 Phyllis Spencer
All rights reserved.
ISBN-10: 1478308311
ISBN-13: 9781478308317

Library of Congress Control Number:
CreateSpace Independent Publishing Platform
North Charleston, South Carolina

To my dear family:
Jenny: for your inspiration
Greg: for your insight
Heather: for your encouragement
And to my Clyde: for your support.

DISCLAIMER

The use of the words "retarded" and "mongoloid" in this book is personally offensive to me. In fact, it just about killed me to write them. However, they are used in an effort to be accurate to the language of the era. No offense is intended in any way by the use of these words, and the terms "intellectually challenged" or "developmentally delayed" are the phrases of the present era and the ones I choose to use in my daily life.

The four-leaf clover image you see throughout this book is special to me for two reasons. First, because I have always had an uncanny ability to spot a four-leaf clover and collected them for the good luck they promise. Secondly, the four-leaf clover has something extra which makes it unique, in the same way that the extra twenty-first chromosome present in Down syndrome creates a special human being.

PROLOGUE – 1944
The Twins

Eleanor Cole was never sure if she remembered her twin or if she just wanted to so badly that she conjured up the images and called them memories. Her parents said that she would have been too young to remember her. Still, there seemed to be something, or the shadow of something, that she knew for herself. The pink sweaters, for one thing. She could picture them, the color of candy floss, hanging from pegs in their room, the same bedroom she'd had all her life. She remembered two beds, her own big-girl bed and her sister's crib. She was almost three years old.

She'd strain to recall more, but it was like trying to catch a voice in the distance. Her parents told her there was nothing more, but she had a feeling they were mistaken. She was sure if she tried harder, the details would come to her, and occasionally they did. But she couldn't tell whether to believe what she had seen with her own eyes or what her parents told her was true.

The girls wore identical sundresses, yet couldn't have been more different from one other. One bounced as if on a trampoline when her mother came into the bedroom. The other, the one the mother reached for, lay on her back and pulled her toes to her lips. The mother clasped her and swayed in tight, grief-filled movements. The girls' father came to the door and steadied himself against the frame.

"Car's ready," he said in a husky voice.

His wife shook her head. "Gib, I can't. I thought I could, but I can't."

He moved past her and whisked the bouncing child onto his shoulder, but she kicked and wiggled to get down. He knelt to her level. "Here's your sweater, Eleanor; let Daddy help you put it on."

The child snatched the pink garment from him. "Do it myself." Which she did and then brought an identical sweater to her mother. "Help 'lizabet." Her voice was gentler this time.

"Gib, Gibby, we don't have to do this. You know we don't." Joyce Cole pleaded with her young husband.

"It's been all set up," he answered. "You know what the doc said."

Of course she knew what he had said. She'd heard it the day the girls were born and every day in her mind for the past two and a half years.

"She'll be dead by the time she's five-ten at the outside," he'd told her bluntly. That was the way everything had been for Elizabeth. Blunt as a blow from a sledgehammer. Not for Eleanor, though.

Eleanor, in the backseat. Her lacy ankle socks fringing her Buster Browns. Shoes that were dusty and scuffed across the toes, the same, but different completely from her sister's. Elizabeth's were perfect. No wear on the bottom. She'd never stood in them for more than five seconds at a time, let alone walked. Eleanor was her sister's legs, running to bring her a toy or fetch a sweater like she did today. She was the real reason they were making this trip.

"Best advice I can give is to take her to a hospital and don't look back. Give your normal girl a chance. Go home and tell the neighbors the baby died. Shoulda done it by now, if you ask me."

That was Joyce's mistake. Asking. That was why she and Gib were driving past the golden barley fields of southwestern Ontario from Faderton north to Orillia. She looked at the plate-round face that smiled up at her from the crook of her elbow. The almond eyes that held both a knowing sparkle and a vacancy that could not be explained. With every concession road, Joyce's ability to speak diminished. Gib glanced at his wife as he drove. In Faderton, her face had been merely sad, and then it had progressed to strained and past desperate, and by the time they reached Lake Simcoe—panicked.

"Stop, Gib. Please, let's take the girls for a walk along the lake before we...before."

Gib sighed raggedly. "You're making this harder than it already is."

Joyce's response was to look at him with hollow eyes. From the backseat, Eleanor shouted, "The lake! Baving suit?"

Joyce left the car door open and walked with the drowsy twin in her arms. She made straight for the water, picking up speed in spite of the sand that sucked at her feet. Past a picnicking family, she strode through a carefully built sand castle, moving hypnotically toward the water. *Three minutes. It'll all be over in three minutes. Why wait five years, ten at the outside? It'll be now. I have to go too.* Elizabeth couldn't leave without her. It was as inconceivable

3

as reaching down her own throat to pull out her heart. *No, it'll be fine. Gib with Eleanor and her with Elizabeth.*

The water was touching the hem of her skirt now, and she slipped on a smooth rock, jerking Elizabeth awake. The cool Lake Simcoe water moved up past her knees, and she held the child closer, wanting to plunge her in all at once, so there'd be just the one shock to get over. By the time the water reached her thighs, she tried to run, working against the weight of her wet skirt and struggling to keep her footing. Only a few more feet and they'd be free. She could go back with Elizabeth to wherever she had come from, and they would be together forever in a few marvelously countable seconds.

Behind her came sloshing sounds, shouts, the family—mad, probably, about the sand castle. Maybe Gib. Didn't matter. The solution so close, she was surprised it had taken her this long to figure it out. The baby she held chest high, so they'd submerge at the same time. She fought the instinct to hold her own breath. Blessed relief as she dipped below the surface and forced a stream of bubbles out her nose. She would never need air again. She tipped forward in the water, curving over the baby to protect her on the journey.

Her foot snagged in something, and she tried to pull loose. She was pulled slightly backward toward the shore, and automatically snorted water into her lungs. Then her hair was yanked up and out of the water, and strong arms propelled her and the baby above the surface. She twisted and fought with sharp kicks, and she raked her nails along the arm that encircled her and Elizabeth. It broke her grip, and Elizabeth was pulled from her, sputtering but calm, always calm, as if she understood and accepted her mother's intentions.

Later, in the waiting room at the Huronia Regional Centre for the Mentally Retarded, the jowl-faced matron didn't comment on the mother's damp skirt or the lines of blood on the father's forearm. Joyce's single response during the admission was to raise her hand long enough to write a feeble signature in the space Gib pointed to on the page. She heard Gib ask the questions.

"When can we come and see her?"

"Absolutely no visits for at least six weeks. It's easier for the child if you see her infrequently. Better for you to be unbonded."

"Will she be with other children?"

"Mr. Cole, we try our best. This facility is designed for only a thousand people, and we have stretched that to the limit and beyond. We were not designed to accommodate children under the age of six, yet here we are, taking your daughter and many others like her. There is a waiting list of several hundred families who want their children to be cared for here. Do you want the space or not?"

"We just want to know, like, what can you do for her here that we can't do for her at home? Like you said, you have so many here—"

"We can give your other daughter a normal life. Out in the world, retarded children are taunted. And this child," she indicated little Eleanor with a prim smile, "will be forced to defend and care for her sister. Even her chances at marriage will be compromised if it's known this condition exists in your family."

Gib nodded grimly. "Yeah, that's pretty much what the doc said too."

"Better to get this over with now, before the children are old enough to remember each other," the matron assured them, getting another resigned nod from Gib and nothing at all from Joyce, who sat clutching Elizabeth as if she could graft her to her body.

Eleanor believed that she had another recollection of that day. As the three of them left the red brick building, Gib held Eleanor's hand. When the little girl reached up for her mother, to form a chain of three, Joyce moved beyond her daughter's reach and wrapped her arms around her own shivering body. Her mother wouldn't reach out to close the gap that was left between them. Every time Eleanor thought about it, her footing seemed to shift under her, as if the surface she was standing on were about to drop out from under her. Or maybe her parents were right, and she had just imagined it all.

CHAPTER ONE
Eleanor: November 1961

I felt my intestines go watery the moment I stepped inside the Kingston Penitentiary. I'd read about the metallic clang of the prison door and had braced for it. But the portal that shut behind me was a piece of timber, five inches thick. Like a piece from a puzzle dropped into place, the door closed with a settling sound, the softness of it more cruel than I'd expected.

Everything inside the KP, as everyone around here called the penitentiary, had had the color leached right out of it. That included the visitors, and there were a dozen of us—all women, except for one man. He wore a pastor's white collar and looked as sad as a basset hound.

The women all knew each other, and they huddled together, leaving the man off to one side. I stood on the other side of him.

I tipped my head back to notice architecture that in another place would have struck me as majestic, maybe even holy. The massive pillars and vaulted ceilings were made of rock carved from the Canadian limestone. But it didn't feel majestic—more like demeaning. I felt puny and overpowered in the face of so much rock, and then there were the procedures, petty and ritualized and meant to put us in our places and remind us that in here, the Canadian Corrections System was in charge.

I wished I hadn't worn my best shoes. Every step I took drew attention to their businesslike percussion against the stone floor. There was a routine to prison visitation, and I tried to follow it by watching the women in the line ahead. They placed their purses on a table, and the guards locked the bags away to prevent the sneaking in of contraband items. Every one of the women had smoke stained hands, and when I risked a glance at their faces, I could see that their teeth were an exact color match for their fingers. Then we came to another table, and everyone but me knew what to do. They peeled off their drab coats, revealing another washed-out layer of bargain clothes. I was dressed completely wrong for the occasion. I felt too young for this, even though I'd been twenty for almost a month now. Not just too young: a couple of the girls looked to be my age, but their worn expressions suggested they'd already learned more about the world than I'd ever want to know.

"I'd like to keep my coat," I told the guard.

"Coats stay here, miss." He was one of those stiff-spined types who saw my clothing request as a radical departure from the rules.

I was wearing one of my two best outfits. It was a suit, deep red—a color the Simpson's catalog called "cranberry." Whatever color you called it, I knew it would be too bright, and it wasn't going to make me popular with the wives and girlfriends who couldn't move on until every one of us cleared through inspection. The guard waited too, hands on his hips. His posture told me he'd get paid the same if I took all day to remove my coat. I gave up, put the coat on the table, and fished out a small parcel, wrapped and tied with a bright ribbon, from the pocket. I heard one of the women huff in exasperation.

Now what have I done wrong?

"You'll have to unwrap that." The guard's voice was as flat as the table that separated us.

"But...it's a gift."

"I see that. We have to inspect the contents before you can proceed."

I tried to edge the tape off to preserve the wrapping.

"Just rip it off, honey. Visiting hours will be pri-tin-ear over by the time we get in."

It was a woman with big arms who said it. She was wearing a sleeveless housedress, even though it was October. My insides had been starting to settle a bit, but now I was all rattled again, and I handed the gift, a book, to the guard, hoping no one could see my hands tremble.

I tried to sign the visitors' record quickly. First my own name, Eleanor Cole. In the column marked "Organization," only the preacher had scrawled a title. I wrote in "Pentecostal Assembly, Faderton, Ontario." Under "Inmate," I wrote a name I only knew through letters, and my heart hit a staccato rhythm when I looked at what I'd written. George Knowles. Finally I was going to meet him.

The regulars led the way through a series of doors and hallways. Behind them, the preacher and then me, the misfit. We couldn't go through one door until the one behind us was locked, so at every turn, we had to stop, wait, lock, unlock, and proceed. We did that four times, and when I figured we must be close to the visitor's area, we were met by a guard, peeved at the inconvenience we caused him. He gave my suit the once-over and then started in.

"There are ten of yous here who declared smokes." He held a paper grocery bag aloft, and I guessed it held packages of cigarettes. "Each visitor is allowed to bring two packs, but in here," he rattled the bag for emphasis "we have twenty-one packages of cigarettes. So do you mind telling me which one of yous don't know the difference between two and three?"

He snickered, but his joke didn't get a laugh. No answer either. He pulled at his jaw a little with his free hand and waited. The women kept their eyes on everything but the guard. Circles of sweat had formed under the big woman's arms. She was old enough to be the guard's mother, yet she turned her eyes toward the floor like a scolded puppy.

"Apparently you didn't understand," he tried again. "There are ten of yous who declared. You can each bring two, which means twenty packages, but somebody's trying to sneak in an extra one, and I want to know who that is."

No answer.

"Reverend, you bring these smokes?"

"I'm afraid not."

"You bring 'em, miss?" He looked right at me, and I could feel my face go red as my suit. He smirked as if he enjoyed this, and he took my red-faced silence as a sign of his success. He had the sneer of a bully. His words were solicitous, but his tone mocking. His question was leading, like the one asked just before the punch line of a joke. I could tell he'd been talking to people this way for a long time. It was a style common to thirteen-year-old boys.

"Why two?"

The way his head snapped back, you'd think I'd spit in his face. "What did you say?"

"I said, why two?" If I left it at that, I was bordering on smart alecky, so I softened my tone to show I was posing a legitimate question. "Why can't we bring in three or four?" The minister swiveled my way, and I backed off. "Or one?"

"It's policy." He snarled the answer at me, as if that should explain everything.

"So, miss, did you bring the extra package? Cause until I know who brought 'em, none of yous are going through that last door." He paused to let that sink in. The women shot frightened glances at one another. Every one of them looked like they had had a lifetime of experience dealing with jerks like this.

"The rules clearly state-"

"I brought them," I cut him off. There were a couple of muffled snorts from the regulars, and the guard made a sucking noise with his upper lip.

"I didn't know I was supposed to declare them. I just put them in with the rest."

"Is that a fact?" Prudent words, if he had to write them, in a report for instance. "What kind did you bring?" he challenged.

I was lying. Never once have I bought a package of cigarettes, but right now I wanted these women to win this skirmish. Someone was trying to bring in an extra pack—big deal. If I claimed it, whoever that was could get it from me once we were inside, and policy-man here might back off. But at this moment, I would have traded a week's pay just to see through that bag. I could picture my landlady's pouch of Daily Mail tobacco on the kitchen table. But the ones in the bag were probably tailor-mades. The guard's expression showed he thought I was an unworthy opponent, to be so easily ambushed. The preacher looked heavenward. I hoped he was praying for me.

"Lucky Strike."

It was the only name I could think of, and I regretted the answer instantly. Lucky Strikes were American, sweet smelling prizes that occasionally showed up on our side of the border.

He rooted around the sack. "Well, well…" He held up a white package with a red circle on it; the find didn't improve his humor. "Lucky guess is more like it."

When we walked through the final door, everyone else knew exactly where to go. I dawdled, waiting to see what the others did so I could follow. The guard emptied the bag on a table, and each visitor claimed the packages she'd brought. I took the Lucky Strikes and held them loosely in my left hand, waiting for whomever they belonged to. In seconds they were palmed away, and a skinny girl shouldered past. I thought I heard her say "Thanks," but I might have just been hoping for it. I went looking for George Knowles.

The first thing I noticed about the visitors' area was that it was a lot like summer school back in Stratford. The windows were too close to the ceiling to let in any more than a feeble light. Heavy wooden tables were pulled tight to a glass panel, with an identical table and chair on the other side. There was a neat circle, about four inches across and cut out of the glass, for people to talk through. The women I came in with hurried as if trying to get the best seat in the house. The ones at the ends were taken first. I was the last one to sit down, in a spot at the center of the row.

Men in denim jeans, the color of creamed coffee, filed in, found their visitors, and pulled up chairs. Each table was flanked by wooden partitions, so I couldn't actually see anyone else. But I could hear them, and I realized that being in the middle, my conversation would be the easiest of all to hear.

More men arrived. Each of them wore a cotton shirt of narrow blue and white stripes like the overalls worn by train conductors. I wondered if people kissed through that hole in the glass or at least intertwined their fingers, desperate for the comfort of human touch.

Suddenly he was in front of me. Boyish—that was the word that popped into my head. The shoulders on the conductor shirt drooped, and the seams caught him midway down his thin biceps. He was average in the height department, but he hadn't filled out yet. Not enough to wear a prison uniform, anyway. Not unusual, I guess, for a nineteen-year-old, but the boys in Faderton were generally more robust.

"George?" I asked.

He looked nervous and brushed the knuckle of his index finger across his lips and sat down.

"Yes. Yes, I'm George."

He reached his fingers toward the glass, as if in another setting we might shake hands.

"I'm Eleanor."

"Yes, I figured."

The tattoos on his forearms looked infected, as though his skin was too sensitive for the quality of ink and needles smuggled in to jail-house artists.

"It's nice to finally meet."

"Yes, yes it is." He nodded agreeably.

Neither of us knew what else to say.

"So," I felt like I was chirping, "they treating you all right in here?"

That was my father's phrase. The one he used when he made hospital visits. Lay ministry, it was called, and he never took to it. Lay misery, he called it. But he did it because the pastor said it was our Christian duty.

"Treatin' me all right…considering." He thought it over once more. "Yes, they are."

Always yes, not a "yeah" or a "yup" even once. Our conversation lurched along like my first driving lesson, neither of us able to coordinate the clutch, brake, and accelerator well enough to proceed smoothly. We kept trying, though.

"You're prettier than your picture," he said.

"Thank-you."

"I like girls with dark hair."

"Thanks, you look nice too."

He shrugged up one shoulder. "Surprised ya come to see me."

"I said I would."

"People say a lot o' things. Doesn't always mean it's gonna happen."

He flustered me. I wanted to reassure him that some people keep their word, but I didn't want to seem like a Goody Two-Shoes.

"I brought you this," holding up the book. "They made me take the wrapping off, though."

"A book." He sounded disappointed.

"It's about cats. You said you like cats."

"I said I like cats?" He sounded like he was trying to recall a hazily remembered conversation. He suddenly looked sheepish.

I felt like he was laughing at me or at least at a joke that he got and I didn't. I imagined him going back to his cell and telling his buddies, and them all having a big guffaw at my expense.

"Now I remember. Yes, I did." He clasped his hands together between his knees and rocked forward. "I said somethin' like that, yes."

"Anyway, I hope you like it."

"I like it fine."

I was pretty sure he was lying just to be polite. If I had met him anywhere else, at a dance, maybe—not that I'd have been allowed to go—I would have liked his looks. Probably talked with him for a bit. He kept his eyes down most of the time, but when he screwed up an instant of courage, he peered out from under long, thick eyelashes you don't usually see on a man.

He used his finger to trace the lines of graffiti etched into the tabletop. Eventually he spoke.

"I can't read it, though."

"They won't let you read a book about cats?" I was filled with righteous indignation. In my mind, I was already hotfooting it to the warden's office to demand an explanation.

Something between resentment and despair shot out from under the eyelashes.

"I didn't say they wouldn't let me read it. I said I can't read it."

"But, but...you answered my letters," I protested.

"Didn't. The chaplain reads the letters from the church girls. A buddy o' mine helped me write back. Blame him for writing about the pussycats."

Embarrassed, I turned away and looked down the hall toward the guard. He was talking with a tall man wearing a navy suit.

"What are you looking at?" George asked. He couldn't see around the dividers that flanked us at the visitors' table.

"Just some guy talking to the guard."

George sniffed and ran his tattooed arm along his nostrils. *That explained the infection.*

"I'm teaching my students to read. Maybe I could help you too."

"Students?"

"I teach grade two."

"Where?"

"Limestone Elementary."

"Here? North o' Princess, ya mean?" His attention sparked.

"That's the one." Suddenly not sure if I should have told him that.

"I didn't know you was livin' in Kingston."

I turned back to see the visitor, who didn't appear to belong either to the regulars or the do-gooders like the basset hound and me. He had blond hair and tugged at his white cuffs so the same precise half-inch protruded from each sleeve. He and the guard were looking my way, wearing puzzled expressions.

"Why'd you come to Kingston?" George asked from the other side of the glass. He reminded me of my grade two students.

"For my job—at the school."

"Long way to come for a job, if you ask me." He sulked as if let down that he wasn't my reason for coming to Kingston.

The navy suit was closer now. He was young, as men in navy suits go, probably around thirty. Handsome too. I half hoped he was coming to talk to George, so I could leave. He carried a briefcase. It was soft-sided and collapsed inward as if it was empty, yet he moved as though it weighed him down.

"Guess if you was teachin' me to read, I'd see you a whole lot." George interrupted my thoughts. He'd edged closer to the glass, and he held his hands together like he was praying. He'd moved them to within an inch or two of the open circle. He kept talking. "I'd like to see a whole lot of you."

I eased back in my chair and was saved from having to say anything by the pressure of a hand on my shoulder.

"Miss Cole? Excuse me for intruding. My name is William Buchanan."

The face of my rescuer looked sincerely regretful for interrupting my conversation with George. I glanced at George, whose scowl showed he wasn't exactly pleased. I'd already figured out that coming to see George Knowles was a bad idea, so it seemed that I was the only one of the three of us glad to get this visit over with.

I didn't have time to question who he was or what he wanted before William Buchanan finessed his way to the answers. The fair-haired man leaned deep into the visitor's booth so George could hear his voice as well as I could.

"I apologize for barging in like this. I'm the pro bono lawyer assigned to this case." His blue eyes darted back and forth, including George and me equally, each time he made contact.

I caught the effort and instantly liked the lawyer for that. The confined quarters made it necessary for us to be physically closer than we would normally be. He was freshly shaved, and the hair at the back of his head formed a line perfectly parallel to his collar. Stars from the sapphire stones in his cufflinks winked when he leaned down, his hands braced on the visitor's table. George's eyes narrowed, and he pulled his arms off the desk and folded them across his chest.

"What happened to the guy I had?"

"The court figured you needed someone with a little more experience this time."

George snorted. "What's the dif?"

The lawyer turned to me. "I've arranged for an interview room for the three of us. Once we're there, we can speak privately."

He touched the back of my chair and motioned with an open hand at a door he wanted to escort me toward. This visit was starting to get interesting again. It might make up for the disappointment I felt when George turned out to be a skinny kid with delicate skin.

At the same moment, a guard on George's side of the glass stepped up behind him. George stood up quickly; the angry scrape from his chair was loud enough to be heard on the visitors' side. My heart pounded as I entered the interview room. It was bare and windowless, and in the center was a round table with four chairs. The lawyer pulled out a chair for me.

"Thank-you, Mr. Buchanan."

"Call me William."

"Thanks."

He stayed on his feet, waiting for George and his uniformed escort. There was a picture of Queen Elizabeth on the wall, but nothing else that I could use as a starting point for some small talk.

"I really appreciate your indulgence here, Miss Cole."

"Eleanor," I corrected him.

There wasn't time for any further talk. George was at the door. He looked as skittish as a stray cat. I was surprised to see he wasn't handcuffed, and I tried not to show my relief when the guard planted himself squarely inside the door. Next to the navy suit, George didn't compare too well. I felt a pang of pity for him—a boy trying hard to be a man.

But George looked like he was feeling very much like a man at that moment. His gaze didn't leave my body, and he inhaled deeply when he stepped toward me. He watched me like a man trying to memorize every detail of a mirage before it vanished. This cranberry outfit was causing me more grief than I ever knew could come out of a Simpson's catalogue.

The lawyer extended his hand toward the prisoner, but George ignored the gesture. In a surly move, George jerked his chair closer to mine and sat down. I felt queasy, knowing that to a casual observer, George and I looked like a young couple about to consult with their lawyer. The legal tone of the questions put the scene into its accurate perspective.

DIVISIONS

"Eleanor, you're here on a compassionate visit, I understand."

"That's right."

"How often have you met with George?"

"This is my first visit."

"Yes, but me and her have been writing back and forth for a long time now," George volunteered eagerly.

Whatever else was lacking in his elocution, he had held on to some long-ago lesson about using "yes" when speaking. He looked at me, and I could tell he wanted me to back him up by saying something like, "Oh yes, a long time."

I said nothing. I was busy trying to remember what exactly I had written in those unsanctioned letters, penned by candlelight in my Faderton bedroom. Could I be in trouble? I shifted an inch or two away from him.

William pursued the point. "So your visit today is a result of your church correspondence, then. There's no personal relationship."

"What's it to you?" George's tone was belligerent, and I was embarrassed that he was trying to make me his ally.

"It's nothing to me. Except your situation has changed, and I may need someone to act as a witness to your character. Someone who's known you for some time."

"You mean in court?" my voice sounded tremulous even to me.

Before I got an answer, George spoke.

"Whaddya mean, my situation's changed?"

"George, there's no easy way to tell you this—" William started.

"It's about my ol' man, isn't it?"

"It is. George, he passed away this morning."

I gasped. "Oh, I'm so sorry." With my right hand I reached over to touch George's forearm, careful to avoid the infected part.

George shot William a smug look as if he had scored a point in an undeclared sparring match. My touch ranked a notch higher than the news of his father's death.

The lawyer opened a file folder.

"George, there may be details here you'd prefer to discuss privately. You can anticipate that this is going to change things significantly for you."

I liked the way he moved into delicate subjects smoothly and with no trace of self-consciousness. His hands, elegant and ringless, played with the edges of the folder as he waited for George's reply.

George squinched up his eyes as if he was confused. I helped him out. "He means, would you rather talk to him without me in the room?"

"No, it's okay. You can stay."

"You're sure?" William sounded doubtful.

"Yes. I might need her to understand all the fancy-ass lawyer talk."

William checked his watch, unfazed by George's rudeness.

"Not much fancy-ass about this. You're looking at a beefed up charge from simple assault to manslaughter or maybe murder—second degree." I snatched my hand back.

"I'm going to do my best for you, but any way you cut it, you're going to be looking at more prison time."

"How much more?"

"Best case," the lawyer shrugged, "less than two years, paroled in less than that."

"Worst case?"

"Closer to six."

"Six years!" George exploded. "No, I don't deserve that. Two, I can do. And worth every minute to get rid of that son of a bitch."

DIVISIONS

I was beyond lost in this conversation. Baffled by the prison lingo, I hadn't followed what was happening.

"Wait—I thought we were talking about your father dying."

"I'll explain later," William offered.

"She can hear it from me." George leaned into the table like a combatant. "It's me she come to see. I'm the one she's been writin', not you."

The guard's hand went to the baton at his waist, and he took a step toward us. William shook his head.

George pushed back from the table and started pacing. Each step wound him tighter.

"We are talking about my so-called father." George's mouth had gone tight and menacing. "That's why I'm here—because I beaned him with a two-by-four. The ol' bastard wanted my help to prop up a wall, but it wasn't working. So he starts puttin' me down, swearin' at me. 'The board's got more brains than you,' he says. 'Give it to me.' So I gave it to him all right, right upside the head." He knocked his own head a couple of times to demonstrate, his words coming so fast that he actually had flecks of foam at the corners of his mouth. "Nothin' worse than he done to me lots of times, 'cept the son of a bitch never woke up. Now this guy," he jerked his head toward the lawyer, "tells me he's dead."

A drop of George's saliva landed just below my right eye. I was afraid that if I reached up to wipe it away, the movement might spook him.

"Which just figures," he went on, "'cause if my old man could find one last way to fuck up my life, he'd do it."

The last pronouncement was uttered with so much fury that I mentally measured how many steps it would take to get from my chair to the door. Four. Then one more to get out. I just hoped the floor would hold up long enough for me to make my escape. It was already shifting under my shoes, and I couldn't tell if I could trust it. The kindhearted young man from the letters had evaporated, and instead, a repugnant individual raged in front of me. George's outburst appeared to move the lawyer and the guard about as much as the limestone slabs that surrounded us.

William slapped shut the file. "We'll have to see exactly what charges are laid, and once we know, proceed with a defense. I expect this can be handled in front of a judge."

"When'll they charge me?" George's anger seemed to be giving way to something else. *Resignation? No, something more than that.*

He stood with his back against the far wall, all the fight gone out of him. *Defeated—that's what he was, and he looked to be in familiar territory.*

"Probably later today or early tomorrow. I expect we'll hear from the police any time now," William responded. "O'Donnell was the arresting on this. He'll be the one to bring the new charges."

He nodded to the guard, who approached, ready to accompany George back to his cell.

"Eleanor, I think if you wait here with me, Chuck will escort the two of us out," William said.

"The two of you? Wasn't you she come to see." George was getting riled again and repeating himself.

If I hadn't been so terrified, I would have sprinted from that room. What kept me there was the knowledge that 399 other guys, all probably just as volatile and a lot stronger than George, were on the other side of that door. I was with the guard, Chuck, and my new savior, William, and I wasn't going to let them out of my sight. What had I been thinking, coming to a maximum security federal penitentiary? I'd never even heard a grown man say the F-word until just now.

DIVISIONS

"George-" I started.

"Don't bother. I can see how it is. Now that you got a choice between spending the afternoon with a murderer or leaving here with a bigwig lawyer, church girl's starting to backslide."

"George, this is not a competition." I sounded pathetic.

"Sure it is. I can see what end I'm coming out on too. Don't worry I'm used to that. 'Short end of the stick'—that's what my old man used to say. 'Boy, you always wind up on the short end of the stick,' he'd say. Well, I guess I showed him what I could do with that stick, didn't I?"

"C'mon, Knowles." The guard stepped in close, cutting off any further objection.

"George, I'll be in touch." William stood to indicate that the interview had concluded.

George's dark eyes cut to William and then drilled into me.

"I'll be in touch too. Eleven Main Street in Faderton, ain't it? That shouldn't be hard to find."

My lunch moved up my esophagus, and I felt both hot and cold at the same time. The impact was obvious to George and to the guard, who pulled George's arm into a straight-arm lock behind his back and pulled him roughly from the room. It didn't stop George from running his mouth.

"'Course, you just made things a lot easier." His feet barely touched the floor, but still the words spewed from him. "I know exactly where Limestone Elementary is—so do my buddies."

A foul taste rose in my mouth, and before I could do anything about it, my vomit covered the floor. William Buchanan was at my side, holding my hair away from my face. My eyes ran with tears, and I tried to quell another heave that was forming just below my ribcage.

"That's my parents' address," I choked out. "What's he going to do to them?"

William Buchanan pulled a square of white silk from his pocket and handed it to me. I pressed it to my mouth and limped out, leaning against him. My new suit wilted, my good shoes spattered, and me, terrified.

"Don't worry about Knowles." William spoke low and reassuringly. "He's a nineteen-year-old kid with the most asinine ideas. He gets into more trouble than he knows how to handle."

We didn't talk while we retraced the route back to the entrance and the threshold I'd crossed less than an hour earlier. I concentrated on keeping my stomach contents under control. I managed by forcing my mind to anything other than my nausea. I counted my steps, and when that stopped working, I conjugated French verbs. *Je suis, tu es, il est, elle est, nous sommes, vous êtes, ils sont, elles sont, je suis.* When the bile threatened to rise again, I changed tenses. We were delivered out of the penitentiary and on to the affluent streetscape of King Street West, just as I got to the *plus que parfait.*

When I finally stepped outside the prison walls with my navy suited knight, I expected to feel free. But I didn't. The flat-bottom clouds reminded me of the low ceilings of my basement bedroom. Thunder rumbled, and the clouds threatened to release a deluge at any moment.

William Buchanan handed my purse to me. I didn't remember stopping for it on the way out. He helped me into my coat, the first time anyone besides my dad had done that.

"I feel like such an idiot," I said.

"Don't." It was a command. "Your first time in a prison, I assume."

"You assume right. Thanks for getting me out of there."

"I've never been able to get used to it myself," he confessed. "That's why I want to unload these pro bono clients. That and the money."

I wasn't sure what to say, so I said nothing. The first drops of rain pelted the concrete at my feet, and my mind went to the bus ride and the four block walk between me and the room I rented from Mrs. McMullen. Mrs. M, as I called her, would be worried about me out in this weather. I just wanted to get going. The sick feeling passed, carried on the wind beyond the ramparts of the KP, and dispersed over Lake Ontario.

"I'm giving you a lift home," he announced.

I tried to protest. "No, you've done—"

"I'm insisting. You still haven't found your sea legs." He cupped my left elbow and steered me across the street and up a set of stairs toward a stalwart stone house that could've been the baby brother of the penitentiary.

"The warden's house," he answered before I asked. "I'm parked beside it."

He picked up our pace as the cold rain began to fall in earnest.

He herded me toward a dark Buick that looked like it had just come out of the showroom. He was too young for a car like that, but I was just happy to get into a vehicle. We ran the last few yards to the car, and I hoped that my post-retching breath wouldn't be too vile in the enclosed space.

The lawyer fussed with the settings on the defroster and the heater. Between sweeps of the wiper blades, the world outside disappeared. Lightning slashed the sky on the lake side of the prison and pulsed into the whitecaps on Lake Ontario. Cars on King Street pulled over, waiting for the downpour to ease. William

Buchanan seemed to be pondering more than the weather that had us entombed for the moment in this luxurious Buick.

"Where's Faderton?" he asked abruptly.

"Near Stratford."

He nodded.

"West of Toronto," I elaborated.

"I've been to Stratford. My parents took me to see Romeo and Juliet."

"I saw one of those plays in grade eleven. The one with Ophelia; we had to memorize her speech. 'The quality of mercy is not strained, It droppeth as a gentle rain from heaven…'"

"Merchant of Venice."

"Yeah, that's it," I said.

"So how did a nice girl from Faderton Pentecostal Assembly get into the Kingston Pen on her own? Usually the pen pals only get prisoners' first names."

His abrupt shift in direction caught me.

"I, uh—" The lightning sizzled over the lake, and thunder clapped hard behind it. "That was a close one," I said, trying to stall an answer.

He ignored the weather and the commentary. If I told him, I would reveal the most underhanded thing I had ever done, and I just knew that judgment resided directly behind those blue eyes. Which way it would go, I wasn't sure, but it was there as surely as thunder follows lightning. So I started to tell him, editing as I went, because it didn't occur to me to simply refuse to answer.

"I was part of a young adult Bible class, and we wrote letters to prisoners, you know, 'lend comfort to the afflicted' and all that stuff." He nodded as if this was familiar. "And like you said, we were given first names only. But," I hesitated, "I wanted to know more. So when the pastor was out of the room, I sneaked a look in his file. He had the full names and the address for the prison—so I just memorized it fast and put the paper back in the file."

"That's it?" he asked.

It sounded trivial, childish even. Nowhere close to the brazen undertaking I had thought it was.

"Not quite. I started writing to George on my own. And he, at least I thought it was him, wrote back to me—you know, privately."

"So was he like a boyfriend?"

I didn't think a Buick-driving lawyer, even a youngish one like this, would understand if I told him I lit candles and dabbed perfume on the paper when I wrote to George from my slope-walled bedroom in Faderton. I thought about the wicked tingle of pleasure that coursed through my body every time I read George's letters. I was pretty sure that was what the pastor meant by worldliness. Whatever George had been to me, it produced a feeling so delectable it just had to be some kind of a sin.

"No, he was just a friend."

"But you took a job here, and Kingston must be what, a couple hundred miles from home?"

"About that. But I just happened to get a job offer here—it had nothing to do with George."

"But you must have applied here to get the job."

His logic shone a harsh light on my—not plans, exactly—my longings.

"That's true—I did."

The rain was beginning to let up, and the thunder had retreated into low growls and distant rumbles. The lightning came in semi-transparent sheets instead of vicious stabs.

"So I guess seeing George for yourself and having him turn on you like that must be pretty upsetting."

I felt my bottom lip start to quiver, and my own tears spilled into a world already awash with more liquid than it could absorb. This stranger had summed up my own situation better than I could have done in a month of Sundays. In a way, it was a relief to have someone supply such accurate words—like a human *Roget's*—to describe my disillusionment. My shoulders slumped in defeat. He might have been just about to reach over to touch me, when there were five sharp raps at my window.

I gasped, and my heart rate vaulted for what felt like the hundredth time today.

A policeman signaled a circular motion to lower my window, which I did with my pulse still recovering. A stocky young officer leaned his forearm against the Buick's door and looked past me to the driver.

"William Buchanan?"

"Yes?"

"I'm Frank O'Donnell. I'll bet you and I are here to see the same inmate."

"George Knowles?"

"That's the one. Our boy Georgie seems to have landed feet first in this one."

The squared-off hand of the cop contrasted with the lawyer's when they gripped in a handshake, inches in front of my chest.

"I've seen your picture. Running for the Grits, I understand."

"That's right, but I'm wearing my lawyer's hat at the moment. Nice to meet you, Frank. And this is another of George's visitors—"

"Let me guess," Frank interrupted. "This must be Eleanor Cole. Who, I'm happy to see, doesn't look anything at all like I pictured."

"How in the world did you know my name?" I wasn't sure if I should be flattered or worried.

"You're the one and only visitor on Knowles's approved list," Frank replied.

"You've been doing your homework," William commented, without enthusiasm.

"That I have."

The policeman tipped his flat forage cap obligingly toward me, a mannerism I found quaint, especially since it was the first time it had ever happened to me.

"I'd like to get a statement from you, Miss Cole. It might be relevant to the case."

"Not likely," William intervened. "She just met him today."

"That's okay," said Frank, pulling out his notepad and holding it close to keep it from the rain. "I'll get your address and come by later this week for a statement."

I gave him the address and telephone number at Mrs. McMullen's. The cop snapped shut his book and winked. "I'm telling you, if it wasn't for this uniform, I'd never get a pretty girl's number."

His dark eyes twinkled, and I realized he was flirting. In different circumstances, I might have responded. I guessed him to be in his early twenties. He moved as if he was mildly surprised with how well he'd turned out now that he'd reached his full height and weight. But right now, male attention was the last thing I needed, and I didn't give him back so much as a smile.

"George was a little rough on Eleanor in there."

The cop frowned and leaned in solicitously. "What'd he do?"

"He threatened her. Intimated he might contact her parents—he knows their address. Personally, I think he's all talk no action."

Frank O'Donnell closed his jaws hard on some gum he rolled around in his mouth. "No action? What would you call killing his ol' man?"

The lawyer tugged at his cuffs again.

"Yes, well, his father has what you'd call a history. Whole family does, for that matter. You're a Kingston boy, so I'm sure you're aware of that."

"Long history," the officer said, as if he knew a lot more than the lawyer did about it. Then, looking at me, he said, "I'll talk to him about what he said."

I squeaked out a thank-you in a voice that sounded like my mother's. Insipid. When I had discovered that word in my *Roget's*, I had thought it was invented to describe my mother.

"Okay." He slapped the door, and the drops of water splashed up from the metal. "I'm off to see my old friend Georgie."

"Go easy on him," William counseled. "He's young."

"He's old enough to know if you're gonna go after a drunk with a two-by-four, you aim below the neck."

"Cops," the lawyer shook his head as he eased the car around the potholes. "They know just enough about the law to be able to break it without getting caught. Where to?" he asked, gliding the Buick along the shoreline east of the Penitentiary.

"Over to Queen, then up Montreal, past the coin laundry two blocks, and turn right."

I felt like William Buchanan was sizing me up. Not the way George had done, openly salivating, but as if I'd applied for a job and he was trying to figure out if I'd be a good candidate. Twice he started to say something, ask me something, I think, but he stopped himself. Maybe small talk didn't come easily to him. As for me, it was one of the few things I could do well.

DIVISIONS

"Have you seen our city hall?" He gestured toward a grand structure with a massive clock embedded in an imposing dome.

"A bit grand for a place like this, isn't it?"

"It's a sad bit of our history. Kingston was destined to be the capital of Canada, so when city hall was built, it was meant to be in keeping with the national prominence that would soon be ours."

"What happened?"

"The queen picked Ottawa as the capital, so we now have a beautiful but oversized city hall to heat and maintain. We got the penitentiary as a consolation prize."

"Some prize."

"In a way, it is. It provides a lot of jobs around here. But it also makes for divisions in the population. People who work for the government get decent pay, pensions, the whole deal. Then there's another class of people who move to Kingston to be close to someone who's been put away."

"Sounds like you know a lot about it."

"I should. I've lived here all my life. Went to Queen's. Decided to hang out my shingle here when I graduated."

"You missed the turn."

"I did? Oh, sorry. I thought it was a couple of streets up."

He turned left, back toward downtown.

"Hard time finding your way around? Let me guess; you don't get over to this side of town very often."

"Yeah, I'm on a bit of a short leash all right. Home, the office, the courthouse. Then there's church on Sundays. Pretty boring stuff, isn't it?"

He drove languidly, coming to a complete halt at every stop sign. At one corner, a young woman slowly pushing another in a wheelchair approached the intersection, and I touched his sleeve to keep him from pulling out in front of them.

"They want to cross," I said.

The stout girl pushing the chair kept her head down, single-mindedly in her determination to propel that chair across the street safely. It was difficult, to be sure, but both girls looked to be about my age—and so was George Knowles. I shivered to realize how very different people's lives could be, and how little I had seen of the world beyond Faderton.

"You see more and more people around like that these days," he commented.

"Not in Faderton, you don't. My place is up here on the right." I pointed to a frame house with a listing porch.

"So what's your family think of you being so far from home? And how do you like Kingston?"

I was grateful for the second question, so I could ignore the first. "I liked it fine up until today. Now I'd just like to paddle back to the sand bar."

"Feel like you're in over your head?"

I nodded.

He pulled the car off the curbless street, not even attempting Mrs. M's rutted driveway. The length of the car was longer than the width of her front yard.

"So why did you get yourself mixed up with George?" he asked. "Just impulsive by nature?"

"No, just looking to do a good deed, I guess."

He gave me a skeptical look. I wanted to ask him something, and decided I had nothing to lose, since he'd already seen me at my worst.

"Do you think George will be all right?"

William shrugged. "All right compared to what? He's had a rough life, and more prison time isn't going to shape him into a model citizen."

"I suppose not. But do you think he's dangerous? To other people, I mean."

"Like to you, maybe?"

I nodded.

"He knows you teach at Limestone, doesn't he?" He laid the sentence out like a snare.

I nodded.

"My campaign manager's wife teaches there too, by the way. Nancy Buckley. Do you know her?"

"Nancy! She's just about my only friend in Kingston so far."

"Your only friend? We'll have to do something about that." He cleared his throat and said, "But about George, he did kill his father, which means he's a guy who can't control his temper. Men without self-control? They're always dangerous to someone." He shook his head in disapproval.

I could actually feel the color draining from my face.

"Until now, he's done mostly misdemeanors. You're probably safe enough, but keep your eyes open, just the same. This last fracas of his was quite an escalation."

"Nice to know he has some ambition." I opened the car door. "Thanks again for helping me."

"My pleasure. If you ever need rescuing again, I'm a phone call away."

I smiled a thank-you. As he drove off on a street unaccustomed to Buicks, I wondered if he saw me as someone who might need rescuing on a regular basis.

CHAPTER TWO
Betsy

The wheelchair bumped into the bottom step leading to May Wilson's front door. The thump of the chair's pivoting front wheels on the aging steps signaled to May that the girls were back from their walk. May finished transferring oatmeal chocolate chip cookies from a hot tray onto a sheet of waxed paper before she responded.

"Hey there, girls, how was your walk?"

"Cookies ready?"

"Yes, Betsy, I just took them out of the oven."

Betsy pushed through the blistered door, leaving May to contend with the wheelchair and its occupant.

"Not so fast, Betsy. We have to get Annie inside."

"Cookie first."

"No. Annie first, then cookie."

Reluctantly, Betsy returned and helped May pull Annie to her feet. Wobbling, teetering, and with enormous concentration, Annie managed to scale the steps and flop into a couch that had been placed by the front door. The moment Annie's bottom touched the seat cushions Betsy made a beeline for the cookies.

"How many are you allowed to have, Betsy?" May called after her.

"Five." Betsy splayed her hand to indicate the number.

May laughed quietly, and Annie grinned, not because she comprehended the humor, but because she understood the mood of laughter.

"Two, Betsy. You're allowed to have two." May struggled to pull Annie's twisted limbs out of her coat sleeves.

"Two," Betsy muttered, placing one cookie on top of the other. "Two," she said again, duplicating the low-rise tower. She put the cookies on a plate, placed it on the table, and sat in the spot she'd been occupying at May's table for the past year and a half. Quickly, she pushed one of the cookies into her mouth and then another. When May came into the kitchen, she found Betsy with full cheeks, a trail of chocolate dribbling from the corner of her mouth, and on the plate in front of her were two cookies. Betsy shifted her irises to the right and to a spot about three feet wide of May.

May shook her head in mock exasperation.

"How do you like the cookies, Betsy?"

"Cookies," Betsy replied, her mouth full. She picked up the plate by its edges, solemnly displaying it for May. "Two."

May had caught on to Betsy's ways awhile back, and she called the girl over to the counter.

"How many cookies are here, Betsy?"

Pointing at them one at a time, Betsy counted. "One, two, three, four, five, six, seven, eight."

"Right. And there were twelve here a minute ago. So how many cookies are missing?"

DIVISIONS

Betsy, unaware that the results would incriminate her, trotted for a paper and pencil. Concentrating hard, she wrote "12" and then a heavy subtraction sign, with an "8" beside it. Carefully she drew a line under the number. She leaned in close to examine what she'd written, and then laboriously wrote the number "1" for the answer. May held her breath, waiting, and Betsy didn't disappoint, but added an intersecting right angle, to form the number "4," and held up the paper triumphantly for May to witness.

"You're right!" May praised her. "But that tells me you took four cookies, not two."

"Sorry, May."

"It's okay, Bets. I'll let you off because you did so good with your arithmetic. Do you remember when you first came here, you didn't know how to count?"

"I count now. And add and do takeaways."

"You sure do. You're learning every day."

"Not Annie. She not learning."

"Not yet, Betsy, but we're not giving up on her."

"Maybe I-I-I could teach her," Betsy offered.

"I think you'd make a darn good teacher. You're soon going to know more than me—then who's going to teach you?"

"Dunno," Betsy answered, back at the table again. "Find somebody, May."

"I'm trying, Bets, I'm trying."

CHAPTER THREE
At Mrs. M's

I had to warn Mrs. M that a police cruiser might show up for me one day this week. I waited a day, and then I mustered my courage and went up to the kitchen to tell her what had happened.

I found her sitting at the kitchen table, the seat of her chair completely smothered by her own bottom. The room was spotless, but as smoky as my father's workshop back when my father had a life and when everyone still thought my mother was just going through a stage. The usual package of Daily Mail tobacco and roll-your-own papers was on the gray Formica table. The big woman was working with a needle and embroidery floss, creating a trail of lace. The contrast of her thick fingers and the delicate strand they created fascinated me. There had never been any mention of a Mr. McMullen.

"Mrs. M?" I said timidly. "Can I talk to you?"

"Can't you always?" She smiled and motioned to the chrome chair across from her. The fat on her arms wobbled from the movement.

Once I started talking, I couldn't stop. I spilled the beans about reading the forbidden list and writing letters to George in prison. I told her about the visit and about George's threats. I finished by telling her I'd gotten a ride home from William Buchanan.

"Buchanan? You're rubbin' elbows with the high and mighty, are ya?"

"High and mighty? Because he's a lawyer, you mean?"

She wasn't a woman who moved quickly, couldn't, probably, but she stumped across the kitchen, extinguished her cigarette under the tap, and leaned against the counter.

"That and more. The Buchanan name has been around a long time. They're what you call 'people of means.'"

"Huh. And I was riding around in his fancy Buick. Not bad for a humble country girl." I brushed my fingernails across my chest as if to polish my manicure. "He asked me what my family thought about me being so far from home."

"Wondered that myself. What'd you tell him?" she asked, making her way back to the table to sit down.

"I kind of ducked the question. He's not as easy to talk to as you are."

She smiled at the roll-your-own she was rotating and settled into the overtaxed chair. I knew from her silence that she'd give me all the time in the world to explain. And knowing that, I poured out the whole story.

It was the last week of August when the job offer to teach at Limestone Elementary had arrived. I'd been waiting all summer for a letter like that, and I wanted to whoop with delight before I read to the bottom of the page. But I didn't, because in our house, nobody whooped. Ever. Until then, I had had no idea that one small piece of paper could carry so much weight. It was my passport out of Faderton, but even better, it was my ticket away from the first door on the left off the living room.

I wanted to slam out the screen door and go for one of my long walks. I used walking the way some people use cigarettes; they light up, but me, I light out. I'd been walking a lot that summer. Heck, if I'd kept going in a straight line, I probably could've walked to Kingston—saved myself the bus fare. But I knew I'd have to stop at that door first. With each step I moved toward it, a few more pounds settled on my shoulders. I knocked quietly and went into my mother's bedroom to tell her the news.

"Mom?" I spoke softly, although I knew she wasn't really asleep.

"Mmm…"

"Mom, I got a job. A teaching job."

"Oh…doing what?"

"Teaching, Mom. Grade two."

She rustled in the bedclothes and propped herself up on one elbow.

"That's great, honey. Is it at the central school or out in the country?"

"It's in Kingston. A place called…" I pretended I couldn't remember the name and held the letter up in the doorway, ostensibly to catch the light, "Limestone Elementary."

I thought that if I made it seem so offhand that I couldn't quite remember the name, then this wouldn't be such a major event. I might be able to slip away without anyone seeing me for the deserter I was.

The dim house, silent except for the ticking of the mantel clock, seemed to close in on me even more than usual. The smell of stove oil and old wood, bearable in the winter but choking in summer, compressed my lungs until I could hardly breathe.

"Kingston? I didn't know you applied to work in Kingston."

Her voice was actually sharp, accusing even. That was a surprise. Usually my mother spoke in a soft voice that petered out by the end of a sentence. She also sighed—a lot.

"What's wrong with Kingston?"

Mom paused, gathering her thoughts like dropped stitches of knitting. "What's wrong with Kingston is that it's not here. The course you took at Stratford was so girls from this area could work at the country schools."

"But I didn't get a job at a country school."

"Because you didn't apply to any. All the schools are looking for teachers. You have guaranteed work, right here."

"That's just the point, Mom. I don't want to be here."

"What do you mean by that?"

"Exactly what I said. I want out. Out of Faderton."

"Out of our family?" My mother's voice was trembling now.

"Out of this house."

"No."

"What do you mean, 'No?'"

"Your dad and I want you to stay here. You're our only one, Ellie. We want you with us until…until you make a home of your own."

"That's what I'm trying to do, and you don't want me to go."

She had no answer for that, so she slumped back on to the pillows. "We'll talk about this when Daddy comes home."

The exchange had worn her out, and in a few minutes, she was sound asleep in the center of a double bed she hadn't shared with my dad for as long as I could remember.

I'd always wished we had a name for the condition that kept my mother in bed during the day and prowling the house with insomnia at night. Whatever it was, it made her dreamy and sluggish, even when she was out of bed. "I'll be up and around in just a minute," she'd say. Then she would sigh and push her way out from under the blankets. Soon I'd find her at the stove, preparing—no matter what hour of the day it was—breakfast. Usually peameal bacon and soft-boiled eggs with toast. Occasionally it would be sausage links and a bowl of Cream of Wheat with a dollop of red jam in the middle that always reminded me of the Japanese flag. My mother was up, yes. But not really around.

Of course, I knew why she was like that. It was because of the baby. The baby they lost. My twin sister. *But my God, Mom, that was twenty years ago, well almost. You still had me. Didn't I count for something?* The daughter she had, me, wasn't enough to compensate for the one she'd lost. Eleanor and Elizabeth. We were supposed to match, like a pair of gloves. But I think we were more like a twin set. Two parts with the same color and texture, but one has long sleeves and buttons while the other one is simple and plain.

I stood in the doorway, my head tilted against the frame, and watched my mother's slight form rise and fall with her shallow breathing. On the wall above the bed, a black and white photo showed my parents on their wedding day. Joyce and Gib Cole, 1939. Her dark eyes sparkled back then, and they gave her a knowing look. *Where did that girl go, Mom?* My grandparents and aunts said I looked exactly like my mother when she was my age. When they said that, I actually felt sick, terrified I'd turn out like her.

"How did your mother tell you about your sister?" Linda Silver, who was the closest thing I had to a best friend, asked me when we were about twelve and eating Popsicles on our back steps. "I mean, what did she say, exactly?"

Linda didn't know she was treading close to forbidden territory in our world. Any mention of my sister caused my mother's eyes to flutter closed and that vein in my father's neck to start bulging. I wanted to protect them from anything that set them fluttering and bulging.

"I don't remember," I answered. "It's one of those things I've always known—it's just always been. Kind of like knowing you're a girl—you just grow up knowing."

"Were the two of you identical?"

"Yes," I answered promptly, although really, I had no idea. I knew almost nothing about my twin, except that she was named Elizabeth, she was born, and she died when we were almost three. I had been desperately curious about her, far more than Linda, even, but every time I asked about her, I got a heavy sigh from my mother or a gruff reminder from my father to stop asking.

Sometimes I imagined what it would be like if she was still here, my mirror image, walking and talking exactly like me. But I didn't do that very often any more. Elizabeth wasn't just off-limits as a topic; she was the family curse. She was the reason my mother was eternally sick. If it wasn't for Elizabeth, I wouldn't be stuck on double duty, trying to make up to my parents what they had lost.

"If she was still alive, do you think she'd wear the same clothes as you?" Linda asked.

"We don't talk about her," I answered primly and went back to devouring my Popsicle.

More than anything, I wanted to pull my mother out of the quicksand where she was mired. But I felt like a lifeguard who can't get too close to a drowning person, for fear of also being pulled down. A job in Kingston would give me just the distance I needed.

DIVISIONS

That night, the first things I packed were George's letters and my *Roget's Thesaurus*. I collected words. I liked the struggle of ferreting out just the right word for something—not something close, but the precise word for a situation. I wanted my *Roget's* close by. I remember snapping shut the clasps on my suitcase and hearing an urgent pounding on my bedroom door. Pounding and snapping were not familiar in our house, where most sounds were muted and muffled.

It was my father, in an unusual posture for him. His hands were on his hips, and his jaw was set in a way I had never seen. I'd been waiting a long time to see him like this. I just didn't want his newfound resolve to be directed at me.

"What's this I hear about you goin' to Kingston?"

"I got a job, Dad. I leave tomorrow morning."

"What's got you so het up about going to Kingston, of all places?"

"Dad, it's a job. I've been waiting all summer to get an answer."

"We sent you to Stratford so you could get a job near home."

"But I want to go somewhere else, somewhere, you know, bigger, more exciting."

"So why not try London, Toronto, even?"

"What have you and Mom got against Kingston?"

He ran a hand through his thin hair. "We just think it might be dangerous."

"Well, I'd rather face a little danger than die of boredom in this pathetic place!"

"You're not going. You can keep looking for another job."

"What?" His words jarred me. I had never seen my father this angry or so determined to make his point.

"You heard me. You are not going to Kingston!"

This was exactly the decisiveness and strength I had longed to see in my father. Moxy, I think it was called. But why, of all times, did he wait until now to finally take a stand on something?

I knew only one thing with bedrock certainty. I would not let this opportunity disappear. The absence my twin had left was not simply a void. It had become a repository for every sadness and disappointment that crossed the threshold of our house. Today's news would not be added to that sinkhole. I wouldn't let it.

"Dad, I've already made the arrangements. I'm going."

"If you do, buy yourself a one-way ticket, because you are not coming back to this house." His finger jabbed the air hard, pointing in my direction.

"Why, Dad? Because I want to see a little of life? Experience something more than you have?"

"You have no idea what I've experienced." His voice was low and menacing, and that vein punched out a quick rhythm.

"Then you should understand why I want to get out in the world. I want more. I want a better life than this!"

He took a step toward me and did something he hadn't done since I was seven. He grabbed my shoulders and shook me—not hard, but enough to get my attention.

"You want a better life?" he repeated. "You want to see what it's really like in the world you think is so wonderful? Fine—go. But when things get tough, don't plan on coming back to this—what did you call it?—this pathetic place."

"Dad, I just want something more."

"What do you have to complain about?" He was defiant now and unshakable. "What did you ever need that you didn't get? Did we ever miss your birthday or Christmas?"

That was when I remembered. I had seen him like this once before, one Christmas, when I was seven.

DIVISIONS

I remembered crawling carefully into the closet, trying to be quiet. I had to go right to the back, where only beams from my flashlight could penetrate. I had spied a promising set of lumps hidden under a blanket. In fact, I could have stomped in, singing "Jingle Bells," and no one would have known. My mother was deep in sleep, and dad spent long hours at the post office, sorting and stamping holiday packages and letters. But creeping preserved the pretense of having a home where parents wrapped and hid gifts in an elaborate effort to surprise and please their children. I had fancied myself to be daring and audacious because I ventured deep into the shadows of the closet, where the ceiling sloped so low that even as a seven-year-old, I couldn't stand upright. Crouched and moving ducklike on my feet, I inched within reach of the blanket that covered shapes of irresistible intrigue. And for the first time in a long while, I longed for my sister. This was the kind of prank that was pointless when done alone. A sister, especially a twin, would have been beside me, egging me on, checking the stairs to be sure no one was coming. We would giggle and shush each other, and together we could have pulled the blanket off the shapes and called dibs on the gifts.

When I pulled back the edge of the blanket, I discovered a set of new toys, waiting to be wrapped. There was a stuffed French poodle the color of blue candy floss; it came with a rhinestone studded leash. A spinning top, painted with a train design that held the promise of whistling like a locomotive when it reached its dizzying apex. But best of all, there was a soft doll with an oversized round head. She had dimples painted on her cheeks and long curling eyelashes. Her face was made of soft, touchable plastic that felt almost like real skin. I turned her over, and best of all, she had a zipper along her spine that opened into a secret pouch, meant for storing pajamas. She had a name tag,

"Cuddles." Although I left her in the closet, I took her into my heart and started counting the sleeps until Christmas day.

On Christmas morning, the three of us finished opening gifts and my mother shuffled back to bed. Dad noticed my eyes brimming with tears.

"What's wrong here?" he asked.

"I wanted Cuddles," I wailed.

"Cuddles? What's a Cuddles?"

"The doll in the closet. I saw her in the closet. You gave her away, didn't you?"

In my entire life, my parents only went away for two nights a year, one in September and another just before Christmas. This was when they did church work, delivering toys to what they called unfortunate children. Now I hiccupped and struggled between words, as I realized that they must have given my Cuddles to one of those children. I expected my father to feel sorry for me. I was so caught up in my own self-pity that I clamped shut my eyes to squeeze out a few more tears, just to punish him.

"I hate those stupid children!" I screamed.

I didn't understand that Gib Cole's emotions were subterranean compared to a child's temper tantrum. He waited, motionless except for that vein, for me to calm down, and when I did, his paucity of words sobered me.

"The children who got those toys are not stupid. You got gifts that develop your mind. Be grateful for that."

"But—"

"And don't ever say you hate somebody you don't even know."

With that, he walked out the back door and didn't return until late afternoon, when the three of us ate turkey and stuffing in silence.

I'd plunged so deeply into my memories that it took me a moment to realize that Mrs. M had stopped tatting and was waiting for me to finish the story.

"There were a lot of silent suppers in our house," I said at last.

"I imagine so." Her voice was as neutral as her comment. "And since you're here, I take it your dad wasn't able to convince you to stay closer to home?"

"I didn't give him another chance. I left the next morning before the sun came up, bumping my suitcase against my leg all the way downtown to the bus depot. I was hours early, but I had made my mind up to get on that bus. I intended to leave Faderton without a backward glance."

"And did you?"

"Glance back? Yes, I did. The last I saw of Faderton was Mom and Dad trying to see into the windows of the Greyhound bus as I passed our house."

"And you haven't heard from them since?"

"I've sent nine letters to them, one every week I've been here, but nothing back so far."

"Give it time, honey. They'll come 'round."

"I hope so. I'm doing everything they'd want me to do. I'm playing piano at the church. I've got a teaching job. I tried visiting a prisoner, which didn't go too well."

"About that—you're not the first young girl, and you won't be the last, to think she's going to rescue some poor misunderstood victim in the pen. Don't kid yourself—there's a reason they're in there." Her fingers were in constant motion. "Anyways, you're trying too hard."

"What's that supposed to mean?"

Her fingers never stopped. She drew the floss from the ball with her left, hooking it around her pudgy pinky, and guided it to the tiny latch hook in her right. Her hands followed a mysterious rhythm, producing lace, like a fat spider spinning a web.

"You're looking for something."

"I am?"

"Everybody is, in their own way. But you're looking for a way to show the world you're worth it."

"Worth what?"

"Worth it!" she shrugged. "Worth everything that parents do for children. Worth worrying over and providing for, educating, loving…you name it."

"I think I am worth all of that."

"So this tizzy of do-gooding. Who's it for?"

"Well, for the people I'm helping. Why else would I do it?"

She took a long draw on her cigarette, closing one eye against the smoke. "Let me ask you this. If you did all these good deeds and your folks never found out about any of it, would that be okay with you?"

"Yeah, I guess. But I'd like to tell them what I'm doing."

"So you write nine letters and get nothing in return. Anyone ever tell you, 'You can't push a string'? Means you can't make people feel the way you want them to, no matter how hard you try. We all have to find it for ourselves, by ourselves, and in our own time."

"Find what?"

"Whatever it is that's missing. And it's different for everybody."

"So how will I know when I've found it?"

She was tatting as rhythmically as a metronome now. "How do you know when you're done sleeping? You just know."

CHAPTER FOUR
Learning

Betsy sat cross-legged on the floor in her room, her face pressed close to the book in her hands.

"Whatchya reading, Bets?" May asked, trundling a laundry basket of clean clothes into the room.

"Riding Hood."

"Little Red Riding Hood? Good story. Here's some clothes to fold."

Betsy nodded, but didn't move from her position on the floor.

"Think you might read that book to Annie? She'd like that story."

"No."

"Why not?"

"What's this, May?" Betsy pointed to a picture on the page.

"That's the big bad wolf. See right there, it says wolf."

Betsy gave May a skeptical look. "Wo-luf," she enunciated slowly. "There's an 'l'."

May smiled in surprise. "There is, but you don't say it. It's silent."

Betsy put the book aside and reached for the clothes. "Reading too hard. I fold."

"You and I are the same that way, Bets. Meant more for doing things than reading about them."

Together they folded Betsy's garments, faded from too many trips through May's wringer washer. As Betsy opened drawers to put things away, she began singing, barely loud enough to be heard.

"A,B,C,D…"

"Where'd you learn that song?"

Not to be interrupted, Betsy answered by raising her voice. "E,F,G,H,I,J—what next?"

"K," May prompted.

"K." The next letters came out in a lyrical jumble, with Betsy nodding along unperturbed.

May supposed it didn't really matter where she'd learned it; the point was that she knew it, and she wanted to know more. May hadn't made it much past grade five before she was pulled out of school to help at home. She didn't know how to teach a regular child to read, much less Betsy.

Annie cried out in the next room, and May went to see to her, Betsy eagerly following along.

Annie, who had slipped down in her chair, was unable to pull herself up and was stranded precariously close to slipping to the floor. Betsy and May helped her up, and May looked around for something to occupy the girls.

"Want to look at pictures with Annie?"

Betsy pulled a well-worn photo album from under Annie's bed.

DIVISIONS

"Pictures? I show Annie."

There were only six of them. Half a dozen photos taken over nearly twenty years. Betsy poked a stubby finger at each one and translated for Annie, like she had done almost every day since coming to May's.

"See—that's Annie—you, me." Betsy took Annie's twisted hand in her own and helped her turn the page. "This one Betsy. Just me."

May knew the ritual by heart. They would look at the next four photos. May had no idea who had taken them, but Betsy provided the narrative. Betsy saw only the subjects of the photos, her and Annie, but it was the background that May saw. Paint peeling off the walls and beds jammed so close together that the headboards touched. While Betsy turned the pages slowly and showed Annie her image in the photo, May couldn't help but see the weary face of the attendant who tipped up Annie's chin, trying to get her to look into the camera.

May had only visited the place once, but that had been enough. What couldn't be shown in the photos was the overpowering smell of the place. Too few bathroom facilities for the twenty-seven hundred people who needed them left an indelible memory in May. Whenever she thought she wasn't doing enough for the girls, which was every day, she had merely to think of the hospital school they'd come from, and she knew she was giving them a life so much closer to what they deserved. But it was a street that ran two ways. May had had a brief, unhappy marriage that had produced no children. Annie and Betsy had become like girls of her own who would always remain children in their minds. She felt a deep contentment when she brushed Annie's hair or read a book to Betsy. It was as close to motherhood as she'd ever get, and for May, it was good enough. She watched as the girls finished flipping pages, and then she checked her watch.

"Time to change Annie now." She laid out a thick wad of material that was Annie's clean diaper.

"Diaper," Betsy pointed. "Starts with D."

CHAPTER FIVE
Frank

It was Thursday before a Kingston police cruiser pulled into the same spot the Buick had occupied in front of Mrs. M's. I thought I had covered the bases by telling her about the visit I was expecting from Frank O'Donnell, but when she pushed back the curtain to see the black-and-white out there, she became silent and reached for a box of Ganong chocolates she kept on the TV tray. I decided it might be better if I met the policemen out on the porch.

There was something about Frank O'Donnell that I wanted a word for. Back in Faderton, they would have said "built like a brick shithouse," but there had to be a better description. "Strapping" came to mind.

The October wind whipped at us, but he seemed not to notice it. When I was nervous, my kneecaps did a kind of vertical dance, and out there on that sloping porch with the peeling paint, my kneecaps were tracking north and south like matched pistons.

"You look cold." He smiled the same way he had over at the KP, flirting but staying close enough to friendly that I couldn't be sure which it was. "Why don't I get your statement in the cruiser. We'll be out of the wind."

Why don't we? Because if my knees keep up this action in the car, you'll see that I'm nervous and not just cold.

"I'm fine here," I lied.

"Well, I'm not," he replied. "Besides, Stan, that's my partner, will ask me a thousand questions about your statement, so I'd rather just do it where he can hear everything you say."

Stan turned out to be at that age when men go thin on top and thick in the middle. There was something familiar about him, but I couldn't place what it was. He had decided the seating arrangement—Frank at the wheel and me on the passenger's side, while Stan slid into the backseat and pulled out a notepad. This was Stan's car, and the two of us were temporarily allowed to use it. The air in it was dry and smoky. I would have given anything to crack open my window, but I was too nervous to reach out my hand. Everything scared me in this bare-knuckled world of metal and strange switches that activated heaven knew what. I wiped my palms on my skirt.

"First time in a cruiser?" Frank asked.

I nodded. "A lot of firsts for me lately."

"Oh yeah?" He had his own narrow notebook in his right hand and quickly wrote the date and street address on the heading. I noticed his neat, back slanted penmanship. Without intending to, I remembered George. *"I said I can't read it."*

I watched the man beside me move confidently through his paperwork, his sausage shaped fingers directing his pen across the page. I imagined what it must have been like, him arresting the undernourished George. Still, George had waited patiently and turned the odds against his father, his slight body fortified with nothing but rage.

"So tell me what you know about George." His voice was flat. I wasn't sure if this was conversation or if we'd moved into official statement-taking mode.

"There isn't that much to tell," I began, and really, there wasn't.

By the time I answered his questions, he knew my age, where I worked, and my parents' address and telephone number, but he knew very little more about George Knowles. "The letters he wrote. Do you have them here?"

"No." It was the second time I had lied to him in less than five minutes. I wasn't sure why I was doing it, but something protective seemed to have reared up inside me.

I was surprised at how easily lying came to me.

"Where are they?"

"The letters?"

"That's what we're talking about."

"Why? Do you need them?"

"You never know. It might help to show his state of mind. And whether or not he felt any remorse."

"Oh," I said. Still not willing to offer up the only part of my life that wasn't a completely open book. "There's nothing like that in them anyway."

Frank switched tacks. "I hear George made some threats toward you the other day at the prison."

"He did say some things," I hesitated. "But he wouldn't really be able to do anything. Not while he's in prison…would he?"

Our eyes met. My fear beamed like a beacon on a snowplow. But his expression stayed neutral, betraying nothing.

"Well now, Miss Eleanor Cole…" he emphasized my name, and the rumble of it drawn across his rough vocal chords was unexpectedly pleasing to me. "I don't know the answer to that. I do know George is no stranger to the inside of a cell, and neither are his friends. If you have any problems, give us a call."

With a tilt of his head, he included Stan in the invitation. The older cop nodded in a way that could have meant that he too invited my call or that Frank had hit a point being reviewed on an invisible checklist.

O'Donnell wrote his name and number on a card and handed it to me. His fingertips grazed mine in the process. At least, I thought they did. The touch was so feathery and surreptitious, I wasn't sure if I'd imagined it, because in every other way, the flirtatious cop seemed to be all business now.

Was it because his partner was seated close by, or had I misread his signals all along?

In the house, I swept past Mrs. M, who waited with an eyebrow raised, clearly expecting an explanation. I mumbled an excuse and hurried straight to my room. I thumbed quickly through my *Roget's*, wanting a word to capture my feelings. I looked under "C" for "confused."

Okay, here it was. I whispered it a couple of times into the mirror. I liked the way the syllables bobbled between tongue and lips, like the unpredictable bounce of a fumbled football. Apparently, I was discombobulated. I just wasn't sure why.

Limestone Elementary School

On Monday morning, the familiar site of Limestone Elementary School greeted me. The school was constructed of jaundice-colored brick, and it squatted in the center of a parched field. For a teacher, it was the kind of place you didn't go to so much as end up at. It was like getting the runt of the litter, then finding that it grows on you. That school had become my daily touchstone, the one place where I could cross the threshold and forget about my perpetually grieving parents, the threats from George Knowles, and the chronic struggle to both eat and pay the rent in the same week. Mrs. M had said, "Every picnic has its ant," and at Limestone, that insect was the principal, Edwin Wallace. He wasn't any better-looking than the school and was not nearly so sturdy. He was lanky, and his arms and legs looked as if they'd been stuck on to his body at odd angles. Most days, he wore a brown jacket over a brown vest, an ensemble that would've looked swell on his grandfather. But I guessed that Mr. Wallace—who hadn't invited the staff to call him anything else—to be only slightly older than myself.

One day, when only Nancy Buckley, the grade five teacher, and I were left at school, I asked her about it. The two of us were stapling colored leaves to the bulletin board.

"Uh, about Mr. Wallace, our principal…"

"Sadly, yes, our principal," Nancy's eyes were alive with mischief.

"Well, I'm surprised at how young he is." I was deliberately cautious. With my luck, she'd turn out to be his sister.

"Surprised? Why? I think he's been shaving for at least a year or two now," Nancy answered.

We laughed conspiratorially.

"So how old is he?" I asked, pursuing the point.

"I'm not exactly sure. But not more than twenty-five."

"So how did he get to be a principal already?"

"Well, he has all the qualifications."

I looked at her dubiously. "Really?"

"Well, let me see." Nancy held up two fingers to inventory our boss's credentials. "He's male, and he can fog up a mirror."

"Fog up a mirror?"

"Yeah, I think the school board has an official mirror they hold up for all the male teachers to breathe on, and if it fogs up when they exhale—well, you got yourself a principal!"

Laughter exploded out of me.

"Hey! You laugh at my jokes! I think we're going to get along just fine."

And we did. By the middle of November, we had our classes practicing together daily for the upcoming Christmas concert, the first in the school's low-watt history. I did my best with the school's out-of-tune Heintzman piano, playing Christmas carols for the primary classes while Nancy turned the sheet music on my cue. The concert was Mr. Wallace's idea, a surprising development, because he worked in perpetual distraction. Every day I saw him leave the school at morning recess and again at lunch and then hotfoot it out the door as soon as the kids were gone. He never offered a word of explanation about where he went or what he did in his personal life.

One gloomy afternoon, Mr. Wallace came to my classroom door with two little boys and their parents. Despite their different heights and age the boys' faces were identical to each other, and both were junior versions of their father. All three had black hair, carefully clipped and combed in the same style. The boys smelled like Ivory soap. Behind them, their mother nudged them to step into the class.

"Two more little Eye-ties," Mr. Wallace announced in his nasal, stringy voice. "One for you, one for Mrs. Buckley."

"You boys come on in." Nancy held out a hand to each of them. I shifted aside to let them pass. They both looked to their parents to see what to do, and the father, dressed in a dock worker's coveralls, motioned them to go inside. The taller boy led the way, but the little one made a dash back to his mother and wrapped his arms around her. Mr. Wallace huffed impatiently, as if he had somewhere else he had to be.

"So you're Italian?" I directed the question to the father, because the mother was still trying to peel the little one off her midsection.

"Scooza?" he said, surprised, I think, that I spoke directly to him.

"Italy. You're from Italy?"

"No Italy. Portugal."

"Azores," the mother added. "This Joseph," she pointed to her older boy, "and this Carlos." She licked her thumb and jabbed at an invisible spot beside the boy's mouth.

She shot one last instruction to the big brother in Portuguese, and whatever she said, it was enough to make him grab the little one by the hand and pull him into the class.

"Mr. & Mrs. Arruda have two older girls too." Mr. Wallace spoke slowly and clearly so they could follow the conversation. "One in grade six and one in grade seven."

The parents nodded proudly, but I didn't trust this solicitousness. Something more was coming my way. I didn't have to wait long.

Mr. Wallace muttered quickly, "The whole school will be full of these DPs pretty soon."

The thick features above the coveralls tightened just enough to signal that the other man had caught the tone, if not the precise meaning, of Mr. Wallace's words. His calloused hands clenched into fists, but Mr. Wallace nattered on, oblivious to the fact that one swat from Mr. Arruda could send him into tomorrow.

"Some fine fellows in Ottawa got the idea that it's up to the Dominion of Canada to provide an education to every immigrant off the boat with a passel of kids."

"Mr. Wallace." I could see the father's swarthy complexion going purple. "I'm happy to have little Carlos in my class." I turned to the parents, but I sure wasn't about to get between those ham-sized fists and Mr. Wallace. "I think your children will get along fine at Limestone Elementary."

The mother offered me a nervous smile, but the father, his work boots rooted to the floor, glowered in the direction of Mr. Wallace.

My principal sealed his fate with one final question. "I wonder if these little wops speak any English at all?"

The boots moved this time. One quick step, and the lapels of that overworn brown jacket were in the clutches of one of Canada's newest citizens. He lifted Mr. Wallace off the floor, the bulging forearms shaking with fury.

"My kids—they got the rights, Mr. Wallace." The mother pulled at the fabric stretched tight across her husband's broad back, but he didn't seem to feel it. Mr. Wallace's brown shoes pawed the air helplessly, one sock settled around his ankle.

"They got the rights," the big man repeated.

Mr. Wallace's thin fingers pulled at the hands clamped on his jacket, but he might as well have brushed feathers against iron. He pushed fruitlessly against the broad chest of Mr. Arruda and went to his only real defense.

"Miss Cole, call the authorities!" His voice was elevated an octave, but even in the clutches of a stevedore, Mr. Wallace wouldn't abandon his formalities.

I didn't move. Partly because he didn't look like he was in any real danger, dangling from Mr. Arruda's grasp. But mostly because he was getting what he deserved after that "wop" comment, and Mr. Arruda was the only one who could make him pay.

"The police!" Mr. Wallace quavered. "Call the police."

DIVISIONS

The word "police" struck a chord with the father. The powerful arms went down and deposited Mr. Wallace on his heels. Judging from Mr. Wallace's trembling chin, it would be a while before he took on another immigrant parent.

Without another word, the father turned and strode from the building, as if satisfied he'd made his point. His wife hurried to catch up, and then she paused and shot a glance at me. I saw a measure of resolve in that woman's eyes that brought tears to my own. I envied them their strength. I felt a childish jealousy of those little boys, because they had parents who would take on whatever battles turned up for their children.

Mr. Wallace completely misread my emotions. "Don't worry about me—I'm fine." He smoothed down his lapels and retucked his shirt. "I've been through plenty worse than that."

That seemed hard to believe. He was about as familiar with brawling as I was with prison.

"I didn't even understand what you meant," I said through my sniffles. "What did you say—DPs, or something?"

"Displaced persons," he huffed, batting at his clothes. "People who have nowhere else to go, so they end up here. Canada takes in the strays of the world. And believe me, a lot of them find their way to Kingston, Ontario."

He had a point. The same thing was happening around Faderton. Farms were bought up by the Dutch and Belgians and worked by their enormous families. But it was part of the reason schools were so desperate for teachers.

"I wouldn't have been able to get teacher's training if we didn't have so many foreigners coming to Canada."

"Don't I know it." His chin had settled down, and he was trying his best to regain his composure. "The province pushes you girls through a six-week program, then calls you teachers, just to give people like them," he jerked his thumb toward where the Arrudas had stood, "a free education. I don't object to that, but there are a hell of a lot of Canadians who could use some help from the government too, but they don't get any."

"Like who?" I asked.

"Like who?" He had taken off his jacket and was folding it, prissily matching the shoulder seams. He draped it carefully over his forearm like a butler with a linen cloth. "Lots of people." He wasn't about to elaborate on the point, but he did go on, talking to himself more than to me. "I never even wanted this job. I should've gone to the University of Guelph to be a veterinarian. I was accepted, you know."

He wanted me to hear that last point, as if he wanted me to know that in other circumstances, he could do better. He checked his watch nervously.

He started to move in the direction of his office and then suddenly whirled on me.

"You know I took a chance, hiring you," he fumed. "You fast-tracked grads were supposed to go to the rural schools, but the shortage of teachers is so severe...I had to hire someone, credentials or not. But it does mean you have to be supervised by a principal for two years before being granted your permanent certificate."

"Of course, I know that."

"Good. See that you remember it. I had to go to bat for you with the superintendent, just to hire you. I expect you to do the same for me when I need your support."

DIVISIONS

"What was I supposed to do? Did you think I might wrestle him to the ground?"

"See if you can restrain yourself when it comes to welcoming people like them."

And with that parting shot, he stalked off toward his office.

I watched him speechlessly, my face still flaming red, my hands clenched. I didn't know what had gotten into Mr. Wallace, but evidently, I had somehow just made an enemy.

CHAPTER SIX
Campaigning

May Wilson's back ached from bending over to bathe Annie. She knew the worst of it was yet to come, when she had to lift the dead weight of the girl's contorted body.

"Betsy, Annie's ready to get out now."

"'kay. I coming."

May waited, knowing there was a fifty/fifty chance she would have to summon Betsy again. More than that, because the girl was immersed in looking through her photo album. She held the book close to her and puzzled over pictures of places she'd lived and people she'd lived with. She spent long hours touching and looking at photos of her parents—people who visited at her birthday and Christmas and who invariably left in a welter of tears that annoyed May and confused Betsy.

"Now, Betsy."

"Cooooming."

"Boy, oh boy, I don't know what I'd do without you Betsy," May said. "I can't lift Annie by myself any more. If it weren't for you…"

Betsy beamed with the praise, and reached under her friend's arms to hoist the girl out of the tub and onto the thick pile of worn towels that May had spread for Annie to lay on.

"I know. I'm your right heart."

May smiled at the latest Betsyism. She grunted from the effort of moving Annie up and out of the bath. Together, they set her gently on the towels, and May covered her for modesty. When she caught her breath, she spoke to Betsy.

"You mean you're my right hand."

"Right hand," Betsy amended, delighted to make the connection.

"Come to think of it," May added, "you are my right heart too."

The doorbell rang, and before May could comment on the rotten timing of the caller, Betsy trotted out of the bathroom, head and shoulders lowered to a determined angle. Visitors were rare, and Betsy welcomed any change in routine bringing someone new into their world. A world that could remain intact as long as the strength lasted in the muscles of May's middle-aged body.

"May-ay." Betsy's voice traveled back to the bathroom. "Guy from paper here. Wants to see you."

"Guy from paper?" May muttered. She had no intention of rushing through the job of tending to Annie. "I'll be a couple of minutes," she called back. "You talk to him, Bets."

May continued toweling Annie dry, smiling and talking quietly, "She'll have the poor guy's life story out of him by the time I get to the door."

When that moment arrived, she saw a handsome man awkwardly trying to fend off Betsy's interrogation.

"Name's Buchanan," Betsy informed May, proud to be the one in the know.

"William Buchanan," he introduced himself and reached a tanned arm toward May to hand her a pamphlet. "I'm the local Liberal candidate trying to scare up some votes."

She thought he looked relieved to see her.

"Mr. Buchanan, we saw your picture in the newspaper this morning."

"Ohhh. The paper guy," he said, clueing into Betsy's earlier announcement.

May decided to leave him standing on the step holding the door.

"Yeah, Betsy and I saw you in the paper. What I haven't seen in the paper, and believe me I've been looking, was an announcement about help for the less fortunate." She glanced meaningfully toward Betsy, who had planted herself by the door, unwilling to miss the excitement of a visitor.

"Do you mean more spaces in the, uh, hospitals?" Buchanan offered.

"They're called institutions, and Betsy here spent most of her life in those places," May answered flatly. "She's been with me a year and a half, and the last thing she needs is to go back into one of those hideous places. Institutions treat them like they're sick. Does this girl look sick?"

"No, she looks healthy to me," Buchanan smiled.

Betsy was charmed; May wasn't.

"Right, and she'll stay that way as long as she has me. I care for two girls here, and I love them. But I'm the only thing that stands between them and one of human warehouses the government is so het up on building."

"So what do you suggest?" He took out his pen and notepad to record May's concerns.

"I suggest the government could save a whole lot of money by paying people like me a little more. They could cough up for families to hire some help. They need a break. There's a lot of families out there willing to look after their own, if they could get a hand now and again. It's cheaper than building an institution."

"So what do you do now when you need time off?"

"What's time off?" May responded bluntly. "I tell you, if it wasn't for the church putting on a get-together once or twice a week, I'd be a basket case."

"Are there many people doing what you're doing?" Buchanan appeared honestly puzzled. "I haven't heard anything about this problem."

"There's more of us than you'd think. I know one young man has to leave his job two or three times a day to go home and check on his brother. I tell you, the one doing the looking after is just about to drop."

"Well," the politician hesitated, "I admire what you're doing for people."

"Bully for you," May answered, "but admiration doesn't pay the bills. As long as I have Betsy here, I think I can look after Annie. But I don't mind telling you, things are tight. The skimpy allowance I get for the girls is my only income. I'm alone here."

May's mouth was set in a line as straight as a prairie horizon.

"You married?" Betsy piped up, asking the man. "May needs a husband."

It was enough to deflate May's anger, and she and the politician broke into laughter.

"No thanks, Betsy," May said. "I had one once—believe me. That's one thing I don't need."

"And I haven't been able to find a girl who'd put up with me," Buchanan answered with a shrug.

*****

It wasn't until he stepped away from the house that he realized how accurate that answer was. He pulled the notebook back out of his pocket. He wrote "Ray – arrange date with that teacher" and snapped the lid back on his fountain pen. He'd been intending to get to this matter for weeks, but now that it was on his list, it wouldn't slip his mind again.

The Date

"William Buchanan wants what?" I shrieked at Nancy over the phone.

"He wants the four of us to go out to dinner together tonight at the Cataraqui Golf and Country Club."

"So I'd be…"

"Yes, you'd be his date. What do you say?"

"I'd say he should have asked me himself."

"He's busy. He and Ray are out at a campaign meeting this morning. The election hasn't even been called yet, and William is so organized, he's got a whole campaign in place. Ray says he's never seen anything so well put together in his life."

"I don't know anything about politics. What would I talk to him about?"

"Don't worry. Ray and William talk enough about politics for all of us; your job is just to sit there and look pretty."

I snorted.

"So besides a smile, what should I wear?"

"How about that red outfit?"

"He's already seen me in that."

"Well, put on your next best thing, because this place is as swanky as it gets in Kingston."

"Oh great. I hope I don't throw up again."

My next best thing was a beige linen skirt that I topped off with a scarlet sweater. That's what I was wearing when the Buick pulled up in front at 7:30 p.m. I invited William in to meet Mrs. M. Inside the little house, he seemed to fill more space than his frame actually occupied. Mrs. McMullen struggled to her feet, patting at her hair and wiping her palms on a tissue.

Mrs. M's breathing was coming in short little huffs, and I wasn't sure which of us was more nervous about my date. She mothered us out the door. Just as it was swinging closed, I turned to gauge her reaction to my escort. She put her finger under her nose and tipped it up slightly, as if to put her nose in the air. Then with a broad wink, she closed the door and left me looking at paint blisters.

The Cataraqui Golf and Country was a right-angled brick and block structure with a valance of symmetrically matched boards. The whole place looked top heavy, like someone wearing a toque pulled too low on the brow. William nodded at a middle-aged couple leaving the club, and as he opened the door for me, said, "Oh, I forgot to mention. Nancy and Ray can't join us tonight. Nancy's not feeling well."

"Again?" I asked. "She missed a couple of days of school last week."

I had counted on Ray and Nancy to help move the conversation along. Then again, I kind of liked being on my own with William. I liked riding in a Buick to the country club to have dinner with a lawyer. I had just enough time to wonder what my parents would say if they could see me now. Thoughts of Faderton yielded to tables glowing with candlelight that winked and glinted off the crystal glasses. A man wearing the first tuxedo I'd ever seen in real life approached us with a wide smile.

"William, wonderful to see you," he gushed.

"Johnny!"

The two men shook hands, clasping one another at the elbow, and I felt like I had stepped into a movie.

"And your lady...?" Johnny asked.

"This beautiful woman is Eleanor Cole." William beamed in my direction. Johnny actually bowed slightly.

I don't remember walking; I must have let the high voltage carry me to the table. Heads turned in our direction, William gave a little wave to a group in the far corner, and an elderly woman at another table touched her husband's hand and they smiled at us. William was the youngest man in the room by at least a decade.

We sat down at the table set with two forks, a knife, and three spoons. I hoped I didn't make a fool of myself by using the wrong one. Talking was always my strong suit, so I decided to take a stab at conversation.

"Do you have any brothers or sisters?"

He cracked up laughing, and it took me a moment to realize that he probably hadn't been asked that since public school.

"Sorry," I blushed furiously, "that's what happens when you spend your days with seven-year-olds."

He grinned at me like I was a charming puppy. "The answer is no. I'm an only child. And you?"

"Same, except I had a twin. Unfortunately, she didn't make it past our third birthday."

"I'm sorry," he said and used the sympathy as a reason to touch my hand. I didn't pull away.

"Thanks," I said, "but I don't actually remember anything about her." I promptly started chatting about Limestone Elementary, a change in topic that caused William to withdraw his hand from mine. That hadn't been my intention. Nor did I deliberately intend to avoid talking about Elizabeth—it was a reflex, learned from my parents. Yet before the salad arrived, William brought the conversation back to my twin and his fingertips to mine.

"It must have been a blow to your parents, losing a child."

"My mother never got over it."

"What do you mean?"

"My mother has been sad all her life, or maybe just all of my life. Distracted, I guess you could say."

He moved his hand back to his side of the table.

"Has she ever been hospitalized for it?"

"For being sad? Heavens, no. In a way, I wish she did have something that could be fixed by going to a hospital. I'd love to be able to help her. I just don't know how."

Over dinner, I told him more about Faderton, the Normal School in Stratford, and what it meant to get through teacher's training and with it, to get passage out of my boxed-in life.

"So you didn't go to an actual teacher's college." There was that snare again, a question made to sound like a statement.

"Just the six-week program at the normal school. The province has been trying to churn out teachers as fast as they can."

"Why's that?"

"There are so many kids now. They call it the baby boom, you know, once all the servicemen came back from the war. That, and all the immigrants have eight or ten kids."

DIVISIONS

I thought about the Arrudas and knew they would never see the inside of a club like this. Of course, I wouldn't have either, if it hadn't been for my date.

It was posh beyond anything I'd ever seen, and I wondered what it would be like to have a life like this. Going to the country club for dinner, not once in a lifetime, but every Saturday night? Every table held an arrangement of flowers, and not just carnations, but roses, different colors at every table. The lighting was soft, and the atmosphere was hushed as if we were all too important to have our conversations interrupted by lowly waiters. How did I get into a place like this? My own efforts had yielded up a rented room and two outfits decent enough to get in the door here. No, William Buchanan was my ticket into this elegant world.

"So when did you become a politician?" I asked trying to get the conversation flowing as easily as the wine.

"I'm not there yet. I have my cap set for the spring election."

"I didn't even know there was an election coming up," I confessed.

"No one does. But rumor has it, Diefenbaker will go to the polls by June, and I want to be ready. In the meantime, I practice law. Have done for seven years now."

"So when you said you're trying to get away from legal aid clients, was it so you could become a member of Parliament?"

He looked impressed. "Great scot, you have a first-rate memory. That's a real asset in politics, by the way. No, I want to run because think I can help people more if I'm involved higher up the ladder. I'd like to be up there where the laws are drafted, not just at the point when they're applied. I want to make a difference, and I think I can if I'm in Ottawa."

"What kind of laws do you think would have helped a fellow like George?" I asked.

"Good question," he said, and I glowed in response. I liked that a man like him would think I was clever.

"George's whole family could have used help early on, before the children grew up and got into trouble."

"Are you talking about the baby bonus?"

"Something like that, sure. When mothers get a little extra money, research shows they spend it on practical things like milk, coats, boots for their kids. That money goes right back into the economy—everybody wins."

"Sounds like more Liberal bafflegab to me." A man with gold-rimmed glasses and wavy hair was now beside us, his wife, vigilant, hanging back a couple of feet.

"Is that your professional diagnosis, Dr. Williams?" William offered his hand, but the doctor ignored it.

"In my professional opinion..." The way he slurred his way through "professional" made me think the Cataraqui Club wine had influenced that opinion. "You goddam socialists are going to ruin this country. Tommy Douglas nearly ran off all the doctors in Saskatchewan, and Lester Pearson will do the same damn thing if he brings this medicare foolishness to Ottawa."

"But, Dr. Williams, people are losing their homes and farms, trying to pay their medical bills. You must have seen that with your own patients."

"If my patients can't pay their bills, we work it out."

The doctor was getting agitated, and his wife focused her eyes on something in the distance, as though waiting for a familiar rant to run its course.

William rose to his feet. He was half a head taller than the doctor. "Don't you think we need a system where every citizen, regardless of ability to pay, gets the same treatment? And doctors should receive fair compensation for every patient they see."

"If I wanted to be a civil servant, I wouldn't have gone to medical school!" The doctor was angry now, and he brought his hand down hard on our table. The force of it tipped my wine glass, and the red liquid splashed into my lap before I had time to move. It spread across the pale linen like a bloodstain. The sight of what he'd done sobered him.

"Terribly sorry, miss. Terribly sorry." The doctor, his wife, William, and even Johnny started hovering and fussing over me, almost knocking over the water glasses with their efforts.

"It's fine, I'm fine," I said, trying to reassure the obviously embarrassed man.

"Allow me to pay to clean your garmentsh," he said, and peeled twenty dollars from a roll of cash. "Hell no," he rocked in a circle, still peeling twenties, "buy a whole new outfit."

In the end, he left a hundred dollars on our table. Johnny whisked around, getting the doctor out of the predicament, and uncorked another bottle for us, a consolation for a dining room incident gone awry.

"Are you sure you're all right?" William asked for the third time.

"Hey, I teach at Limestone. A bit of wine on my skirt is hardly the end of the world."

"Are you sure you want to be seen in public with a politician?"

Does this mean he's going to ask me out again? "Why wouldn't I?"

"It could be dangerous," he teased.

"Could be profitable!" I countered, pointing at the twenties. William nudged the cash toward me.

"Take the money. You heard what he said; buy another dress."

"Are you sure I should?"

"No question about it. The fool had too much to drink. He knows better."

He sounded like a father chastising a wayward teenager. I folded the money and put it in my purse. *New skirt? Forget it. It was enough to pay two months' room and board at Mrs. M's.*

The time flew past, and by dessert, the spilled wine was forgotten.

"You talked about your family earlier." William picked up the thread the doctor had snapped. "I can understand your mother; it's very difficult to lose someone." His blue eyes grew serious. "I was twenty-six when my parents died in a car accident."

"Oh, now I'm the one who's sorry."

"There are days I walk into the house, and for a moment, I still expect to find my mother in the kitchen or my dad reading the newspaper."

"You still live in the same house?"

"They left it to me. It's too big for one person, but it's home," he shrugged.

The waiter cleared our plates. I was silent while he poured coffee from an elegant silver service and moved on.

"How long ago was the accident?"

"Six years now." His voice sounded low and sad.

We both stirred in silence.

"Figure it out yet?" William asked me.

"Thirty-two."

"You got it. And you?"

"I'll be twenty-one next September."

He brightened considerably and took a long drink of coffee. He nodded approval, as if the drink was unusually good. "Perfect," he proclaimed. "That's absolutely perfect."

"What's so perfect about being twenty-one?" I asked.

But his only answer was a smile. I'd have to check, but I thought a smile like that was called enigmatic.

CHAPTER SEVEN
Faderton

The letters arrived at Eleven Main Street in the shelter of Gib's corduroy coat. He placed them on the sideboard, unopened and with no comment. When Joyce opened the first one, she said, "Oh Gib, listen to this—"

"Keep it to yourself," he ordered.

"Gib, it's from Eleanor, and she's doing really well."

"I don't want to hear about it."

"Why not? It's good news." Then she added, "We could use some good news—couldn't we?"

"I don't need any 'I told you so's' coming from Kingston. If she's doing good, fine—she can stay there and do good. I'll keep bringing them letters home, just stay quiet about what's in 'em."

So that was what Joyce did. She understood Gib's anger, even if she'd rarely seen it in over twenty years together. So she learned to keep an eye on the sideboard and retreat to her shadowy bedroom to read the letters silently. She even started to look forward to them, and that was rare too. It had been a long time since she had looked forward to anything. She thought maybe she'd forgotten how to enjoy life. But she could do it; the letters showed her that.

One week, Eleanor wrote about a chubby little girl who wasn't getting on well, either in the classroom or at recess: "The little dear often slumped over her desk and couldn't follow what was going on. In the schoolyard, she'd sometimes trip or stumble, and one day I saw her get hit in the face with a dodge ball. She didn't see it coming at her. That's when it struck me—she can't see. Long story short, she's got glasses now and is doing much better."

Joyce would shake her head in bewilderment, perplexed that her daughter could make that kind of difference in someone's life. After reading her letters, Joyce always offered the same comment, to the same empty room, "Isn't that something?" Then, without fail, she would answer her own query. "It really is something."

She only hoped her husband would come to his senses before Christmas and let their daughter come home for the holidays. Joyce thought she might bring it up to him tonight. She felt a shiver of, she wasn't sure what, but it stirred inside her. This coming weekend was their overnight to do their benevolent work, as they called it. She'd remind him about that too. So much to remember. The two things. She wrote them down on a piece of paper by the telephone. Usually it was Gib who reminded her of what to do, even what to wear. But she felt stronger lately, and she knew it was because of the letters. *I might even peel a few potatoes, and Gib would like some pork chops done up in that mushroom sauce I used to do.*

When Gib Cole stepped into the kitchen, the light over the stove was on, and supper, a real supper, was cooking. Joyce had even shifted some papers to one end of the table, clearing a spot for plates and cutlery. Gib smiled gently at her.

"Well, what's all this?"

"Oh, a little supper. I thought you'd be hungry," Joyce answered, as if it hadn't been fifteen years or more since she'd last made a proper meal.

"Okay then," Gib answered. "It smells real good."

The telephone rang, and Gib went to answer it, circling out of his wife's way as she removed the platter warming in the oven.

A rough voice asked, "Are you Eleanor Cole's ol' man?"

Gib hesitated. "Who is this?"

"A friend of your daughter's."

"What do you want?" Gib was terse.

Eleanor had never had a boy call her, but this was a man's voice, and it put Gib on guard.

"I want to let you know, your pretty daughter better watch herself."

The vein in Gib's neck was bulging. "What the hell's that supposed to mean?"

It was the first swear word Joyce had heard him use since the day Eleanor had left.

"It means that some boys here in Kingston plan to pay her a visit. That walk to Limestone school can be dangerous for a girl by herself."

Gib's face turned a mottled white and pink, and he brought his hand to his chest.

"Who—"

The phone line went dead. Joyce looked up from stirring the sauce, just in time to see Gib slump into a chair, the receiver still in his palm.

"I'm not feeling too good, Mother." He tried to move the telephone receiver toward her. "You better call the doctor."

My return to Faderton was several weeks earlier and a lot less noteworthy than the homecoming I'd imagined. I had pictured myself coming back at Christmas, toting brightly wrapped presents, and my Dad would greet me with an all-is-forgiven embrace.

Instead, I came on the first bus I could get after Mrs. M relayed the message to me about my dad. "Your mother said he's had some kind of a spell."

"A spell? I had asked. "Mrs. M my mother uses that word to describe everything from a bout of diarrhea to a stroke.""Well there was a telephone call. And it scared your dad," she'd said. "Caused him to have some sort of a spell with his heart."

"A telephone call? From who? What was it about?"

Mrs. M was shaking her head before I finished firing my questions at her. "I don't know the details – but I think it had something to do with you."

So, here I was—home at dusk in the ugly nonlight of November. There was no one to meet me, so I had to walk to my parents' from the coffee shop that served double duty as Faderton's bus station. It was a street I had traveled countless times, but it didn't look like the same place I had left a few weeks earlier. The houses on Main Street were smaller than I remembered and not much better than my own rundown neighborhood in Kingston. It took coming home to realize that I thought of Mrs. M's area as my neighborhood. I had discovered it and staked a modest claim there. For the first time, I was seeing Faderton as the place I came from, not the place where I lived.

"Mom?" I called from just inside the kitchen door. No response.

"Mom, where are you?"

I heard a murmur of voices that led me into the living room. The muffled words were coming from the bedroom. The house was hot, stifling, really. Some sort of sauce was congealed and fissured in a pot on the stove. I didn't bother taking my coat off. I wondered why sounds in this morose house always sounded like they were coming from under water. One half of the conversation was my mother, and the other voice was familiar. I paused outside the doorway, trying to place it.

"You've been through so much, Joyce. Now this, with Gib's heart attack, being in the hospital and all…"

"We'll survive. We've been through worse." That was my mother talking, beginning and ending each sentence with a sigh, as if she'd get marks for consistent punctuation.

"Worse? You mean, when you lost the baby?" It was Linda Silver speaking. They still didn't know I was there. I could picture Linda's face, eyes wide, pulled close to my mother's, pleased that she had navigated past the fortifications around the topic. My mother would not speak of it, though. I smirked in the shadows; my mother, for all her fluttery ways, could turn to ice on one subject. And Linda had just brought up the forbidden subject: my twin sister.

"Yes, when we lost the baby, that's what started it, I suppose. But really, it wasn't just losing Elizabeth, although I thought I would die, wished I could die, when that happened."

My God, she was talking about it! I'd never heard her say so much on the topic.

"It seems daft, but losing Elizabeth turned out to be the easiest part of all. The years after were much more difficult—each one harder than the year before. Still is.

When the girls were born, it was all such a surprise, you see. We didn't know we were having twins. Not like today, they can tell you all these things ahead of time. So there we were, I was twenty, Gib was twenty-two, kids ourselves, really, with twin girls."

"Eleanor and Elizabeth," Linda injected, as if our names might have slipped my mother's mind.

"Eleanor and Elizabeth. That's what we named them," my mother confirmed. "Anyway, Dr. Fredricks told us right away that something...," she took a ragged breath "...something was wrong with Elizabeth. She was so weak, we weren't even sure we should name her. They say it makes it easier on the parents if you don't name the baby, but I don't know."

"Did Dr. Fredricks say what was wrong with her?"

I felt sure Linda had gone too far now.

"Just about everything, it seemed. She had a bad heart. She was such a sleepy, droopy baby. No strength to her at all. She was too feeble to nurse, so Gib and I had to feed her one drop at a time."

"But Eleanor, she was healthy?" Linda coaxed.

"As a horse."

"That must have been a relief to you and Gib."

Mother was silent at that. A drop of perspiration rolled down the inside of my arm toward my elbow. I would've waited a week for her answer.

"It should have been. Eleanor was a robust child, and I should have been grateful, but to be honest, she was the one that made things so difficult. Always has."

"Eleanor?" Linda gave voice to my surprise. "What did she do?"

"She was normal. She grew, she walked, she talked. She surpassed her sister in every way. Everything she did was like a cruel yardstick held up beside Elizabeth. When she accomplished something, it pointed out exactly how far short her sister had fallen."

"I suppose it must have been easier when Elizabeth was gone," Linda sounded like she was commiserating, but I knew that voice well enough to recognize that she was wheedling out more information. Sweat ran between my shoulder blades, but I wouldn't dare move to loosen a button, when I was finally getting the lowdown on the big family secret.

"It was supposed to be easier," I could hear mother's sadness, "but it was just the opposite."

"The opposite?"

"Everything came so easily to Eleanor. School, piano lessons, good looks, her health. You know she didn't miss one day of school in twelve years?"

"But Joyce, surely you don't blame Eleanor for what happened to Elizabeth."

"Blame. No, I didn't blame her—not exactly. You see, it just would have been easier to have one or the other. One healthy child—what we expected. Or even one sick child, and then we would have been able to take care of her better—maybe we'd still have her. But the way it was, it was the cruelty of it all. Every time Eleanor succeeded at something, it pointed out how much Elizabeth had been cheated. So no, it wasn't blame, that's the wrong word."

"What's the right word then?"

My mother responded quickly, as though she'd been keeping the answer warm for a long time, just waiting for someone to ask for it.

"Resentment. I resented everything that Eleanor ever did. Her piano recitals, her perfect report cards, all those choir performances—I resented every one of them. I'm not proud of myself, but that's how I felt. God help me for saying this, but it would have been better if we'd lost both of them. Then Gib and I could've started over, with a clean slate."

Linda fell as silent as I was. Mom's confession must have stunned both of us. But the silence didn't last long; Mom had opened a floodgate, and the words, more words than she'd strung together in twenty years, came flowing through the sluices. I reached to the wall to steady myself.

"Don't get me wrong. I love the girl, always have. It just seemed spiteful of God to give us two girls, and then leave us with one to show us, day after day, what we'd lost."

"But that isn't Eleanor's fault."

"I didn't say it was. It's God's fault, and sometimes I get angry at God, but I stop myself because I know it's wrong. But I just slip back and can't get past the sad truth that God let one of our girls go down one path, and kept the other one from doing the same. All I can think about is that one has to travel alone, and the other didn't get to go at all." She was crying now. But she was pushing on, as if once started, she had to say her piece.

Linda tried to comfort her. "It's all right, Joyce. Everything will be all right."

"It's not all right. It's too late for all right." My mother's voice worked its way out from behind the tears, and just as she said, she could edge her way into anger, if only temporarily.

"I've ruined everything. There's nothing I haven't failed at. I couldn't help Elizabeth, and I couldn't enjoy Eleanor. Gib—he didn't know what to do with me. He married a bright-eyed girl with some gumption to her. He expected a life, a real life together. He and I used to go out for Sunday afternoon drives. We'd take a picnic if the weather was nice. We did that a few times after the girls were born. But after Elizabeth was gone, I felt nothing but pain. Excruciating pain. Trying the old things that used to make us happy reminded me of the way things were, but doing anything new felt like we were betraying Elizabeth by moving on without her. So I just stayed put—and now look what's happened."

DIVISIONS

In the dark and heat of the living room, the truth hit me like a fist. My life counted for nothing. Worse than nothing. I was the source of the grief in our home. Me. The twin who lived, brought more sadness than if I'd died. I sagged inside my coat, and although I stayed on my feet, I had the sense that beneath me, the floor was starting to sag. The boards underfoot felt as if they were breaking apart, and I wobbled, feeling like I was standing on carpet stretched over nothing.

All this time, I'd done double duty to make up for Elizabeth, and it was exactly the opposite of what my parents needed. I had spent my life trying to make them happy, and they had acted like they were proud. They praised my report cards, applauded my recitals, and paid for more lessons. Why? Why do that if I was bringing them more grief? If resentment, not pride, was behind their smiles, why didn't they tell me? I could have backed off, and they might have found a way to, maybe not love, but at least not resent me.

"But-" Linda's voice strained and I could picture her simple face trying to puzzle together the pieces of what we'd both heard. "Joyce, you didn't act like you resented Eleanor. You and Gib seemed proud of her."

"What else could we do? If we encouraged her, she'd go her own way, eventually."

"Her own way?" Linda asked. "What are you talking about? You were the ones who didn't want her to go to Kingston."

"I know. We always figured she'd teach for a year or two and get married, and she'd be busy with a family of her own."

That was their strategy. Endure me for as long as they could, then marry me off. Didn't even matter to whom—just so long as he took me off their hands. My whole life was without value. The floor was firming up now, enough for me to move, anyway.

87

I shifted around by degrees, took a step, and faltered, my nylon coat hissing against the hassock. Silently I hoisted my bag. The snow from my boots lay puddled on the mat. I stole out the back door, seared by my mother's revelation.

I crept out the door and stood in the darkness. My mother's words washed over me in cruel waves until I felt as if I was drowning from the weight of them. *"Couldn't enjoy Eleanor...easier to have one or the other...resentment."*

In the dark night outside my parents' house I wanted to be rescued. I wanted to be pulled up and away from the crush of those words, and taken to safety. It had happened once before, and I remembered it clearly.

I was twelve when I went swimming, with our Sunday School class, at the quarry in St. Mary's. I had jumped from the stone ledge into water, bracing and deep, deeper than I'd ever experienced. It was my first time there, and I plunged in, feet first, with innocent abandon. I felt my body knife deep into the quarry waters, and I started to think, "I'm further below the surface of the earth than I've ever been," and I was still going deeper. I tried to keep my toes pointed and wait for the water to bob me back to the surface, but my composure was fleeting, and I began flailing my arms and legs in a panic to climb back to the top. My hair was long, and it floated up around my nose and mouth, and I worried that even when I broke through the surface, I might suffocate on my own hair. I began kicking wildly. My hands windmilled, grasping for something to push against. I was exhausted, fighting against water and gravity. Then suddenly, I surfaced, and I was delivered into the Sunday afternoon sunshine. No one heard my coughing and choking above the whoops and shouts of the rest of the swimmers. Except for one boy. He'd been sunning himself on the ledge where the swimmers hoisted themselves out before flinging their goosefleshed bodies off the precipice again. He noticed my ungainly progress back to safety, and he had reached a thin white arm down to me. His honey-colored freckles formed a splattered contrast over his pinked up skin. I had never seen anything so beautiful in my life.

But there was no helping hand reaching out to me now. All I found was Linda's car with the keys in the ignition. I took it I gunned out of town. Served her right, she had my life story, I could take her car for a while. I needed to talk to someone. But who? William Buchanan was tempting, but he'd ask too many questions, trying to find the logic in it all. I abandoned Linda's car outside the bus station in Stratford. I had three minutes to make a call before the last bus pulled out.

When Frank O'Donnell answered the phone, he didn't get a chance to do much talking. I sniffled and hiccuped my way through an explanation about the threatening phone call and how it caused my dad to have a heart attack. Frank didn't offer much solace, but he promised to look into it.

When I hung up, I realized I still had a couple of minutes. So I placed another call. I needed to tell someone what had really happened, what I'd learned by overhearing my mother's conversation. Mrs. M's voice, gravelly with sleep, answered on the third ring. I told her where I was and that I was coming back that night.

"But why? You only just got there."

My response was a plaintive wail and a few words, garbled by sobs.

"It's all right, darlin'. Don't try to talk. Come on home. You can tell me all about it then."

CHAPTER EIGHT
Christmas Concert

My students were stamping star shapes onto green paper Christmas trees. When they finished, I planned to rehearse—for what seemed like the thousandth time—the singing of the Huron Carol. Since I was the only one on staff who knew how to coax music out of the old Heintzman piano, I became the accompanist for the Christmas concert. Nancy, who could read a little music, would turn the pages.

My grade two class, with their innocent, pure voices, would be the hit of the concert. I rehearsed them to perfection. The piano was stowed in the hallway just outside my classroom door, and every day we had to roll the heavy thing into the class.

When I asked for two volunteers to move it, the boys and girls competed mightily for the job. Bony little arms shot into the air, eager to help me with whatever I asked of them. I resorted to posting a list of assistants, so every child would have two chances to push the piano. It was supposed to make everything fair, but I encountered a flaw.

Early in December, Carlos Arruda, who was acquiring English at an astonishing rate, came to school coughing and swiping his sleeve across his reddened nose. He laid his head on his arms.

"Carlos, why did you come to school today? I know you're not well."

"I'm okay."

I crouched by the boy's desk and touched his forehead.

"You're not. You're burning up!"

"Today is my turn, and I don't miss it."

"Your turn? What do you mean?"

He lifted his head with an effort. "To help with the piano. I did it one time. Today is last turn. I'm not miss it."

He planted his chin on his forearms and fixed his dark eyes on a point on the chair in front of him. I couldn't hold back my smile, but I did need a solution.

"Carlos, if I let you have your turn early, would you like to go home after that?"

He nodded his head without lifting it off his arms.

"Boys and girls," I called to the group. "We'll be practicing our carol this morning and doing our arithmetic pages this afternoon."

Excited whispers went around the room as the students snapped and zipped shut their pencil cases. Carlos's watery eyes turned adoringly toward me, and I had the feeling I had just become the first girl Carlos Arruda would ever love. In moments like these, I felt I was born to be a teacher. In fact, if Mr. Wallace had walked in right now and cut my pay in half, I would have said, "Fine."

On the night of the concert, parents and grandparents trooped in and sat in the folding chairs set up in the gym. We had half the gym filled with chairs, but so many people were showing up that Mr. Wallace and two boys in grade eight were scurrying to add to the number. My stomach clenched, then relaxed, then clenched again. I don't think I'd felt so queasy since that day in the KP.

I peeked out from behind the makeshift curtain to see Mrs. M seated as comfortably as she could be, considering that a good deal of her spilled over the edges of the chair. Beside her, Nancy's husband Ray, who had chauffeured us to the concert in his ancient Plymouth, waited for the show to begin. Ray had a friendly, encouraging look about him, and I scanned for more faces like his. I found the Arrudas, with a brown-eyed toddler bouncing on his father's knee. Just as I turned to go back to the dozens of details that kids and concerts present, I caught sight of a familiar form entering the auditorium. My knees turned to slush.

Frank O'Donnell paced like a cop on a beat to the back of the room and stood, hands behind his back, against the rear wall of the gym. *What in the world is he doing here?*

"C'mon, it's time."

Nancy's voice interrupted my churning thoughts, and I had no choice but to put Frank O'Donnell aside for the moment and get back to what I'd been working on for two months.

"The kids are dying to know what the surprise is," Nancy said.

"Think they'll like it?" I asked, checking on one more aspect of the evening that was giving me the jitters.

"Only one way to find out," Nancy answered with predictable practicality.

She had already assembled the children into the rows they would be performing in.

There they were, all twenty-eight of them. All dressed the same in white tops and dark bottoms, outfits that had been assembled with some difficulty. Two children had temporarily shortened their sleeves by carefully tucking them at the wrist. More than one pair of pants, probably purloined from an older brother, was folded and safety-pinned at the waistband. The children stood perfectly aligned by height, but keeping them still was out of the question. They chattered, the boys slapped and pushed at each other, and the girls gripped each other's hands and scolded the boys to be quiet. Twenty-eight excited second graders, and among them there wasn't one jot of patience left. It was time to deliver the surprise.

Mrs. McMullen had taught me how to make bow ties for each of the children from red satin fabric. I did my best, hand stitching every night past midnight, but Mrs. M could see that I wouldn't be finished till spring and had pitched in to help. She spent the entire week leading up to the concert sewing, turning, and pressing the fabric into perfect scarlet bows. When I presented the twenty-eight bows to the boys and girls, their angelic faces lit up. I was already ridiculously proud of my little ones, and they hadn't yet sung a note.

Bows on, backs straight, and without daring to step out of the order they were placed in, they paraded to the gym, and the concert was underway.

I purposely saved my class until the end. When they filed into place, Nancy whispered to me, "And now for the pièce de résistance."

"Don't talk like that. I can only worry in English," I whispered back.

"Not a thing to worry about!"

Easy for her to say. She didn't know that Frank O'Donnell was in the audience. Though I wasn't sure if he was, myself, since the lights had been lowered. Our footlights were a pair of mechanic's trouble lights on loan from someone's uncle who ran a garage. They bathed my class in a harsh glare that made them shade their eyes as they tried to see their parents in the audience.

I struggled to gain their attention. Only Carlos Arruda didn't have to be asked twice. His gaze didn't waver from me, and I felt pretty good in a slim-fitting black velvet skirt. My own white top was adorned with a Christmas corsage Mrs. M had pinned on me just before we left home. I wasn't sure who was more nervous, me or the children. They resisted—then succumbed to—the temptation to waggle their fingers in greeting to their parents, and for a moment, I fervently wished my own mom and dad could be there too. But at least I had someone; Mrs. M, Ray, and maybe even Frank O'Donnell were out there waiting to hear what we'd all spent weeks preparing.

I had arranged to have the lights dimmed just as I struck the first haunting chords of the Huron Carol. The audience was silent.

"'Twas in the moon of wintertime…"

The children's voices rang pure and true.

"When all the birds had fled."

Pause for one full beat. The children stopped precisely, and waited in silence.

"The mighty Gitcheemanitou
Sent angel choirs instead.
The wondering hunters heard the hymn
Before the night the stars grew dim."

Then the rumbling base notes, and I pushed the aging Heintzman to capacity as the sweet voices rose in confidence and volume when they settled into the familiar throb of the chorus.

"Jesu your king is born,
Jesus is born
In excelsis Gloria."

Nancy turned the pages at her cue, and we exchanged a triumphant glance, knowing that our young prodigies were turning out a flawless performance.

I played through the balance of the pages in a state of bliss, letting my fingers hold chords and trill arpeggios without any conscious thought on my part. I had practiced until I could let memory guide me. It was a powerful pleasure to let the music flow through me, my nerves and muscles the conduits for melody.

When the last note sounded, a moment of almost reverential silence fell over the gathering. The lights came back up, and the applause began and didn't stop. I could feel my eyes fill with tears when I surveyed my talented little group. I had never been more proud. When I rose from the piano, the applause quickened, and in one movement, every member of the audience stood to acknowledge me.

A standing ovation. In Limestone Elementary. Our "stage" was plywood sheets supported by cement blocks. The walls were stained where the Canadian cold and damp had permeated them. The piano bench wobbled, and the E flat in the second octave stuck when it was played. But for this moment, I couldn't have been more elated if I had been at a concert grand in Carnegie Hall. But when I turned to find Frank O'Donnell, he was gone, and my moment of glory lost some of its luster.

While chairs were being folded and put away, the children hugged me with abandon, and parents thanked me for the best concert the school had ever produced. The round little girl I had written to my parents about waited for me, wiping at her new glasses, steamed now with emotion. When I hugged her goodbye, she whispered into my hair.

"I love you, Mith Cole."

"I love you too, sweetie."

Later, when the school was nearly empty, I hurried toward the door to ride with Ray, Nancy, and Mrs. M that was when I was stopped by the nasal drone of Mr. Wallace.

"Miss Cole. A word with you, please."

I had avoided Mr. Wallace as much as possible since the Arruda bout in the hallway, an easy enough feat considering how often he was away from Limestone Elementary.

"That was quite a performance," he said.

It didn't sound entirely like a compliment, so I didn't say thank-you.

Instead I said, "I think people enjoyed it."

"I'm just a little curious about the selection for your own class."

"The Huron Carol?"

"Yes." He drew out the vowel sound and managed to make the word three syllables long. "That's an Indian song, I think."

Wherever this was going felt dangerous to me. "You're right," I answered, trying to sound both neutral and confident.

"Did you really think that was an appropriate choice?"

"Well, yes I did. It's Christmas, it's Canadian, and it fit the children's range beautifully."

"But it is an Indian song. Considering the trouble those people give us, just in this neighborhood alone, don't you think a song like that just encourages them?"

"Our children, Indian and otherwise, could use a little encouragement, Mr. Wallace."

Edwin Wallace drew a deep breath that caused his nostrils to flare.

"You're a new teacher, Miss Cole. And like most new teachers, you think you can change the world."

"I don't think—"

"I'll thank-you not to interrupt me. There are a lot of our own people who could use help too, as I think I've mentioned to you. Instead, we pour scarce education dollars into these people, and it's like pouring sand down a rat hole. Using their music as part of a Christmas celebration just gives them one more chance to try to reinvent history from a bunch of lies. Jesus was born in a stable, not a lodge of broken bark. He was not found by wandering hunters, but by three wise men."

I could feel my hands trembling, and I clenched them tight in my gloves, determined not to satisfy the pencil-necked tyrant. For some weird reason, my mind flicked to Frank O'Donnell, and I would have given anything for his gift of inscrutability.

"Wondering," I finally retorted.

"What?"

"Wondering hunters, not wandering." I tried to make my words drip with disdain.

"Don't quibble with me, Miss Cole."

"So you didn't enjoy the concert?"

"All but that piece. I think you should have asked for my judgment on that one."

"I would have, if I could ever find you."

Mr. Wallace's long neck turned red, blotting up from his collar and ending at his earlobes.

"Where do you disappear to all the time, anyway?"

"Where and when I am away from the school is none of your concern, Miss Cole. What you need to remember is I'm the principal, and you're the one who needs my supervision for two years if you want a permanent teaching certificate."

I slammed the Plymouth's car door so hard, the trio waiting for me jumped. I tried to tell them of my encounter with the principal, but emotion strangled the words when I tried to speak. Instead, I simply allowed myself to be folded into the corpulent bosom of Mrs. M and sobbed all the way home.

CHAPTER NINE
Attacked

There was no word from Faderton over Christmas. Which was natural, considering that they didn't know I'd ever come home to help out after my father's heart attack. As far as Mom knew, she'd called Mrs. M with the news, then never heard another word.

But I had heard words: the cruel ones my mother used when she spoke to Linda about me. I worked hard to put them out of my mind, but rarely succeeded. Every day when I walked home from school, I thought of them. I felt betrayed for the façade they'd spent a lifetime trying to keep up.

Resented my piano recitals! If she'd have told me that, I would have gladly given up the damned things. I liked playing in public under the cover of choir voices, but at a recital, there was nothing and no one to hide behind. I hated getting all prissied up in some scratchy dress and being so nervous I couldn't eat for three days before. Weeks of practice and playing the same forgettable conservatory piece over and over, just to have it all performed in about two minutes. I had done it for my parents. Thinking on some ridiculous level that they would be comforted to see how outstanding I was, and maybe it would be a small comfort for losing Elizabeth. At least, I thought that was why I had done it. Things had just became a pattern, and if anyone had asked, I probably wouldn't have been able to tell them why I was pushing myself to please them.

As I trudged through the snow, I tried to distract myself by looking at the surroundings, but the low sun of March was not kind to the street in front of me. The frame houses crowded close to the curb, like homely spectators at a county fair, waiting to see something spectacular. But there wouldn't be anything spectacular, or even mildly interesting happening here, and the facades of the houses were frozen into permanent disappointment. The flat front houses were gaunt and plain, like old maids who'd conceded to an unloved life. No shutters, no cornice pieces to soften the right angles where soffits met the walls. Most of the front doors opened to stoops no more than one stride off the street.

At the odd house, long dead chrysanthemums poked through the crusted-over snow. But mostly, people along here didn't do much with shrubs or flowers to relax the rigid lines of the street front. A few had roofs that had sagged under the heavy snowfall of Kingston winters. Some of the porches were furnished with rusting kitchen chairs and, at one, a ratty armchair had been commandeered for outdoor reclining. One house displayed a forlorn Christmas wreath, the plastic leaves bleached at the edges by more than one summer season.

Even with the doors and windows shut tight against the wind from the lake, I could occasionally get a whiff of life inside these homes. I sniffed boiled cabbage at one place and cat urine about a block further down. As if my dreary surroundings and the betrayal from my mother wasn't enough, I was beginning to worry about George Knowles again.

William Buchanan had told me he'd been successful in arguing for an early release date for Knowles.

"Why on earth would you do that?" I had asked last Saturday at the Cataraqui Club.

"Eleanor, prisons do not rehabilitate people. All they do is punish and make men angrier than they were when they went in."

"The last time I saw George, he was pretty angry, all right. At me. I don't want him out on the street. He might come after me."

"I'll protect you," William promised, and if we hadn't been sitting with a table between us, he looked as if he might have kissed me.

"Leave him in there. That'd protect me."

"He won't be out for a few months."

"What do you mean—a few months? At the prison, you said a couple of years. Now he'll be out when?"

"Probably the fall. You don't have to worry about anything. He'll be so glad to be out early, he'll walk a straight line. A guy like George isn't meant for prison life."

"William," I answered, wishing I could afford to be as ignorant about life north of Princess, "a guy like George probably couldn't draw a straight line, let alone walk one."

I hurried as fast as the snow and gloom would allow and tried to figure out which bothered me more, the thought of George being out or the image of him without visitors inside that prison. I tried to imagine what it must be like without the comfort of written words to transport a person, mentally at least, to the outside world. It was as if he was walled up inside two prisons. I forced George out of my thoughts and focused on the comfort of the hot meal Mrs. M would have waiting for me.

The other person I thought about was William Buchanan. Every Saturday night, I had gone out with him, and it was an arrangement that I couldn't quite explain, although I tried when Nancy asked me about it.

"Here's what my dates with William have been like; he picks me up after he's been doing political stuff all day—"

"Like campaigning, you mean?"

"Guess so," I shrugged. "Anyway, he's hungry and doesn't like to eat alone, so we go out to eat. To the country club," I pronounced "country club" with an English accent to mock its sophistication. "I tell him about my week, you know, trying to avoid spitballs and Mr. Wallace. Then he tells me about his week. He makes speeches, meets with Ray to plan strategy, and talks to voters. At night he either has meetings or work to catch up on at the law office. He brings me home by nine o'clock, asks me to go out the next weekend, and drops me with one—just one—really spectacular goodnight kiss."

"So, do you like him?"

I hesitated. "I like...being liked. He seems to think I'm clever, and funny even. But..."

"But...?"

"He's a lot older than I am. I think he's lonely and just wants a dinner companion."

"Are you sure? Because he told Ray you would make an excellent asset."

"An asset? What's that supposed to mean?"

"It means that if you play your cards right, you just might be living on Kensington Street someday."

"Play my cards right? I told you—he doesn't even call or try to see me between dates."

"That doesn't mean he isn't interested," Nancy insisted. "Ray says he's the most intellectual man he's ever met. He thinks so far ahead, he's probably choosing universities for your children."

But I wasn't thinking about "someday" as I approached Mrs. M's little stucco house, eager for the warmth I knew lay just behind the front door. As I reached the worn front steps, I had pulled my key from my pocket when a pair of hands shot out of nowhere and grabbed my arm. I was jerked hard to the right, and my school books fell into the snow while I fought to stay on my feet. I tried to scream, but a rough hand pushed up on my chin and propelled me backwards against the porch wall. My head hit the wall hard, and I could hear the sound of my own skull thud against the unyielding porch wall. The pain was searing and the attack so swift that I wasn't able to fight back. All I could think about was the man pinning me against the wall, when I saw a second man emerge from the bushes.

"Hey there, church girl. A friend of ours wanted us to say hello. His name's George, do you remember him?" The man holding me asked. He stunk of liquor.

I could only nod my head in response. The movement sent a bolt of pain down my spine. His friend leered at me through decayed teeth and moved his face close enough that I could feel the heat and stench of his breath on my mouth. I pulled back reflexively and pushed against the one holding me. The movement was enough to make him stumble, and that was when I realized the alcohol could work to my advantage. But the gap-toothed one moved to help his buddy. He clutched the front of my coat with one hand, and with the other, brandished an empty bottle of Jack Daniels as if he meant to bludgeon me with it.

"We ain't gonna hurt ya." His foul breath made my stomach turn. "Georgie wants to know if you're gonna come back for a visit."

"No, I'm not," I spat the words at him. I should have thought about whether the answer would get me out of trouble or into more with these revolting characters.

I prayed that someone might drive by and see my predicament, but few cars traveled the side streets, and no one was out walking on dreary March days. I felt my key clenched in my right hand, and without a second thought, I brought it up fast and hard into the cheek of the creep with the bottle.

Instinctively, the hand he held me with went to his face, and he yelled loud, drunken curses at me as I tried to wade through the snow away from him. My freedom was brief, because his accomplice, in a boozy stupor, tackled me and dragged me down into the snow. I was fast to get to my feet, but just as quickly, my arms were pinned tight to my sides by the one with the fetid breath, who clinched me from behind. I spied the empty bottle lying in the snow where he'd dropped it, too drunk to realize what happened.

Somewhere in my throbbing head, it registered that these two were slipping and sliding, not just from booze, but from boots so worn and cheap that they couldn't get a grip in the snow. That thought and pure terror guided me, and I planted my feet and pushed backward, shoving my captor's back against the porch wall. I screamed guttural, angry sounds, loud and confusing to the tough guys whose courage came from the bottom of a bottle. My arms were still useless to me, and the one in front of me was out of kicking range. I brought my heel back hard and scraped down the shin of the goon behind me. He bellowed, but the pain didn't cause him to let me go; in fact, he gripped me even tighter as his friend staggered toward me.

DIVISIONS

No one in the imbroglio heard the screen door bang open or saw Mrs. M thunder out her door, brandishing a cast iron frying pan. Mrs. M crossed the porch in two fiery steps, leaned over the low wall, and powered by her full and ample weight, brought the frying pan down on the head of my attacker. The resounding metallic gong and the instant release of my arms were all I needed to make my escape, past the lout who was still standing trying to figure out why his partner in crime was moaning, face down in a snow drift.

I scampered up the steps to Mrs. M, who was leaning hard against the porch wall. The black frying pan hung heavy from her free hand.

"Mrs. M!" I wanted to pull her back into the house. "C'mon, Mrs. M, let me help you." I glanced over the wall. The figure on the snow was struggling to get up. His friend had already disappeared. A siren wailed in the distance, a wake-up call to my attacker, who staggered off down the street as fast as a wounded drunk could go, which is pretty fast when the cops are closing in, because he was out of sight within seconds.

I tried to wedge myself against Mrs. M as a brace, but I wasn't even sure she noticed. She was panting, short shallow breaths, as if it hurt to breathe. The skin between her eyebrows was pleated tight, while her mouth sagged open as much as the flesh below her chin would allow. The police car slid to a stop in front of the house, and Frank O'Donnell came sprinting up the walk.

"Help us, Frank! Mrs. M can't breathe."

The iron pan clanged to the floor, and its force split time into two simultaneous streams. One stream was fast-moving, and through it, I watched Frank bound toward us. The other part was languid, and time stretched into wispy thoughts that drifted through my mind even as Mrs. M sagged into my arms. The best

I could do was help break her fall. Her knees crumpled while I struggled to hold her.

That was what an onlooker would see. But in my mind, all I could see was Mrs. M's embroidery floss looped around her fingers. The measured movements of her hands tatting, drawing out the floss, pausing for a long pull on her cigarette, then back to the rhythm of her work.

She listed off to one side, and her hip landed on the porch. Frank's boot pounded on the bottom step. But my eyes saw Mrs. M sewing and pressing red satin fabric in the glow of a trilight floor lamp. She licked the tips of her fingers, coaxing the material into exact positions and then securing it with the slow hiss of a steam iron. She sealed the corners into perfect right angles, and hand stitched a finish on each bow.

Frank's foot thudded onto the second step. He reached toward us to help me slide her heavy form to a lying position. He may have spoken, but I heard another voice.

It was gruff from too much smoke, and there was just enough wheeziness so you'd know there was a toll to every word spoken. "You'll have to find it by yourself, for yourself, and in your own time."

"Find what?" I'd asked her.

"Whatever's missing," Mrs. M had said.

Time stretched and flexed like a cat waking from a nap.

Frank was beside me now on the porch. His dash must have taken less than five seconds. He fumbled around her neck for a pulse and dropped an ear to her chest.

"She's gone, Eleanor." His expression told me he was stricken. But still on high alert, I noted more. Guilt, as if he might have saved her if he'd moved faster. But then he said, "She was probably dead before she hit the porch."

DIVISIONS

Like an elastic band, time snapped back into form, and I cried out. She was gone.

Problems

I couldn't believe she was gone. Mrs. M had become my friend, my confidant and the person I looked forward to coming home to at the end of the day. She had died trying to help me. The smell of her tobacco, the half-finished tatting project on the kitchen table were like silent prongs of guilt prodding me that she was gone, and it was my fault.

In the days following her death I would turn on all the lights in the house to ward off any return of the attackers, then turn them all off in case the lights attracted the very attention I was trying to escape.

Frank O'Donnell gave me a ride to school each morning in his cruiser, but that protection couldn't last forever. I expected his supervisors to put a halt to that soon.

What I didn't expect was the lawyer's letter that arrived by registered mail at the school a few days after Mrs. M's funeral. I waited until after class to show Nancy. She read it while eating an apple and commented between bites. "So it looks like her cousin inherited the house, but he'll let you stay until it sells."

"Yeah, as long as I 'exercise customary care and fiduciary responsibilities.' What's that mean?"

Nancy finished chewing. "You should ask William, but I think it means you have to pay the bills."

"What bills?"

"Heat, hydro, taxes—the cost of keeping the place running. More than rent, that's for sure."

"More? How am I going to pay more? I was barely covering room and board. Now I'll have to buy food on top of it all."

"Could your folks—"

"No." I cut Nancy off. "I'll never ask them for anything."

I couldn't bear to tell Nancy about what I had heard my mother say. Nancy came from a noisy brood of sisters, and she wouldn't understand about a mother who resented her daughter and then spent a lifetime pretending she didn't.

"I'll just have to pay until I can find a cheaper place."

Nancy's shoulders sagged as though my burden was hers too. "What would you think of…" She stopped talking, interrupted by the distinct clicking of Mr. Wallace's shoes coming into the classroom.

"Mrs. Buckley, I'd like to have word in private with Miss Cole." Mr. Wallace pursed his lips, waiting for Nancy to leave.

"Interesting form of transportation you've acquired, Miss Cole," he said the moment Nancy closed the door. As much as I disliked the man, I had to admit that Mr. Wallace was on top of things at school. His eye for detail extended to seeing how and when I arrived at school each day.

"You mean the police car. Yes, I'm getting a police escort from the constable who helped me a couple of weeks ago."

"What happened two weeks ago?"

I didn't want Edwin Wallace to know anything about my life outside of school, but I was trapped into answering.

"I was accosted, you see, and…"

"Accosted? Why am I just hearing about this now?"

"Well, what would you have been able to do about it, Mr. Wallace?"

I regretted the words the moment they passed my lips. I could tell from the instant flush on Mr. Wallace's neck that we were both thinking about his helplessness against Mr. Arruda.

"I'm sure I don't know," he answered in icy tones. "But I do know what I can do about it now. I can ask you not to arrive at school with a police escort. It's..." he paused, as though searching for a sufficiently scathing adjective, "unseemly."

"Mr. Wallace, it's for my safety."

"I want to know your reason for needing a police officer's protection."

I couldn't risk telling Mr. Wallace about the letters, the prison visit, and all the trouble that followed me since. "If I get dropped off around the corner, would that be all right?"

"Miss Cole, an explanation, if you please."

If I tell him, I might lose my job. Then what would happen to me?

"As long as it doesn't affect my job, it shouldn't matter how I get to school."

"So you're refusing to tell me?"

"I'm sorry Mr. Wallace. I don't think it makes any difference to my teaching. So I'd rather not. However, that police escort might just save my life."

"Miss Cole." Edwin Wallace's Adam's apple yo-yoed in his thin craning neck. "If you are really in such grave danger, perhaps your presence here at Limestone is perilous to the children."

My heart stopped. He was leading this toward firing me. I couldn't let that happen. This job was all I had.

"There's no danger to the children."

"Miss Cole, do I have to remind you that your education is not complete until you've taught successfully for two years?"

"The way I get to school has nothing to do with how well I teach," I insisted.

"I'm sure being squired about by young Atlas is highly pleasant for you both."

"Mr. Wallace, it's not that."

"Whether it's that or not, Miss Cole, you refuse to enlighten me on the background, so I can do some refusing of my own. I refuse to continue to supervise you past June of this year."

"Then I'll have to find another principal who will."

"And I also refuse to provide a letter of reference for you. Even with the current shortage of teachers, Miss Cole, you won't find a principal in the county willing to hire you. You'll be lucky to find a job teaching eight grades in a cow pasture, which was, if I recall, what you were trained for in the first place."

Edwin Wallace might not be able to throw a punch with his fist, but his words crushed me. He snugged the knot of his tie up tight to the collar that gaped around his emaciated neck and wheeled out of the classroom.

I sat at my desk, too stunned to move. Mrs. M was dead. I was terrified to stay at her house, and I couldn't afford it anyway. I couldn't get a ride to school with Frank any more, and in a few months, my teaching career would be over. I couldn't go home, was afraid to even call home. All this because I went to visit George Knowles in prison. I couldn't believe the unfairness of it all. I had tried to do something good, and it had all backfired on me. I gave up the tears that I'd held at bay. They spilled off my cheeks and onto my desktop blotter. Nancy came into the room, ready to resume our chat. I tried to wipe my eyes quickly.

"Don't bother on my account," she said, waving a hand in the air to bat away my efforts to hide my tears. "I grew up with three sisters. I know exactly what a weeping woman needs."

Nancy held out a bag of cookies. She had baked them herself and laced them thoroughly with chocolate.

DIVISIONS

I took one and placed it on the splotched up blotter. "Thanks, but I'm going to need a lot more than this," I said, and recounted what had happened with Mr. Wallace.

Nancy let out a long, low whistle.

"You're in a bind."

"Thanks, I already noticed."

"Okay, I can't help you with everything, but you can stay with me and Ray until you find something better."

I ran the tissue back and forth under my eyes.

"I don't want to impose on you guys. I don't know what to do." Fresh tears started rolling down my cheeks.

Nancy brushed the cookie crumbs from the front of her sweater. She sized me up like a horse trader, "Well, I know exactly what to do."

"You do?"

"Yep. You're coming to stay with us."

"Nancy, I can't—"

"Here's why," Nancy proceeded as if I hadn't spoken. "Ray's signed on as William's campaign manager for the election coming up in June. That means I'm not going to see much of him for the next few months, so you won't be imposing, you'll be keeping me company."

"I'll pay you something for rent," I offered weakly.

"Wait till you hear my offer," Nancy held up her hand to stop me.

"Okay." I was dry-eyed now.

"You know I'm a great cook, but lousy at cleaning. If you pay for your own grub and take over cleaning the apartment, you can stay in the spare room. You can ride back and forth to school with me. There's two problems solved. Whaddya say?"

"I say you're the best friend I could ever have found."

Nancy stood to leave, taking the last cookie and crumpling the bag. "One last thing. You'll have to leave by the end of June. I'll need your room for the baby."

She tossed the wadded up cookie bag and lobbed it into the waste can like basketball player, but couldn't resist one backwards glance to see if I'd caught her last comment.

My expression, which must have resembled the gaping of a landed trout, confirmed what she wanted to know. With a wink and a nod, she was out the door and left me to the comforts of my chocolate cookie.

CHAPTER TEN
Kensington Street

"Hi Nance, did anyone call?" The apartment was stuffy and smelled of baking.

"No, Frank O'Donnell didn't call. Just like he didn't call for the last two months. Did you make it to Fort Henry again?"

I nodded.

"That's gotta be at least two miles, then you come up three flights of stairs. How come you're not out of breath?" Nancy demanded from her post at the kitchen sink.

"It's three miles. And it's easy for me, because unlike you, I don't have a bowling ball in my belly."

Nancy snapped a tea towel at my butt. I slid out of her reach and went to the bathroom to fill the tub for a quick soak.

"So you're going out with William again tonight, but you're hoping Frank calls instead."

"Hopeless, aren't I?"

I pulled an outfit from the makeshift closet at the end of the hall. I left the bathroom door open, so we could talk while I got ready.

"More like hopeful," Nancy corrected. "But seriously, what's Frank got that William Buchanan doesn't have, times ten?"

"How should I know? I never talk to Frank. I thought he liked me, but I guess I was wrong."

I ran the soap and facecloth over my body quickly to be ready in time.

"William must like you; he's taken you out every weekend since you moved in here."

"Every Saturday night, just like clockwork. Thing is, I just don't know what he sees in me."

"I guess the real question is, what do you see in him?"

Nancy came in and sat on the closed toilet seat, chin in her hand. For a moment, I could convince myself we were sisters and we'd been doing this all our lives.

"Oh Nance—I ask myself that question every day." I dried and pulled on my underwear. "For one thing, he's so smart, and just being with him makes me think I must be all right, because he wouldn't be with someone who isn't."

Nancy nodded agreement. "Ray says he has exceptional judgment."

"I spent about an hour one night with my *Roget's*, trying to find a word to describe him."

"So what'd you come up with?" she asked.

I sat on the edge of the tub to pull up my stockings and think for a bit.

"Astute."

"Explain please. Ever since I got pregnant, my brain has gone to mush."

DIVISIONS

"He's really good at analyzing things, but he's completely logical. Sometimes I think he doesn't have any emotions, and then other times, I wonder if he squashes them down so no one sees them." I slid the metal rings of my garters into place.

"What do you mean?" Nancy asked.

I pulled a satin dress that Nancy's sister had lent me off the hanger and unzipped the back. I was down to borrowing clothes from anyone I could, so I wouldn't wear my same two outfits over and over again on our dates.

"Well, you should see what happens at the club. People come up to him, in the middle of a meal, and ask for his advice on stuff like life insurance or buying property."

"What's he do then?"

"You should hear him! He always starts by asking them more questions, and he keeps right on eating while they talk. Then he chews." I furrowed my brow and acted out the whole performance. "He puts down his knife and fork, leans back, crosses his arms, and gives them his answer, with an explanation, in about ten seconds flat." Nancy zipped me up.

"My gosh, doesn't it make you feel a bit..."

"Stupid—yes!"

Nancy laughed. "That wasn't what I meant."

"What I really feel is guilty," I admitted. "As though I'm using him."

"So are you?" Nancy asked bluntly.

"Not intentionally. But I wouldn't see the inside of a movie theater or a restaurant again if it wasn't for him."

"How are things in the romance department? Has he moved past his one kiss quota?"

I paused, my lipstick poised at my mouth.

"You're blushing!" Nancy pointed at me. "There must be something going on, or you wouldn't be as red as your lipstick."

"Romance...okay. That's what I mean about emotions. Yes, we've moved to a few more kisses, but just when he's getting a little more eager, he stops."

"That's because he's a gentleman."

"Maybe. Sometimes I think he's more interested in looking perfect than in what he really wants in his own heart."

"Maybe he doesn't know what he really wants."

"I doubt that. I get the feeling he knows what he wants, but he tries to ignore it so he can keep his appearances. If he wins the election, he'll be going to Ottawa this summer."

"Speaking of summer, do you know we only have four weeks of school left?"

Nancy massaged the side of her belly with the heel of her hand.

"Know it? It's all I think about. I told you I'd be out by the end of the month—and I will. God, I wish I had a job lined up for next year."

"Well, as of this summer, I'm no longer a teacher either. I'm a mommy."

"You'll be a great one too, but have you ever thought about doing both? You don't have to quit just because you have a baby."

"I know. I've thought about it. It seems like I'm wasting my education if I'm not going to work. Then again, I don't know if I'd want to leave the baby with someone else all day."

"Maybe your mom could help you," I suggested.

"My mom would hit the roof," Nancy shook her head at the thought of it. "'Mothers and babies are meant to be together'," she mimicked her mother's voice. "'Even animals know that much.'"

I could already imagine the deluge of handmade bonnets and blankets this baby would get from grandmothers and aunts. For the first time, I wondered who, if anyone, would do that for me if I ever had a baby. Nancy's life just seemed to grow fuller, with more people to love and love her back. I had been away from home for almost a year, and I didn't have much to show for it. My parents' lives, which I used to think so stunted, were starting to look pretty good. They had neighbors and friends from the church. My dad had a job he could count on. When I left for Kingston, I had thought I was going to save myself from the disappointment of their—had I really called it pathetic?—life. My stomach growled with hunger, and I was relieved to hear the tap on the door that signaled William's arrival.

"I have two surprises for you," William told me as he waved thanks to another vehicle letting him pull into traffic.

"Is it anything about George Knowles?"

"No, poor Georgie won't be surfacing for a while yet. What made you think of him?"

"Nothing, really."

Nothing, unless of course you count my father's heart attack, getting attacked by thugs, Mrs. M's death, and living in poverty—all surprises compliments of George Knowles.

"Do you like surprises?" he asked.

"Depends." I was cautious, still caught up in the events of the past few months and not willing to let William know the extent of my problems.

So you're willing to go out with him every week but afraid to tell him what your life's really like. So are you using him? It was Nancy's voice I heard, but it was the question I asked myself every weekend. No, I'm protecting myself.

"So why don't you tell me, and then they won't be surprises anymore," I added logically.

"Smart girl," his tone was warm, and I realized that this feeling, right here, was the answer to Nancy's question about what I saw in him. I liked the way he made me feel when I was with him. He approved of me, at least the parts of me that I let him see.

"Surprise number one is that tonight's dinner will be served at 817 Kensington Street, and the unrenowned chef is," he tapped out a drum roll on the steering wheel, "William Buchanan."

"I didn't know you could cook."

"I don't know if I can. Tonight we'll both find out. Besides, I thought it might be time for you to see that I really do have a home.

Unlike me, who will be without one in less than a month.

"Great! And the second surprise?"

"I've been invited to speak to a group of school kids about the election and explain how voting works."

"That's wonderful!"

"Guess where?"

"My school?"

"You got it! Limestone Elementary, Monday morning at eleven o'clock."

"How'd that happen?" I asked, already a bit panicky about him seeing me at my job.

"It was Ray's idea. Teaching civic duty and all that stuff—none of the other candidates are doing it, so we may get a mention in the *Whig*," he shrugged.

"Mr. Wallace agreed to it?" I asked.

"Yeah, once we finally got hold of him, he was all for it."

"That guy disappears faster than Houdini, and then he just shows up again. Never explains where he's been."

"Maybe he's sneaking off to see his girlfriend," William offered suggestively.

"You obviously haven't met Mr. Wallace."

"No, we'll meet Monday morning. Here's my place." He turned the car into the driveway of a substantial red brick home fortified by a foundation of quarried limestone.

Thoughts of Mr. Wallace flew out of my head as William led me up the wide stairs to the generous front porch. Reflexively, I compared it to the sloped and peeling structure on the front of Mrs. M's house, where George's friends had met their Waterloo. Now, standing on another porch, about to enter a different home, I realized how much I missed coming home to a real house every day.

And what a house it was! I entered a vestibule, which opened into a center hall with a heavily patterned oriental carpet over rich dark wood. The word "gracious" must have been conjured for this type of home. Although when I turned to the right and took in the mahogany dining table and twelve upholstered leather chairs the color of oxblood, I thought "affluent" would work well too. To the left of the hall was a wide living room whose focal point was a raised marble hearth under a deep mantle. A bank of tall windows trimmed with heavy moldings gave a view over the porch to the street. I noticed a dark car slowing to a crawl, as if looking for a particular address, or maybe just slowing to admire the elegance that lined the street.

Play your cards right, you could be living on Kensington Street. Did Nancy really believe that? Could she be right?

Trees bright with spring leaves grew on the boulevard that ran down the center of the street, so a direct view to the neighbor's house was discreetly refocused by the greenery. At the opposite end of the living room, a tall pair of French doors with panes of beveled glass opened into a smaller room, a den, I supposed, although I'd never been in a house with a room that qualified as a den.

"Well, here it is," William announced, "the old homestead."

"It's beautiful," I complimented him. I didn't want him to know it was the most opulent house I had ever been in.

"Well, it's home. Come on in, and let's see how the masterpiece in the kitchen is progressing."

"I don't smell anything cooking," I ventured, as I followed him through the dining room and through a swinging door to a more modestly sized kitchen.

"I don't either. I think I should be worried about that," he tried to joke, but I noticed his jaw clench when he said it.

"What are we having?"

"We're supposed to be having roast Cornish game hens, stuffed with wild rice. And," he added, checking his watch, "they should have been finished cooking in another eight to ten minutes."

"That's pretty exact timing for a guy who doesn't cook much."

I spied an open cookbook on the table and pretended to check it out while William looked over the sophisticated dinner. I had a sinking feeling that I wouldn't know how to eat it, even if it was ready.

"There must be something wrong with the oven; it's still cold." He didn't sound pleased. "I put those birds in an hour ago, and they should have been ready—"

"I know," I smiled, "in eight to ten minutes. Does it matter if we eat an hour later? Do you have to be somewhere tonight?"

"No, I don't have to be anywhere." He ran a hand over his hair and down the back of his neck. "Are you always this calm when things go wrong?" he asked, and I recognized what I thought was a touch of admiration in his voice.

"This? This is what it looks like when 'things go wrong' in your life?"

"I just had it all planned, you know." He sounded put out. "Now I suppose this thing has blown a fuse." He turned his attention toward the oven.

"Probably just the shock of actually being used," I joked, moving to the immaculate stovetop beside him.

"Well, I had everything perfectly timed, and now it's all loused up, and I have to find which fuse is burned out, and hope I have the right size to replace it."

"Or you could just turn the oven on," I suggested with a sly smile.

"I did. See, it's set to three hundred and fifty degrees."

"That's the thermostat, but to get it working, you have to actually turn this." I reached for the dial and clicked it into place.

His expression turned from incredulity to disgust. For a moment, I thought I'd offended him by showing him where he had gone so obviously wrong.

"Unbelievable incompetence," he sputtered.

"Oh, don't be so hard on yourself," I said, determined to make light of it all.

"I'm not talking about me. I mean the design of that oven. What kind of lamebrain would build something that takes two dials to turn it on?" he asked.

"I think all ovens are made that way. What's the problem? Now you've learned something, and we can spend an hour or so talking while the chickens cook."

"Cornish game hens," he corrected me. "And just for the record, only a woman would put up with an appliance made that way."

Frank O'Donnell drove his car along Kensington Street for the third time in an hour. When he saw Eleanor get into the Buick with

Buchanan, he'd expected to follow them to some political event. Eleanor lived with Ray and Nancy, and Ray was tied up in Buchanan's campaign—it would make sense if Eleanor went along too. But Ray and Nancy were nowhere in sight, and the Buick had been driven straight to Kensington Street and was staying put. Clearly they hadn't simply stopped in to pick something up and leave.

Would Buchanan be able to get her to go for him? He was too old for her. "Probably in there right now trying to explain the British North America Act to her," Frank muttered and smiled to himself.

Frank tried to reconcile that with the Eleanor he knew. The one who laughed out loud with her mouth open and her head flung back. Then there was the whole mess she had created by visiting George Knowles in prison and then fending off George's buddies. Even at twenty-two, Frank considered himself a pretty good judge of character. He suspected that Eleanor's soft heart would guarantee her a lifetime of mishaps. She really did need someone with a steady hand to steer her through. Whatever attraction she had, if any, to William Buchanan, it wouldn't last long. She wouldn't be enough of a thoroughbred for him, and she would soon see what a nervous Nellie he was.

He drove to the top of Kensington, through the Queen's University campus, instinctively keeping an eye out for pretty students, and then he turned the car toward the familiar turf of the Wellington tavern.

Solutions

"What do we have to listen to this guy for?" Carlos Arruda, whose command of English had grown incredibly quickly, whined on Monday morning.

"This guy is named William Buchanan, and he's going to explain why it's important to vote when you grow up," I explained patiently.

"So I'll hear him when I grow up. I don't want to miss recess for this. I want to play ball."

"I know. Finally we've got some glorious spring weather out there. Maybe we could have our physical training class outside this afternoon. What would you think of that?"

Carlos ricocheted around the class, telling the others that Miss Cole promised they could go outside for PT. I didn't bother reminding him that a suggestion is a long way from a promise, and instead concentrated on herding the group into the gym to hear William.

Mr. Wallace introduced William and then retreated to a seat where he crossed his thin legs, revealing a band of pale skin above the sock line.

"Does William always look this good," Nancy whispered, "or is it just because he's sitting next to Mr. Wallace?"

I elbowed her a warning to be quiet.

The children listened attentively—for about five minutes. Then they began to fidget. At the ten-minute mark, Mr. Wallace warbled a warning and reminded them that Mr. Buchanan was a guest and deserved to be treated well.

I noticed Ray making a discreet slashing motion across his throat to signal William, who was sharp enough to wrap up quickly. "In conclusion, Mr. Wallace, boys and girls, thank-you for inviting me to Limestone Elementary. And I would like to finish by inviting a friend of mine to come up to the front. That's okay by you, Mr. Wallace, isn't it?"

Mr. Wallace appeared puzzled, but nodded primly.

"He probably wants to thank you for getting him in here," I whispered to Nancy.

William's voice, strong from daily speeches on the campaign, called out, "Is Miss Cole, the grade two teacher, here?"

The boys and girls from my class pointed excitedly in my direction.

"Oh, there she is," as if noticing me for the first time. "Miss Cole, would you mind coming up here? I have something I want to ask you."

A man with baggy pants, carrying a large camera, entered the gymnasium by way of the side door.

William's going to corner me into saying which party I'll vote for, I just know it.

The photographer spoke quietly with a teacher who was slouched against the wall and then picked his way through the tangle of students sitting on the floor.

"Boys and girls," William continued when I reached his side. "I came here to ask all of you a very important question. I asked you, 'Will you vote when you grow up?' And what's your answer to that question?"

The children sensed that things were taking a turn for the interesting; even a newspaper reporter was in the building.

"Yes!" they called out, agreeably, if not exactly enthusiastically.

"I didn't hear you. Can you say it louder?" William goaded them.

"Yes!" they shouted in one voice.

Flushed by his success, William put a hand on my shoulder and drew me closer to him. "Well, that's just one question I came here to ask. But I'm sure hoping I get the same answer to my second question."

Smoothly he reached into his pocket and dropped to one knee. I scanned wildly around and found Nancy, and we shared a moment of disbelief as our eyes locked above the heads of the students seated on the floor of the gymnasium.

He can't be doing this. We haven't even talked about this.

I turned my attention back to the man in front of me. William had opened a tiny box, covered in royal blue velvet, and displayed its contents for me. I turned to look at Mr. Wallace, who had moved to the edge of his chair, his right ankle now tucked behind his left shin, looking like he was about to drill himself into the floor. Beneath tightly pressed lips, his neck was covered with blotches.

He is. He's going to ask me to marry him. What am I supposed to say?

In slow motion, as if I was swimming up from the bottom of a pool, I craned to see Ray. He stood, arms folded, shaking his head admiringly with an "I can't believe he's actually pulling this off" expression. The photographer, his face hidden by the camera, was poised to catch the carefully composed shot.

That's when I heard William's voice. Strong, confident, like a director showing an actor how to deliver well-rehearsed lines.

"Miss Eleanor Cole," he paused, and reached for my left hand, "would you do me the honor of becoming my wife?"

"Ah...," I stammered. "I–I don't know what to say."

If William was disappointed with my response, he didn't betray it. Everything about him, from his broad smile to his blue eyes, bright with excitement, told me he expected a positive response.

"Say yes," he answered simply.

The diamond glinted where he held it, a few inches from my hand. The children closest to us heard William and repeated his words. "Say yes," they pleaded, "Say yes." The words gained momentum, and soon every child at Limestone Elementary was chanting and clapping in a primal rhythm.

"Say yes, say yes, say yes!"

I felt like I was riding the crest of the words, afraid to slip into the trough of the waves that were building and moving me inexorably in a direction that shocked me.

Marry you? I hardly know you. How many dates have we actually had?

"Say yes, say yes!"

How would I explain this to my parents? They've never even heard of William Buchanan. And what about Frank? Why was I even thinking of him?

"Say yes, say yes!"

I shot another look at Nancy, who shrugged as if to say "It's up to you," and suddenly I knew she was right. It was up to me. I was completely on my own, engulfed by the chanting. I stood there, dizzy and light-headed, watching every face in the school come into focus only to blur again into a watery mass in front of me. William Buchanan's hand reached out for me in a way that made me remember the boy from the quarry.

There was no more room for me at Nancy and Ray's, no money to afford another Mrs. M's, and my parents hadn't heard of William Buchanan because they didn't speak to me. In four weeks, I would be out of a job. George Knowles would be out on parole in a few months, and it would only be a matter of time before he or his buddies caught up with me again. I seemed to hear Mrs. M saying, "You'll have to find it for yourself, by yourself, and in your own time." So was this "it," or was I just desperate to be rescued? It felt like my survival depended on grabbing this chance.

William Buchanan was on one knee, asking me to marry him. Everything I knew about him told me that if he thought it would be a good match, I should trust his judgment. After all, my own had landed me a month away from the poorhouse.

DIVISIONS

"Say yes, say yes!"

William detected the moment I shifted from hesitation to acquiescence, and he slipped the ring onto my finger. The camera flashed, and the smell of a spent bulb filled the air.

"Yes," I said quietly. "I'll marry you."

He was on his feet. "Could you say it louder?"

I honestly didn't know whether I could or not. It didn't seem to matter.

He folded me into a suffocating embrace, and the children around us cheered. The round little blonde pulled off her glasses and knuckled her eyes. Carlos Arruda appeared to be the lone dissenter in the group. He held his hand protectively against his throat. His dark eyes were narrow, and he shook his head ever so gently.

Reactions

Dear Mom and Dad:
By the time you get this letter, my name will be Eleanor Buchanan. I am getting married on June 16th, two days before the election. My husband-to-be is William Buchanan. He's is the Liberal candidate here, so if he's lucky, he'll become a member of Parliament on the 18th.
Everything is happening so fast, but not because of what you might think. I'll be leaving teaching at the end of June. I really love it, but William says he's well able to support me, and I'd just be taking the food from someone else's table. I suppose he's right—still, I did think I was just beginning to get the hang of it.
I know I went to Kingston against your wishes, and you told me not to come back. But I hope we can let bygones be bygones. As you can see, everything is working out for the best, so I hope

you'll come and see us at our house (I've got to get used to saying that!) at 817 Kensington Street.

Love
Eleanor

"Kensington Street? Where is that, Gib? I don't remember ever seeing Kensington Street."

"Probably over on Snob Hill. More 'n likely that's where a member of Parliament would live."

Joyce looked at the letter again. "Like it says here, 'if he's lucky.'" It was as close as she would get to contradicting Gib.

"Well, the Tories already got my vote today, so I don't know how lucky this Buchanan is going to be." Gib was working out a crossword at the kitchen table and didn't lift his head to look at his wife.

Joyce attempted to step gingerly around the trip wires this letter had laid across their kitchen. One of the few dreams she'd had left had just evaporated. She bit her bottom lip, but the tears came anyway.

"I'll bet she was a beautiful bride."

"Prob'ly was." Gib's chin was tucked tight against his chest, and Joyce saw his shoulders shake, trying to stay strong. She knew him well enough to know he was thinking the same thing she was. The only girl he'd ever be able to walk down the aisle took that walk without him—and it was his own damn fault.

"Will we go to see them?" Joyce asked timidly.

Gib coughed and cleared his throat roughly. He wiped a knuckle under his nose a couple of times. "Maybe in the fall, Mother, for her birthday."

It was early evening before Frank O'Donnell got to the Wellington and settled into his favorite seat to read the newspaper.

DIVISIONS

He had a mouthful of beer when he spotted the photograph. It ran under the headline "Buchanan Wins Twice," showing a grinning newlywed couple emerging from the stalwart doors of Sydenham United Church. The sidebar told how a distinguished young lawyer from Kingston became a bridegroom and an elected member of Parliament all in the same week.

Frank fought to keep his breathing steady and pressed his fingers under his armpits to keep his hands from shaking. He tipped his chair back and rocked it gently on two legs. He caught a movement in the top corner of the grimy window. A spider made its unrelenting way toward a fly, trapped in a web. Frank eased the chair down to the floorboards and took another swig of draft.

"Anything more I can getcha, Frankie?" He looked up to find Kingston's most agreeable barmaid ready to serve him.

"No, Shelagh, I don't think there is." He lifted his glass as if in toast. "I believe I have everything a man could ask for."

The wedding photograph was clipped carefully and placed in leather bound scrapbooks in several fine homes in west Kingston. One reader, deprived of scissors but ensconced in some of Kingston's prime lakefront real estate, creased the newspaper carefully and then gingerly tore it, splitting the image of the bride apart from the groom. He smoothed the clipping carefully and tucked it into the pages of First Corinthians, in the New Testament he was allowed to keep in his cell.

He studied the photograph until there wasn't a detail he couldn't reproduce in his mind's eye. The hand that held the bouquet, dense with white roses, that hand had touched him. The lips, which in the picture were parted in a wide smile—his name had been spoken by those lips, and he felt, more than remembered, the utter joy of simply watching her mouth as she spoke kind words intended solely for him.

The rest of the paper he crumpled into a tight ball and threw it against the wall of his small home.

"Buchanan, you thieving bastard!"

The man quickly paced the length of the room and slammed his fist against the wall.

"She came here to see me. Wouldn't have met you at all if it weren't for me."

"Keep it down in there," a voice called from the next room.

"Shut up yourself!" The man tore the mattress off his own bed and flung it to the floor.

Heavy footsteps approached and stopped at the entrance to the disheveled room.

"If you plan on getting out of here anytime soon, you watch yourself, Knowles."

CHAPTER ELEVEN
Victory Party

I practically vibrated as I walked with my husband of two days toward the entrance of the Cataraqui Golf Club.

"I'm not sure many girls would be as understanding as you've been," he said to me.

"I've been understanding about a lot of things. Which one specifically are you trying to thank me for?" I teased him.

"For agreeing to a victory party instead of a wedding reception."

"Instead of a wedding reception? I agreed to that?" I bantered. "I thought this would do until we could have a reception."

"We'll see," he said, deliberately noncommittal. We arrived just as results from a blaring television set were read by the mellifluous-voiced CBC announcer.

"Prime Minister John Diefenbaker will be returning to Ottawa with a minority government. Lester Pearson, leading the Liberals, has made inroads into the Tory stronghold, but his party remains in opposition. One bright spot for the Liberals has been the riding of Kingston, where William Buchanan, a young lawyer, was elected with a wide margin over the incumbent."

A whoop of approval erupted from the gathering, and William was kissed, backslapped, and embraced in victory.

People I recognized from the club and from our wedding surrounded him. I knew these were the ones who had contributed money or who had stuffed envelopes or walked door-to-door with him. They'd helped him realize his dream, and I wondered what I had to do with any of that. I looked over at him and saw what he must have looked like as a little boy. It felt like a glimpse of how our own son might look, and I warmed to the image instantly. He pushed his hair off his forehead, like a little leaguer taming a cowlick. Then I saw something that was new to me. He looked confused, lost, as though he might cry. I moved closer to him. "What's wrong?"

He seemed to hear my voice as something that came from off in the distance. But he did turn toward me.

"They've all worked so hard for this." His voice filled with bewilderment. "They did it to help me. Why? Why would they do that? I'm just really grateful. Humbled, actually."

Before I had a chance to reply, we were separated by the crowd, who wanted to wish him well and get him to the platform to speak. William worked his way across the room full of red and white "Vote Buchanan" signs. I stayed near the back, and Nancy edged her way to my side. She looked exuberant. "How are you two doing?" I pointed to my friend's belly to include the baby.

"Never better," she beamed. "And you?"

"Overwhelmed," I answered honestly.

A buzz was coming from the front of the room, and I realized that William was up on the platform and signaling to me to join him. Before I knew what was happening, Ray and a couple of other men created an opening in the crowd for me. All I saw on my way up was a blur of red and white and my own feet taking me in a new direction. I stepped up to his side, and a cheer rose from the crowd. William presented me to the mass with a gesture that said "Look what I brought home," and they roared their approval.

I felt like his raven-haired trophy, wearing a dress of Liberal red topped by a white *peau de soie* jacket. I knew there hadn't been a time in my life, including my wedding a couple of days ago, when I felt more radiant. Only one thing could have made it better: if I could have looked into that crowd and found my parents faces staring up at me. William delivered his victory speech with my hand clasped in his own, and I wanted my parents to see that. I wanted to show them what someone else, someone important, thought of me.

I tuned in just in time to hear William's conclusion.

"I know how much each of you has done to help me. You've pounded in lawn signs, made phone calls, and took a chance on me. I just ask that you don't leave until I speak to each of you personally. I intend to be the last one to leave this party tonight. I want to shake every hand in the place before I go home."

When he finished, he pulled me toward him for a kiss.

"You're a political wife now, Mrs. Buchanan."

"I guess I am. I just hope I don't embarrass you."

He winced when I said that. It was just a flicker, but enough to confirm the accuracy of my words.

"You won't."

But it was a tepid reassurance at best, and we both knew it.

I hadn't meant to drill into the nerve William thought he'd kept so well hidden. Not tonight, at least. Not when he was so assuredly at the top of his game. But that was just it. I felt like I wasn't in the game.

Nothing in Faderton could have prepared me for the graces I would need to keep company with women who were raised to be deferential wives of doctors and lawyers. They'd grown up learning to play tennis and golf. They understood the need to comply with the rules of their culture. Rules that, for example, forbade them from using the golf greens during times men claimed them for themselves. They learned the value of volunteering for the right charities. They chose their clothes and words with caution, to earn the approval of the men in their lives. My ways were unvarnished. While I knew it might make me a hit with voters on the streets, I had produced a few sidelong glances from members at the club. Now that he was elected, William had already insisted that we both remember his position when we stepped out into the community. Remember it? I wondered if I'd ever be able to forget it.

Nancy and Ray, flushed with victory, interrupted my thoughts with great, celebratory bear hugs for both of us. "Let's mingle," Ray shouted, and the four of us stepped off the platform and waded into the party. A well-dressed man and woman pushed toward us.

"I've seen these two before. They've never wanted to talk to me until tonight," I said to Nancy through teeth clenched into a smile.

The woman wore a three-strand set of pearls, and her black hair was pulled tightly back from her face.

"Billy! Congratulations!"

William made the introductions to Tom and Cookie Carrothers.

"Cookie and I have known each other since grade one," he said, placing his arm around her tanned shoulders.

"Eleanor," Cookie enthused, "some of the girls and I are looking for a fourth for curling in the fall. Would you join us?"

DIVISIONS

"That sounds lovely. You do realize the only thing I've ever curled is my hair."

Everyone laughed, and Tom assured me by saying, "There'll be lots of first timers when this new rink opens. You'll be fine."

"Do you golf here in the summer, Cookie?" I asked, copying the insider small talk of the other women.

"Tom gets in a few rounds. Me, I pick up the kids on the last day of school, and we cottage all summer in the Gatineaus."

"Well, I'll see you in the fall then," I responded. "I'll be looking for things to do. William leaves for Ottawa in September."

"William?" Cookie repeated incredulously. "Is that what you make this sweet young thing call you, Billy?"

"She can call me anything she likes, just not late for dinner."

Nancy stayed close to me while William and Ray glad-handed the guests and made a stream of introductions. I leaned close to Nancy, "Cookie cottages. You'd think she'd know a verb from a noun wouldn't you?"

Nancy's guffaw was almost lost in the commotion. Almost, except it was just loud enough to catch William's attention, and he shot us a stern look.

"We better behave." Nancy dramatically straightened her shoulders and took on a look of mock propriety.

"You're absolutely right. I mean, I wouldn't want to be caught having fun now that I'm a political wife."

The Home Front

It was almost September. The first since I was six years old when I wasn't counting the days to go back to school. The calendar that governed my life had been overturned, and I had nothing to replace it with. Nothing tangible, anyway.

One Friday evening, William came home from work while I was up on a ladder replacing the tear-shaped crystals on the dining room chandelier.

"What are you doing?" he asked.

"Cleaning your mother's chandelier."

"You did it again."

"Okay, okay, our chandelier. Look how this sparkles and breaks up the light like a prism." I held the dazzling crystal up to the late afternoon sun, enjoying the effect of a fine piece of craftsmanship.

"You shouldn't be doing that," William said.

"Why not? It needs to be cleaned. What am I supposed to do all day if I don't clean?"

"There must be something you'd rather do than clean. Aren't they looking for tournament volunteers over at the club?"

I exhaled in a huff.

"What's so bad about the golf club?"

"Boring. The women all talk about their perfect children and their golf scores and what they bought last week at Jackson Mativier." I exaggerated the name to make it sound more French and cultured. And, if I was honest, just to bug William a bit because he expected me to shop there too.

He ignored my jab.

"So do something else," he suggested. "Whatever you'd like."

"I'd like to teach school."

"We both know Edwin Wallace has removed that option."

I hated the memory of the last ugly encounter with Mr. Wallace in his office, right after the June assembly. He dragged up the subject of the Huron Carol at the Christmas concert, and accused me again of putting the children at risk by not telling him I was being stalked. He dredged up the reprimand he'd given me for arriving at school in a police car. Then he accused me of cooking up the proposal scheme so my boyfriend could get some publicity for his flagging political campaign. Even two months after the encounter, I burned with shame at the memory, and my eyes stung with tears.

"I'm sorry," William said. "Sometimes I forget that everything in the world isn't a legal battle."

I could see he was embarrassed, and I wanted to save him from that. After all, marrying him had solved everything. Nancy had teased me about moving out of their three-story walk-up straight to "Quality Heights." George Knowles and his pals weren't likely to find me now that I wasn't teaching at Limestone Elementary.

"It's okay," I answered him gently. "I just wish I was doing something useful."

"You are. You're making a home for us."

I moved, down off the ladder, and put my arms around William's neck.

"That's one of the things I love about you. You have a generous streak a mile wide."

"Don't let anyone know about it, all right? It'll ruin my reputation as a hard-driving lawyer."

"Is that what you are?"

"Hardly. There's not much I like to avoid more than a courtroom. Too much anxiety and people's lives hung out for everyone to see in a court."

"You don't find that intriguing? Kind of like some juicy gossip?" I asked, folding up the ladder.

"No, I don't. I like a nice predictable life, with a beautiful wife to come home to."

"Good. Because your beautiful wife is dying for some company. Are you ready for supper?"

"Dinner," he paused and smoothed his tie, "is the fish fry with the mackerel stabbers."

"With the what?"

"The Catholics. The Knights of Columbus. They host our lodge for a fish fry the third Friday of every August. I told you about that."

"Yeah, you did," I conceded, anticipating another lonely evening. "I forgot."

"I put it on the calendar," he persisted.

I nodded, picturing the calendar in the den where William's careful block printing filled every square. He was in front of it now, jabbing his finger at a spot in the middle of a sea of black ink. "See, it's right there, Knights of—"

"I get it! You made your point. I forgot; you didn't. What else is new?"

I snapped shut the step ladder and trundled it to the laundry room. I could hear him pound up the stairs, and predictably, he was back down in ten minutes, shaved and changed into a fresh shirt. He tried to kiss me on his way toward the door, but I dipped out of his reach before he made contact.

"Will you wait up?" he ventured.

"Maybe," I sulked.

Just as the oak door closed behind him, the telephone rang.

"So how's life on Snob Hill?" asked a tired voice.

"Nancy! How are you? Life on Snob Hill? Quieter than yours, by the sounds of things. David sounds like he's kicking up a fuss."

"He's hungry—again. I had no idea one baby could eat so much. All I do is feed him, change him, rock him to sleep, do the laundry, and start all over again. Do you know what I did with my time before he was born?"

"We used to be teachers. We could send them home at four o'clock."

"I think I remember that. Seems like a lifetime ago. Anyway, somebody called for you, and I want to pass on the message."

"Frank O'Donnell?" I felt guilty for the quiver of excitement that ran through me at the thought.

"No, and if he did, I would have just told him you're a married woman now. If he'd 'a wanted you, he shoulda moved faster. It was Mrs. Marsh, from the church you used to go to over here. She needs you to play piano once a week for some social group or something."

"I'd love to."

"Good, because I told her you'd do it. I can't stand thinking about you and your life of leisure, when I'm in a diaper pail up to my elbows."

"When does she want me?"

"Thursday afternoon. One o'clock."

"I'll be there, and I'll bring enough sheet music to keep us going all afternoon. Nancy, you have no idea how much this means to me."

There was no response except for David's caterwauling in the background.

"El? Sorry, I gotta run. Oh yeah, about the music? Mrs. Marsh said to tell you to keep it simple."

I rifled through the sheet music I had brought from home and some that William's mother had. Everything I touched looked like it might work for the sing-along, so the music pile kept growing higher. I hadn't thought to ask what kind of people I'd be playing for. In truth, I didn't care. I had something to do, somewhere all my own to go, and I felt oddly lighter than I had in weeks.

In my dresser, one drawer was filled with the kind of nightgowns William liked me to wear. They were all long and sweeping. At the bottom of the drawer, I'd hidden a list, and I checked it every night to be sure I didn't forget anything. I had washed and ironed the sheets. William couldn't relax if the sheets weren't clean. He also liked four pillows on the bed and liked the window shades to be pulled to just the right height. I had actually made a tiny pencil mark on the frame to mark the distance he wanted the blinds to be from the sill. The house was dark now, and I realized how quickly the short days of fall were coming on us. I thought back to the summer solstice, the longest day—and shortest night—of the year, just three days after our wedding. A wedding night that had been a sign, or as *Roget's* put it, a harbinger of things to come.

The honeymoon suite at the Gananoque Inn was splendid. Double doors opened to a balcony overlooking the St. Lawrence River. Brass fireplace utensils reflected the evening sun, and lacy curtains billowed and puffed at the windows.

William ignored the room and tipped the bellhop, generously, I guessed, judging from the boy's reaction. I watched my new husband move his clothes from garment bag to closet, placing each hanger about three inches from the previous one along the rod. He went into the bathroom while I paced nervously in the bedroom, casting anxious glances at the bed and stifling an urge to giggle. I went to the mirror to admire the sapphire earrings he'd given me. They had been his mother's, and they matched the cufflinks I'd noticed the first day we'd met. His parents had bought them as a set in Paris. I could hear the soft sound of glass-bottled toiletries, as he placed them on a wooden shelf. It was the same sound that thimble-sized glasses made when they were put into the wooden holders after communion.

He emerged from the bathroom in navy pajamas.

"Are you prepared for tonight?" he asked earnestly.

"Ready and waiting."

When he didn't respond, I added, "...and waiting."

"What I mean is—did you bring any protection?"

"Protection?" I feigned innocence. "You're supposed to protect me, now that we're married."

I knew he was uncomfortable being direct with words like "condom" and "gel," but so was I. He put a finger and thumb to his forehead as if trying to ward off a headache.

"Eleanor, it's been a long day, and you know perfectly well what I mean."

The tone was unexpected and reminded me of Mr. Wallace.

"Yes, I do know what you mean. Was I supposed to look after that?"

William looked bewildered. Immediately I could tell that he didn't know, and it only took another second to discern that his pride couldn't tolerate admitting it. I felt like asking him what he expected me to do. Go to the drug store and ask someone? I wouldn't even know what to say.

Instead, unwilling to let anything spoil our wedding night, I rushed into the breach. I was pretty sure that if I could smooth over this rough spot, the rest of the wedding night could be perfect. With rings on our fingers, we could do anything we wanted. I quickly created an elegant solution for getting past this moment.

"William," I took both of his hands in mine. "I don't want any protection."

"What do you mean?"

"I mean, I want to have a baby. If we're going to have children, why not sooner rather than later?"

"A baby? Already? Are you sure about this?"

"Well, let's put it this way. Here we are, neither of us with any protection. If we get a baby out of it, is that so bad?"

William threw his head back in relief. That was the first time I noticed anything about his jaw line. It was starting to sag, just a little, but enough to remind me of the twelve years between us. A slow smile took over his face, and he shook his head in admiration for me, his bride.

"It's a fine plan, Mrs. Buchanan."

"Plan? Yes, well I don't have duplicate copies in writing or anything—but would you be willing to go ahead?"

With his hands on my hips, he pulled me into him and asked, "Does it feel like I'm willing?"

"Willing and able, I'd say."

"Great, now you go have a bath and do whatever it is you women do in the bathroom, and we'll both be ready."

Beyond the bath, I had no idea what "we women do in the bathroom," but whatever it was, I must have done something right. My first night as a Buchanan was filled with unexpected pleasures and pantings that left both of us startled at the ease and relief of pleasing one another. William said he felt like a coureur de bois charting new territory through a jewel of a lake he discovered. Over the next few weeks, he took great delight in traveling that lake, beginning near the edges and shallows and then venturing from the safety of shore. He spent his nights moving around my body, which was placid and serene one moment, then turbulent and churning the next.

As for me, I loved to watch William's face contort and grimace under my ministrations. I learned my way around him, using my hands, mouth, and an instinct that came from somewhere deep and primal. I took his reactions for my markers, knowing that a nip here or gentle pressure there would elicit grateful moans and gasps that he was powerless to repress. He returned my attentions with abandon. What made it best of all was when I considered that this might be the night I would conceive a child. It would be the final step off that cycle of defeat that was my legacy from Faderton.

Yet in the mornings, when I would sidle up to him in the kitchen and comment on the previous night, he would pull away from me.

"Eleanor," he asked me once, "you, uh, you don't tell anyone about, you know, what we do, do you?"

"No. Who would I tell? Besides, everybody does it. That's why the population is booming."

"No, Eleanor," he responded tersely, "everyone doesn't do it—not like us, anyway."

"Well," I smiled, "they should. If every man put his—"

"Stop it!"

It was as if he had slapped me. Without another word, he left for the office.

I spent the twenty-second summer of my life living in a house that felt like someone else's. To escape, I did what I'd always done. I walked. Long solitary marches along the north shore, over the Leslie Causeway and into the grounds of Fort Henry. The first time I went, I paid my money and joined the tour group. I hardly needed to, though, because William had told me all about it. The fort had been built more than a hundred years earlier and was intended to defend Canada against invasion from the United States. But the United States never sent any soldiers to the limestone garrison, and the fort's greatest distinction was that no shot was ever fired from it. Inside the walls, I smiled, because American invaders did eventually come to the fort. Every summer in fact, but they carried cameras, not rifles, and they photographed students in scarlet tunics who reenacted military drills that had never been needed.

After the tour, I intended to leave by skirting the south edge of the property. The road curved past the East Ditch Tower, a structure that overlooked the lake and a tiny island. A dry ditch, at least twenty feet deep, led from the fort to the tower, and I paused to imagine soldiers long ago waiting inside for the marauding hordes of Americans who had never arrived. How did that feel? Waiting for something momentous to happen and then gradually realizing it never would.

I discovered a set of stone stairs that led down, through the weeds, to a wide ledge of rock at the water's edge. I followed the stairs, amazed to find foot-sized indentations worn into the steps. Men, probably my own age, must have run up and down this hidden staircase, rifles ready, watch after pointless watch. I sat on the ledge and stretched my legs out on the sun-warmed rock. I tried to imagine what it must have felt like to be recruited and convinced of the worthiness of their cause. Duped into believing that what they did made a difference. I thought about it until the breeze began to blow cool and raise goose bumps on my arms.

Did any soldiers come to this place when they realized their efforts counted for nothing? Was this how they felt when they realized they'd been deceived?

CHAPTER TWELVE
The Church Basement

Flakes of white paint curled like eyelashes along the boards of the Pentecostal church. I carried a foot-high load of sheet music down to the church hall in the basement. People waited in the long open room that smelled of macaroni and tomato soup. Some cups, still on the table, contained the last of some red Freshie. The mottled green linoleum floor was littered with crumbs and remnants of lunch that made it look like there had been a much larger crowd than the ten or so who waited in the hall. The piano, with a stool that I knew from experience was stuck at a level too high for me, was at the far end of the room.

I made my way tentatively into the room. *Was this the group I was supposed to play for?* A man, balding and with his head tilted at an odd angle, was apparently fascinated with something at the window. He shifted his weight back and forth between his right and left foot, as though marching to orders heard only by him. He held his elbows bent so his hands, open and empty, sagged from wrists that he held at chest height. His eyes were trained on a spot about four inches in front of the glass, where, from what I could see, there was nothing at all.

I jumped when I heard a yelp from somewhere behind me, and I turned to see a young girl writhing and twisting in a wheelchair. The girl was unusually pretty, and it was easy to imagine that but for this cruel trick of nature, she would have been lithe as a cat. A tired-looking woman, bent at the waist, was trying to get the girl to make eye contact.

"Are you excited, Annie? Do you like the party? If I go now, will you be a good girl?"

The girl's mouth twisted and gaped open, showing a cracked and swollen tongue. The gums around her teeth were bright with inflammation. She stiffened her back, lifting her pelvis out of the chair in what I thought must be an effort to escape the confines of the seat. Spittle drooled from her bottom lip, and the woman simply wiped her face and chatted to the girl as if she didn't notice anything amiss. With hands turned nearly backwards against the underside of her wrist, the girl batted against the arms of her chair.

I looked away, repulsed and embarrassed. I took another couple of steps toward the piano end of the room, hoping to see a familiar face. A man whose height couldn't have reached five feet clasped shreds of what looked like a towel close to his cheek, like a baby with blanket. Sometimes he dangled it at arm's length, and the grimy fabric, reduced to a series of strings, was marched along a path seen only by the diminutive man, pantomiming the way a child would move a doll through an imaginary adventure.

A kitchen to the side of the hall emitted the companionable clatter of scraping plates and cutlery being washed and dropped into trays. A plump woman wearing a belted dress of blue and lilac flowers bustled out of the kitchen toward me, the piano player. Mrs. Marsh looked as relieved to see me as I was to see her.

"Welcome back!" she enthused.

"Glad to be here." I realized as I said them how utterly truthful those words were. Events at William's church, for that was how I thought of Sydenham United, felt restrained and governed by moderation.

"Our friends here," the woman splayed her hands in the direction of the entire room, "are from different homes in the community." She turned her attention away from me for a moment, "May Wilson—are you still here? You need a break; now get going."

May dabbed at Annie's chin a couple of more times before leaving.

"They're getting together to socialize, and we thought a sing-along would be good for them."

I looked dubiously around at the group.

"But can they? Sing along, I mean."

"Some can. Some just listen and enjoy the music."

I was bewildered. The girl in the wheelchair squealed again, and I moved, careful to get beyond the reach of her lobster claw hands. My own hands gripped the music, and I recognized the same panic I had felt during my first few days at Limestone Elementary.

Mrs. Marsh draped her flowered arm around my shoulder and ushered me to the piano. I was glad no one else tried to touch me as I passed through the group. I arranged my music and settled my hands on the keys. I sounded a couple of chords. Just as I thought. This old beater needed tuning in the worst way, but today's group probably wouldn't care. I swiveled around on the stool, prepared to speak to the little gathering.

"I have song sheets," I began. "Should I hand them out?" A couple more church women, apparently finished in the kitchen, had joined the group, and I directed my question to them.

"Sure, some of us need them." One reached for the sheaf of papers. "But there's at least one person, Betsy, who knows the words to just about anything you can play."

"Really?" For some reason, I felt the need to be jolly. Surely she didn't mean one of the—what was I supposed to call them—patients?

Just then, a flurry of pounding feet came running in from outside, and a short man wearing boys' running shoes came hurtling in.

"Bobby!"

Several voices called out at once, and Bobby managed to look grateful and flustered at his reception, both at the same time.

"Where is Betsy?" the same woman continued as if Bobby's thundering arrival was perfectly normal.

"Here I am," said a voice from behind my shoulder. "You're late," she held up her wristwatch and scolded Bobby.

"Yeah, my brover's fault."

Betsy was an egg-shaped girl who had edged her way up to the piano. I was nervous by the way she had gotten so close to me without my knowing she was there. Yet something about her attracted me instantly. Smooth, almost flat features were perched on a plate-round face, and they gave her an open, innocent visage. Her dark hair, thick and straight, must have been styled with a bowl and a meat cleaver. She was clearly excited for the music to start. Her eyes sparkled uncommonly bright, not with awareness but with something that struck me as pleasant and sweetly simple.

"This my friend," Betsy said pointing toward Annie in her chair. "She listen, I sing."

Her voice sounded like gravel rolling down a hopper. Her tongue was thick, and I wondered how the girl could possibly sing around a tongue that seemed to loll past her teeth and lips.

"You sing and she listens," I repeated. I was glad to have understood that much of Betsy's rapid, breathy speech.

"Yeah. You play."

"Okay. I'll play." I laughed a little too enthusiastically.

"Now," Betsy ordered.

"Betsee-ee," Mrs. Marsh called a warning tone.

"Sorry," Betsy corrected herself. "Now, please."

The flowered dress bobbed in approval.

I hit the opening notes of "Que Sera Sera." The church ladies led off, warbling boldly. From the corner of my eye, I saw one of them try to turn the man at the window toward the action at the piano, but he shrugged her off. She tried again, with the same result, but this time he shouted "No!" Startled, I paused in my playing, and the church women trailed along for another half bar or so. One of them rolled Annie's chair next to Betsy beside the piano.

"Let's try again," I called out with false bravado.

Annie began contorting herself in the chair and making guttural sounds. She flailed her twisted hands and forearms down hard against her thighs. I felt a couple of drops of spit land on my cheek as the girl grunted and chuffed through her drool. Pressing on, I resumed the opening of "Que Sera Sera." Annie let out a primeval wail, and someone tried, unsuccessfully, to quiet her.

I gave the church women a beseeching look, but kept grinding through the music, determined to do my part for the sing-along. I tried using my eyes to communicate a "Get Annie outta here" message, but it didn't work. A tone-deaf good Samaritan stood by Annie, mopping away at the girl's chin, all the while committing serious melodic transgressions. But Annie's noise must have penetrated the wall the marching man had constructed around him. He covered his ears, picked up his pace, and responded with a toneless burr of his own. The little man's towel clutching escalated to flinging it about in wide figure eights, like an exuberant band leader conducting an ensemble using a filthy rag as a baton. The sing-along had degenerated into chaos before we got through the first two verses. On top of it all, Betsy was leaning close to me, insisting on telling me something at this very moment. Her speech, already difficult to decipher, was worse because she was stuttering in agitation. The noise from Annie, the marcher whose every step thumped out a rhythm steady as a metronome, and the tuneless monotone coming from Annie's helper all competed with Betsy and her desire to be heard. I soldiered my way through three verses and four choruses before staggering to the final note.

The cacophony came to a ragged ending. Betsy could not be put off another moment. She reached for my wrist. Her blunt fingers handcuffed my left hand. I looked around for some help, but everyone seemed distracted by their own unknowable mental machinations, while others were distracted by indifference. The church women chatted casually to one another, their charges rocking and crooning contentedly to themselves. I was stunned at the strength of Betsy's puffy hands. I tried to pull my hand back, but Betsy's grip became tighter, and the face that had been unguarded a moment ago took on a ferocity that frightened me. Betsy leaned her face close to mine, and I recoiled, when every instinct I possessed told me she was going to bite me. Betsy's lank hair fell across her face. She growled and seemed to become a creature less than human, but not quite animal. Her fingernails dug into my wrist, and crescents of blood welled through the punctures. Terrified, I vaulted off the piano stool and screamed.

"Stop it! What do you want?"

DIVISIONS

Betsy gasped and drew back, her features a palette of innocence. Slowly her bottom lip protruded. She raised her voice into a thin wail, a noise that irritated like tight shoes on a blister.

Mrs. Marsh rushed toward us and tried to move Betsy away from me. Betsy responded by planting her rear end solidly on the floor, refusing to move. Mrs. Marsh came in behind her and tried to force Betsy to her feet by hoisting under her arms, but the girl was immovable as a parked truck. Tears and mucus spilled from the girl's eyes and nose, creating a slimy sheen across her cheeks.

Annie's neck periscoped slowly in her friend's direction, and she slumped, defeated, into the incarceration of her chair and body. Bobby, with his high forehead and rolling gait, approached the firmly anchored Betsy and tried to comfort her.

"Go away," Betsy snarled at him.

Bobby froze, like a prisoner caught in the glare of a tower search light. Mrs. Marsh stood beside me, both of us helpless to curtail the tantrum Betsy was pitching. Yet when I scanned the rest of the group, I realized that most of them were waiting peacefully or had turned their attention to something else, content to wait out the storm of Betsy's own internal climate system. I was embarrassed, because it was my reaction that had prompted the disintegration of the afternoon. Since Nancy's call, I'd been counting the hours until this afternoon, and now I'd spoiled it. The round girl, still on the floor, decelerated her protests into one, unintelligible word that she repeated like a mantra.

"Jugaboz, jugaboz."

"What's she saying?" I asked Mrs. Marsh.

"I don't know. If only we had more help, you know, people trained in this sort of thing. I thought Betsy would enjoy this more than anybody. Maybe we should just go home."

"Home? No. Sing," Bobby demanded.

"Sorry, Bobby. Betsy is ruining it for everybody. We'll just finish now."

Bobby hung his head.

I felt desperate. For one thing, I didn't want to be the cause of the upset, and I wondered if I'd been gentler with Betsy, maybe we would have avoided this scene. Besides, it was the first time in a month that I'd been excited about doing something, and I didn't want to go home any more than Bobby did.

"Wait," I tried. "Let's at least see if we can figure out what she's saying."

I knelt by the girl, who was sitting cross-legged on the floor. Betsy was doubled over, her face almost touching her thick ankles in a display of alarming flexibility. I touched her shoulder, and Betsy sat up, pouting and blotchy from her crying jag.

"Jugaboz."

"Pardon?" I responded.

"Jugaboz. *Jugaboz*." Betsy said stubbornly. "Annie want Jugaboz."

"I don't know what you mean. Jugaboz—what's that? Bobby, do you know what she means?"

Bobby shook his head.

"You know," Betsy accused me, as if I was being deliberately dense.

Then Betsy began singing and made her message as clear as the crystals that hung from the Buchanan chandelier.

"Jug a Boz, Jug a Boz, Jugga all the way."

Suddenly, I did know. I understood from the flawless melody Betsy supplied. Before she could finish the second line of mangled lyrics, I joined her, singing "Jingle Bells," and Betsy broke into a smile that could have powered the city of Kingston. Annie squealed with pleasure and turned gratefully to her friend who, with great determination, had finally communicated the request. I took hold of Betsy's plump hand, and singing all the while, helped her up and led her back to her post by the piano. Betsy didn't pause, and I joined her where she was, midway through the chorus, and started playing.

I must have done something right. Voices combined, some actually singing, while for others it was more of a moan-along. My sheet music stayed in its neatly arranged pile on top of the piano.

I had to cast back in memory to find the songs I had started out with as a budding pianist. They came back to me as some of the purest music I'd ever played. For the rest of the afternoon, I took requests.

"Row Your Boat."

"Jesus Loves Me."

"Twinkle Little Star."

Voices called out, jumbled at times. Stammering at others, laboring to be heard, but I played until every request was answered and filled in with a few of my own. I couldn't remember when I'd last put in an afternoon so quickly, or when I'd felt this happy.

I was humming "This Little Light of Mine" when Mrs. Marsh approached.

"May Wilson wanted me to give you this." She handed me a plain white envelope addressed to Mrs. Buchanan—Piano Teacher. Inside, a neatly printed note read:

> Dear Mrs. Buchanan: Would you be willing to give piano lessons to one of the girls I look after? Betsy really enjoys music, and I think she could learn some simple tunes if she had someone to show her. I have an old piano,

and I could make sure she practices. Also, how much do you charge for lessons?

May Wilson

"She wants me to teach Betsy to play the piano," I relayed to Mrs. Marsh.

"Betsy does love music," Mrs. Marsh commented.

"I don't know if she loves me, though!" I pointed to the welts on my wrist.

Mrs. Marsh shrugged apologetically. "Betsy doesn't mean anything by that; it's her way of communicating. She tries so hard to make herself understood. Piano lessons," she shrugged and splayed her fingers in the air, "might help her a lot. At least think about it."

I did. All the way home. A group to play for and a new student. I smiled to think that I'd be a teacher again.

Not the way I had thought I would, or to the kind of student I'd envisioned, but still teaching. *So Edwin Wallace, put that in your pipe and smoke it.*

CHAPTER THIRTEEN
Ottawa

William watched the porter swing the luggage up through the September air and into the train that would deliver Eleanor and him to Ottawa for his rookie session of Parliament. The couple climbed aboard and settled into the velvet seats reserved for first-class travelers. Even that sanctuary was permeated with the smell of oil and steel. William inhaled deeply. It was a scent he found thoroughly agreeable for its suggestion of things solid and reliable. Eleanor rested her head on his shoulder. He liked the smell and feel of that too.

"It's going to be nice to sit back and relax for two whole hours," she said.

"It's been a hectic summer, hasn't it?" he agreed.

"I think everybody in Kingston wanted to meet with you at a barbecue this summer. If I had to eat one more piece of chicken, honestly, I think I'd grow feathers."

"So you're discovering what it's like to shoulder the duties of a politician's wife," he teased.

"Yeah, well, there were a few wifely duties I would like to have performed more often, but you're away almost every night. How are we ever going to have a baby? Especially now; I'll only get to see you on weekends."

She kept her voice low for privacy, but he caught the plaintive note embedded in the cautious tones. It rankled.

"So why don't you stay with me for the week? There's no reason you have to be home before Friday is there?"

"Because, I can't. I have Betsy's lesson on Tuesday, and I play piano at the church on Thursday."

"Couldn't you cancel?"

"No. I promised. Besides, it's my work."

William lapsed into silence. The gentle sway of the train and his wife's warm body beside him was the right combination to ease him to the edge of sleep for a few moments. He was awakened by Eleanor, trying to resume the conversation.

"So will you be minister of something once you're sworn in?" she asked him.

William looked at her with a dumbfounded expression.

"I did it again, didn't I?" she said.

"Did what?"

"Said something that showed I'm even more ignorant than you thought I was."

"No, no," he said. "The Canadian political system is kind of complicated. A minister of something is a cabinet member. You only get that when you've been around a long time and you have plenty of clout."

"Oh, sorry."

"Well, I just hope you understand how low I am on this totem pole."

"How low are you?"

DIVISIONS

"If I was any lower, they'd have to cut the grass to find me."

Madelaine

Madelaine Harvey boarded the Ottawa city bus, trudged to the first available seat and wove her blond hair into a braid without benefit of a mirror. She didn't want to see how she looked in the dowdy nylon uniform of the parliamentary cleaning staff. Her family thought this job put her just below the nation's cabinet ministers, even though she had tried to tell them that the closest she got to anyone in power was to clean the latrines of the backbench members of Parliament. At first she thought the job might not be so different from her work at the extraordinary Montebello Hotel in Quebec. But she couldn't have been more wrong.

To an outsider, life as a chambermaid at the Montebello might have appeared drab, but for Madelaine, that hotel was full of companionship and promise—especially compared to the other choices life had offered. One of those choices was a low-eared boy from the next concession, whose family's pig farm bordered that of her father's. The boy had made it clear on their first date that he was looking for a wife—but he wanted a pretty one, not one with broad shoulders and a strong back, like his mother wanted him to find.

Madelaine's other option had been training for the sisterhood at Ste. Anne de Beaupré. More appealing than a life raising litters with low ears, true, but she balked when it came to believing in miraculous cures, no matter how many crutches were abandoned on the pillars of the church.

In comparison, life on the staff at the Montebello was grand. First, there was the hotel itself. Situated on manicured grounds at the edge of the Ottawa River, the hotel was built of massive dark logs, ends whittled to sharp points to resemble a settler's cabin in the forest. But this was no cabin; it was an impressive structure, appointed with rich linens and fine furniture. For Madelaine, it was a refuge where she and the girls on staff shared giddy gossip, whispered in French, about the haughty patrons at the hotel.

Hours spent sweeping carpets and cleaning commodes passed by easily. There was always a story to share over something found in a bedroom that set the girls blushing and giggling over the discovery. One of the bolder girls had one day donned the massive brassiere of a particularly pompous guest and had stuffed it with hotel towels and paraded about while the girls cried and crumpled with laughter.

When another girl's illness got Madelaine promoted to cocktail waitress at the Lobby Bar, she felt sure she had ascended to heaven. Not only did she encounter a whole new clutch of friends, but some of them were young men who charged the atmosphere with anticipation that didn't exist in the housekeeping department. And for the first time, Madelaine got a close-up look at wealth. She'd had no idea waitresses earned such enormous tips! Unfortunately, it was a short-lived career.

"Miss Harvey?" an American guest had drawled, reading her name tag as she served him and his group their third round of Crown Royal.

"Ar-vay," she corrected him gently with the French version.

"Ar-vay? Why'd they put the 'H' there if you don't want people to say it?"

"Hit's French," she had responded patiently.

"Hit's French? Hits?" he yelled. "There's no 'H' on 'Its,' but you say it anyway." He played to his group of fellow Americans.

The men in the group responded with guffaws at their friend's cleverness, and the women with indulgent smiles.

"I can't figure out these Canadians. They stick letters in their words we aren't supposed to say…now the French are addin' in sounds that don't even have letters. What the hell are we supposed to be, mind readers?"

"If I was a mind reader, darling," said the tall redhead closest to him, "I believe I could get through yours awful fast."

Madelaine appreciated the woman's effort, but over the redhead's shoulder, she could see the imperious bearing of Francois, the food and beverage director. He waited to intercept her in the servery off the opulent lobby.

"Mademoiselle Harvey," he hissed at her in French. "It is not our place to correct our guests."

"I thought he'd want to know."

"He doesn't. He doesn't, and I don't, and for that matter, there isn't anyone who cares about your stupid name. You local girls are a disgrace," Francois fumed, while Madelaine waited for the inevitable.

"You came to us from housekeeping, did you not?"

"Yes, sir."

"Well, that's where you belong. You go back to cleaning toilets and making beds, and be grateful I don't kick you out right now."

He'd snatched the serving tray from her. "Make up the drink orders, and I will finish serving these guests myself. Give them the chance to see some sophistication for a change."

The demotion back to housekeeping would have been bad enough, but her father used it as an excuse to send her to relatives in Ottawa and free up another place at the overcrowded Harvey family table.

Now, sitting with slush puddled around her boots, surveying the gray Ottawa landscape, her loss felt sharper. There were no friends to be found on the staff at the Parliament buildings. She worked alone and at night, exchanging only a few odd words of English with the security guards. When she began work, the buildings were emptying of office staff. She recognized the camaraderie of the pretty girls streaming away from their desks while she alone was going into work in the ill-fitting outfit supplied by the government. As for suitable young men, she'd been in town for a month and had yet to spy anything answering that description.

She knew the uniform would soon smell of furniture polish and bleach, and the skin on her hands would become chapped and rough. She looked at those hands, now holding an Ottawa transit map. Elgin Street. Should she say the "g" as in "girl," or "g" as in "gentle?" Probably no one cared; she certainly didn't.

"C'est ma destinée," she sighed as she climbed off the bus outside the House of Commons. With scant English or education, she contented herself wearing the habit of the cleaning staff. But she wondered, when she stepped off the bus, what she'd be doing at this moment if she had gone to the convent or had taken the position of Madame Low Ears. What if this turned out to be even worse?

CHAPTER FOURTEEN
Better than I

In the low light of a November afternoon, Frank O'Donnell caught a glimpse of his own scowl in the Buchanans' hall mirror and deliberately rearranged his features into a neutral pose. Just being in William Buchanan's house made the bile rise, and it burned his throat before he stuffed it back down his esophagus. The sour smell of kitchen garbage didn't improve the place either.

It wasn't simply because his police issue boots were more accustomed to striking asphalt and dirt than brushing across hand-knotted oriental carpets. Police calls usually took him into the hard scrabble sections of Kingston, where the man of the house was either inebriated, absent, or wishing he was. Using nothing more than a uniform that fit loosely at the waist and snugly on the biceps, Frank found it easy to dominate encounters with most men. But William Buchanan, he knew from experience, was not most men.

The lawyer surveyed the damage in his house with his feet planted wide and his hands on his hips. It was the same posture he had assumed in the courtroom when Frank had testified to the nature of George Knowles's record. Frank had listed Knowles's misdemeanors, right back to adolescence, in hopes of putting Knowles in the hoosegaw for a good long time. He recalled the lawyer arguing for a sentence that would see the criminal back on the streets in less than a year. He could still picture Knowles sitting at the defense table, watching William, his own lawyer, with a sneer of contempt. The little weasel had feigned indifference when the judge agreed to the lighter sentence; and Frank wondered why the lawyer bothered to work so hard for the ungrateful jerk. Then again, it was a nice change, seeing William Buchanan struggle for something. He didn't have much practice doing that. When Buchanan had won the case, Frank complained about it to his partner.

The older man had laughed. "What do you care? It's job security for us. Guys like Knowles keep guys like us in a job."

Today, Frank felt a twinge of superiority, knowing that Knowles had been released less than forty-eight hours earlier. A fact he hadn't let Buchanan in on just yet. He decided to focus by asking a predictable set of questions.

"About what time did you come home?" he asked the other man.

William checked his watch. "Exactly twenty-two minutes ago."

"Can you tell if anything was taken?"

"Not that I can see. It's a little hard to determine in all this." He gestured at the bizarre conditions in the Kensington Street rooms. "Who would do something like this? And why?" William asked.

"Maybe you've made some enemies," Frank offered and shifted his chewing gum from one set of molars to the other. He watched the suggestion settle uncomfortably on the lawyer, then resumed with his questions.

"Besides you and your wife, is there anyone who has a key to the house?"

"I don't think so."

"A housekeeper, maybe?"

"No, not since I've been married. I can't think where my wife could be at the moment."

Frank sensed the lawyer's discomfort at being unable to account for his wife. He knew exactly how to form a tiny, knowing smile and then deliberately let a few seconds of silence hang between them in the air.

"So when are you expecting her home?" he finally asked.

"Well, I don't know...exactly. She's usually here when I come back from Ottawa. I took an earlier train today."

Frank left another long pause before picking up with the questions.

"Have you had any unusual telephone calls?"

"Not that I know of, but my wife would know better than I."

Frank paused at the "better than I" phrasing, as if he was about to comment, but let it go.

The Shivaree

I drove home from another Thursday afternoon of playing for "the kids," as I now called them, and glanced at the fingernail scars still visible on the underside of my wrist. It seemed a long time ago. I smiled and hummed the songs, and as I did every Thursday, marveled at the magic of music to transform a mood and soothe troubled spirits. I had tried before to reach out with music, sending it as deep as I could into my mother's world. I had dispatched the notes from my piano, willing them to penetrate where my words could not, but I had failed. These afternoons proved to me that it hadn't been the fault of the music or even of the musician. A willing receiver was required, and the Annies, Betsys, and Bobbys of the world were far more capable in that area than my mother had ever been.

As I drove, I planned the next week's program, when I wanted to introduce more Christmas music. I turned the Buick on to Kensington Street. I was thinking of simple instruments the kids might use to keep a beat with the music. But I was confused for a moment, thinking that maybe I'd turned at the wrong corner. A flashing light from a Kingston Police cruiser was pulsing a rhythm of red light that reflected and refracted in the jagged lead panes of my own front door.

Frank and William turned as one, when they both heard the gritty sound of my shoes stepping on shards of glass from the broken transoms. Whether it was from the shock of seeing the house so obviously damaged or guilt about the flip-flop my heart did when I saw Frank, I wasn't sure, but I stopped, watching them without moving a muscle. For the first time, I saw how similar they were. Both stood solid, like two rocks. One polished and smooth, the other, roughhewn and newly excavated. The thought wasn't fully formed before it disappeared. Why did I think that? They were two men, one tall and fair, the other stocky and dark—totally different. But there was something, a gesture, a mannerism maybe. It was there, and then it was gone.

I crossed the threshold, pulverizing glass with each step.

"Where have you been?" William snapped in my direction.

"What on earth happened here?"

I walked past him into the center hall and tried to take everything in at the same time. I moved like a sleepwalker into the house until the debris on the floor snagged the heels of my shoes. I saw long strips of white fabric scattered about the floor, draped on the chairs, and fluttering from the crystal chandelier. Garbage that I recognized from our own kitchen container was strewn about the house. Coffee grinds, eggshells, grapes that had gone moldy, all were combined with the shredded fabric. A rancid smell that didn't quite qualify as disgusting lingered over it all.

"You haven't answered my question," William fumed.

"Did something explode?" I asked. "I didn't go out and leave something turned on accidently, did I?"

Frank shook his head.

"So what is all this?" I asked again.

There were fabric pieces everywhere. Hundreds of long strands of white cloth. They hung from the stair spindles and lay so thickly on the floor that it was impossible to walk without stepping on the narrow white swatches. In the kitchen, torn strips of material were jammed into the toaster, stuffed into the coffee pot, and forced down the drain. Apple cores from the garbage littered the countertop.

"Who did this?" I asked. "Was it a shivaree?"

"A what?" Frank responded.

"A shivaree. You know, people do this kind of thing to newlyweds."

"Never heard of it."

"Well, friends do it for fun. They sneak in when the couple's away and take the labels off canned food or put itching powder in their bed." I saw William roll his eyes. "Sometimes they unwind rolls of toilet paper and string it about the house like this. But they wouldn't break the windows, and besides—"

"Sounds like something that would pass for fun in Faderton," William interrupted.

"They don't do that here?"

"No, Eleanor, no one does that here."

Frank's eyes danced back and forth between William and me, as if he'd caught the scolding tone I'd heard too often.

William broke in on my thoughts.

"You remember Frank O'Donnell, don't you?"

"Of course I do. Sorry Frank, how are you?"

"Mrs. Buchanan," he nodded, careful to keep it formal. "You were Miss Cole when we met before, I think."

"I was. Now I'm not sure what I am. What happened?" I asked again.

"That's what we're trying to figure out," Frank answered.

His partner stepped into the kitchen from the back verandah.

"What did you find, Stan?"

"Nothing much. Pry marks on the door, nothing else broken that I could see."

My senses must have been on high alert, but there was something about Stan that I recognized, but couldn't quite place. I remembered meeting him in the patrol car at Mrs. M's, when they questioned me about George Knowles. But even then, there was a memory that slipped from me like a bar of soap in the bathwater. I was interrupted just as the connection felt like it was going to happen.

"So, nothing stolen. The silver cabinet's full, the jewelry's still on the dresser." Frank lifted his chin as he spoke and scratched at the dark stubble on his throat. "And nothing broken, except the window, which the intruder probably used to escape through. Yet somebody took time to rip up white sheets or something and strew them around the house like this."

"It's not sheets," I said. I knelt down and picked up the fabric, examining it closely. I darted up the stairs, confirming what I already knew in my heart. I could hear Frank and William start up after me. I met them at the top of the stairs, cradling an empty garment bag.

"Now what?" William asked.

"It's my dress."

"You think someone broke in to steal a dress?"

I lifted a strip of the satin fabric that trailed over the railing.

"This," I held the piece aloft. "All this—it's my wedding dress."

When Stan suggested that they question us separately, Frank agreed and stayed with me. I stood rooted to the landing near the top of the stairs, my hand on the baluster for support.

"Mrs. Buchanan—"

"Don't be ridiculous, Frank."

"Your husband-" he looked around to see if William was within earshot.

"Don't worry. All he knows is we met that day at the penitentiary."

"That's it? Did you tell him about the phone call and your dad's heart attack?"

"Nope."

"How about the scrap over at Mrs. M's?" Frank ticked quickly along what William didn't know.

"No."

"You tell him about the rides to school?"

I shook my head. I got the impression that he was enjoying the sense of collusion he and I shared.

"What would have been the point of dragging it all up?" I asked in a voice just above a whisper.

"Eleanor—what was the point of keeping it hidden?"

The desperation on my face told him all he needed to know. William Buchanan had arrived with a deep, soft safety net for me to land on, and I had dropped into it thankfully. Frank waited for my answer. My shoulders were hunched with tension, and I caught myself fiddling with the rings on my left hand.

"It's hard to explain," I started.

"Try it. You're the one always looking for the right way to say a thing."

"It's just—he's never made a mistake in his life—not that I know of anyway. He already thinks he's married to a dunce. Why offer him any more evidence?"

"Well, in that case, he has made a mistake."

"Marrying me?"

"No, thinking you're a dunce."

Frank's Irish charm had found its mark, and I was grateful to let it work its magic while he got down to business.

"So, back to work here. Would you mind showing me where the dress was?"

I led him up the last couple of steps and toward the bedroom I shared with William. I thought of what we did in that room, and letting Frank in, no matter how detached and formal he was acting now, made me feel awkward.

"It was in our closet," I said, pointing from the hallway.

"Is this your room?" he asked, pausing at the doorway.

I nodded and waited in the hall while he looked around and took some notes.

He came back, notebook still open.

"Any idea who might have done this?" he asked.

"None at all."

We moved to the landing again. Frank didn't look around the house the way I had when I first saw it. He seemed determined not to comment on it. The landing was the size of a small bedroom, and he ran a thick finger along the mahogany banister that I polished to a sheen every week. For people like us, who weren't raised in houses like this, it was hard work to resist admiring the place, but Frank was trained like a poker player not to react. Still, there was that finger straying along the wood.

"This break-in seems specifically directed at you. Have you made any enemies?"

"Enemies? I'm not sure I'd call him an enemy, but Mr. Wallace didn't exactly start a fan club for me."

"Your principal?"

"Ex-principal; he fired me. Then of course, you know all about George."

"And speaking of Knowles, what's your relationship with him now?"

"There's nothing. I haven't been in touch with him since that first day."

"Has he contacted you at all?"

"No. He wouldn't know where I am now anyway."

"He might."

"How could he?"

"Well, your wedding picture was splashed in the paper not too long ago. Don't you think Knowles would take an interest, when the only female visitor he had all year winds up marrying his lawyer?"

"Oh my lord." I sat down on the top step and put my head in my hands.

"Eleanor, he was released two days ago. This incident, within forty-eight hours of George getting out—let's just say it would be one hell of a coincidence if they weren't connected."

He maneuvered his way past me and sat a couple of stairs down, so he could see my face.

"Where were you this afternoon, Eleanor?"

"At the church."

"You didn't meet up with George?"

"Absolutely not. Why would I?"

"Well, I know you were on a mission of mercy, and sometimes people like you wind up helping more than is reasonable—or safe."

"I know. I thought I could help him, but I was in over my head."

William and Stan came from the kitchen, back to the hallway.

"Maybe you'd be better off sticking with your church work," Frank smiled.

"What work is that?" William wanted to know.

Frank and I descended the stairs together.

"The same thing I do every Thursday afternoon, play piano for the sing-along."

"Oh right, for Mrs. Marsh." William looked visibly relieved that I'd finally answered his question.

"What is it you do?" Frank's pen was poised at his notebook.

"I play piano for some people who, well, people who don't think as well as we do."

"What do you mean?" Frank was puzzled.

"Well, some are crippled, but mostly their minds are a little off."

William frowned. "She means they're retarded."

"I guess that's the word, but it seems degrading to me. Anyway, we had quite a time at first, finding the right songs, but once I did, they loved it."

Frank gave me a look that would've melted a glacier. My husband however, was unmoved by my charm.

DIVISIONS

"Do you think you're safe with those people?" William asked me.

"Safe? Why wouldn't I be?" I slid the cuff of my sweater a little lower on my wrist.

"Stan told me George Knowles has just been released. It seems your do-gooding with him may have gotten us into this." He kicked at the remnants of my wedding dress on the floor. Half a tomato rolled across the Oriental carpet. "I just want to be sure you're not headed for another scrape."

Stan took a step toward the door, his boot heel crushing the errant tomato into the wool rug.

"If it wasn't for George Knowles, I wouldn't have met you. Is that what you mean by a scrape?"

Our conversation shuddered to a halt. Frank and his partner used their stock police phrases to extract themselves from our house and were followed outside by William. He thought I couldn't hear him, but he hadn't allowed for the broken windows, and I stayed close enough to hear every word. Through the web of shattered glass that was held in place by the leading, I could see him; I could see dozens of him, in fact. The way a fly must see the world in multiple refractions.

He placed a companionable hand on Stan's shoulder. "I'd appreciate it if you fellas would let us know what you find out about Knowles."

So now they're "you fellas." Nice and chummy all of a sudden.

Frank answered, "We'll do what we can."

William lowered his voice, and through the cracked and crackled glass, I saw a multitude of Williams glancing toward the door and huddling with the policemen as if they were all teammates. He muttered, too low for me to hear the words, but I could catch the tone, and he sounded concerned.

Then I heard Frank. "Don't worry, Mr. Buchanan, I'll be happy to do that."

"Happy to do that." An odd phrase, coming from Frank. What exactly would make a man like Frank O'Donnell happy?

Halfway House

George Knowles and all his assets fit easily into the nine-by-nine-foot room in the halfway house. For lack of options in prison, he'd developed a habit of sitting on his bed. Now his greatest singular pride was the luxury of sitting in a chair with his feet propped against the hot water radiator. But he couldn't settle deeply into that chair. His shoulders stayed clenched from too many years prepared to bolt from his father and then from the keepers and inmates who formed his social circle.

George ground his cigarette into the arm of his chair and flicked it hard toward the open toilet.

He jumped when a fist pounded on the door. Without opening it, he knew the law was on the other side.

How hard did you have to knock on the door of a room so small you could piss across it?

He scrambled out of his chair to push a jam jar of bootleg behind the seat cushion. The door was pushed open by Frank O'Donnell and his partner. George felt his mouth go as dry as an old maid.

"Georgie! Just thought we'd drop by and see how you're doing."

"Yes," George answered, trying to keep his voice steady. "Yes, I can see that."

Frank made an exaggerated visual sweep of the room and pursed his lips.

"Nice place ya got here, Georgie."

George said nothing, but looked to the partner, who stood in the doorway, arms folded across his chest.

"It'll do." George had his back against one of the crumbling plaster walls looking like a housecat stalked by a German shepherd.

"Not quite as nice as Buchanan's, is it?"

"Buchanan's? I wouldn't know."

"Oh, you wouldn't, eh?

"I don't get too many invites from my lawyer."

"What about his wife?"

A vein pulsed in George's temple, and Frank knew he'd hit a hot button.

"What about her?"

"Oh now, Georgie, she's not so bad is she? She came to see you in the pen. That's more than any of your other lady friends did." Frank paused to see if his needling was getting to George. "I know that for a fact, because I checked the visitors' record."

"Yeah, she come to see me. I kicked her out, though."

"Kicked her out with your lawyer, and look what happened. Seems like you're a pretty good matchmaker, Georgie."

"What do you want, O'Donnell?"

"I'm here to tell you to stay away from Buchanan's house."

"I never been near the place."

"Never." Frank, devoid of emotion in either his face or voice, waited for George to respond.

George started scratching at the tattoos on his forearm.

Frank continued, "They've been having a little trouble with vandals. Funny thing is, the problems started right after you got out of the pogie. How do you explain that?"

"I don't have to explain nothin'."

Frank moved menacingly close. "You do if I say ya do," he growled.

George shifted tack. "What kind of trouble they having?"

"Petty stuff. Someone tore up the wife's wedding dress, garbage thrown all around. You know, pissant kind of crap like you'd pull."

"Wasn't me," George answered simply.

"Well, who else would do that kind of thing?"

"How should I know? Seems to me the last time I saw you, you weren't too happy with my free legal advisor either."

"So?"

"So, maybe you done it, and you're tryin' to pin it on me."

"Why the hell would I want to do that?" Frank sounded surly, but curious.

George wanted desperately to reach for another cigarette, but he knew his hands would quiver with fear if he tried to light it.

As if something funny had just occurred to him, George added slyly, "From what I hear, you might have a reason."

If Frank's eyes had been gun barrels, George would have taken two to the head, right there in the halfway house. Even with half a jam jar in him, George grasped that much. He noticed the partner too, taking it all in without comment.

Frank's hand went to his baton, but that was as far as he went. George was pretty sure he had the partner to thank for that.

Finally Frank snarled, "Just stay the hell away from Kensington Street, Knowles."

"Kensington? Is that where the bastard lives?"

CHAPTER FIFTEEN
Parliament Hill

As a new member of an opposition party, William searched for his seat and found that he was assigned one as far from the speaker as one could get and still be in the House. On the first day, he had had his picture taken with Lester Pearson, leader of the Liberal Party, and then was rarely in the same room with the man for the next three months.

When Ray came to Ottawa one night, William was grateful for the chance to unload on his friend. They met outside the Chateau Laurier Hotel, on a bridge overlooking the Ottawa River.

"Do you know this is the final lock in the Rideau Canal system?" William explained to Ray. Without waiting for him to answer, William added "It's remarkable, isn't it, to think of the vision people had a hundred years ago, to build an inland waterway between Kingston and Ottawa. There are sixty-four locks in total, and it's so fitting to think the system ends right here at the base of Parliament Hill."

"You could always give historical tours if you get kicked out of the House," Ray kidded.

The two men walked along the edge of the Rideau, and William looked up the hill toward the clock and the spire of the Peace Tower that symbolized the Canadian House of Commons. He shook his head in disappointment.

"You know what I get to do in the House, Ray? I raise my hand to be counted for votes. I don't make any speeches; I don't bring forward any bills or motions."

"You're a new guy. And your party is in opposition. Your turn will come; these things take time," Ray assured him.

"Time, right. Speaking of that, do you have any idea how long it takes to get anything done in the Parliament of Canada?"

"No, how long?"

"I don't really know; I haven't seen anything get done yet," William conceded. "But I can tell you, these guys make glaciers look speedy."

Ray laughed good-naturedly. The friends walked at a comfortable pace until Ray broke the silence. "Do you remember why you got into this racket in the first place?"

"Remind me."

"To help people. You said you wanted to make a difference, higher up the ladder. So you're not as high as you want to go, but as a member, you have a lot more access to government than any of the people you represent."

"I guess you're right."

"Of course I'm right. Look, I didn't spend the last three years campaigning with you because you're good-looking, you know. Do you still have that notebook you carted around last spring?"

"Right here," William gestured toward the inside pocket of his overcoat.

"Well, dig it out. You have enough notes in that book of yours to fill a filing cabinet. I watched you. You wrote down details of pension screw-ups, immigration problems, income tax disputes…"

William shrugged "It's what people were worried about. They talked to me because I was on their doorstep saying I wanted to help them. Seems to me a really good secretary could look after this stuff."

"Yeah? So do you have one?"

"Not really, no."

"Well, neither does anyone else. So for now—you're it."

William snorted with dissatisfaction, and the two walked on silently. They meandered into the ByWard Market district.

"A bit seedy here, isn't it?" Ray asked.

"Seedy? God no, it's a great area! The farmers come in every day with produce. When I want to remember why I came to Ottawa, I walk through these stalls and remind myself who the really important people are in this country."

"You see—that's the attitude that got you elected. I think people take to you."

"Think so? I'm not so sure. Eleanor is really better at loosening people up than I am. Unfortunately, she'd rather spend time helping mental deficients learn to sing than campaign with me."

"Wait'll she gets a bigger taste of political life," Ray assured him. "Parties, dinners, fund-raisers—she'll like to get dressed up and have some fun."

"I'm not so sure," William answered dubiously. "She really seems drawn to these people. I mean, I ask her, 'Can they tell you where they are? Do they know what day of the week it is? Do they even know their own names?'"

"What's she say?"

"She says people have lots of ways of telling you what they know; we just have to learn to listen."

"What's that supposed to mean?"

"Damned if I know."

Ray changed the subject.

"So does that notebook have enough problems in it to start you off?"

"That it does," William answered.

"Good, because you can make a difference, but you have to start small."

"No wonder I made you my campaign manager."

After Ray's visit, William got down to business applying his energy to his constituents' everyday challenges. In the space of a few months, he developed a habit of attending question period, and then he'd hustle along the underground corridor between the Centre Block and his West Block office, eager to get to his constituents' concerns—which he now considered his real work. One late winter afternoon, his long strides caught him up with a group from the province of Quebec. They spoke French together, and William nodded in their direction.

"Messieurs, bonjour."

"You speak French?" one of the men asked him.

"Un petit peu," William admitted. He held his finger and thumb an inch apart.

The men shrugged and turned back to their conversation. He was ahead of them now in the corridor, and he heard a loud burst of laughter from the group. He felt his ears and neck grow hot as he supposed they were laughing at him.

His secretary, whose time he shared with another member, handed him a stack of messages when he came in.

DIVISIONS

"You know, Mr. Buchanan, you get the prize for having the most messages of any of the MPs I've worked for."

"I do? What's the prize?"

"Long hours, a tight schedule, and the chance to get kicked out of your job on a regular basis."

"Makes the practice of law sound downright tranquil by comparison," William responded. "But I do have a couple of minutes each day I still call my own. Do you know anyone who might give me some French lessons?"

"You're not doing enough already? Now you want to learn French?"

"Well, it occurred to me that this is a bilingual country, and I can't even talk to some of my colleagues."

"Let them learn English, then."

William looked at her wordlessly. She knew she had gone too far. Chastened, she mumbled, "I'll see if I can find someone."

One Wednesday night in March, William finished preparing his to-do list for the next day. He looked out the window to the snow swirling through the air and went back to his desk and opened his French book. He needed to learn a few more vocabulary words before his Thursday tutoring session. The high school teacher the secretary had located had set him the task of conjugating verbs each week. He was not thrilled with either her methods or his pace of learning. The door to his office opened, and a woman in the dull rayon uniform of the cleaning staff entered.

"Hello," he said. "You must be new."

"Yes, monsieur. New to this floor. It's all right…?" she looked around questioning.

"Of course, I mean—*certainement*. You're French?"

"Yes, I am."

She said "am" with a slight "h" sound, so it sounded like "ham" to William. He found her accent charming.

He held up his textbook for her to see.

"I need practice. Will you help?" he asked.

"If I'm permitted," she looked around anxiously, as if a supervisor might appear.

"Don't worry. No one but me and the cleaning staff are ever here at this time of night. Never any bosses."

She smiled.

"Comment vous appelez-vous?" he inquired laboriously, working every syllable.

"My name is Madelaine."

"Où habitez-vous?"

"I live now with my aunt and uncle in Ottawa. Before, I live in Montebello, Quebec."

"Avez-vous des frères ou-" he flipped a page to find the right word, "ou des soeurs?"

"I have four brothers and six sisters."

"Quelle âge avez-vous?"

She hesitated.

"Too hold. Twenty-eight."

"Not old; young, much younger than me. And you speak English well. Where did you learn it?"

"Chateau Montebello. English guests. I know mostly cleaning words: bleach, brush, soap."

William remembered staying at the Chateau Montebello with his parents when he was a teenager. The hotel was built as a replica of a wooden fort. Enormous dark logs formed the walls of the luxurious structure. The grounds were manicured and spacious, running from the hotel down to the edge of the Ottawa River. He didn't remember anything about the cleaning staff.

She moved through the office, running her duster along the shelves of books and sliding a carpet cleaner over the floor. William pretended to be absorbed by the French-English text and the words he had jotted on the page in front of him. He watched her furtively and wished he could think of something more to say in either official language. As she was finishing her tasks, he finally spoke.

"Madelaine."

She turned toward him, and he was able to get a good look at her face. Blond, with wispy bangs, she kept her curly hair back and in place with a dark hair band. She had full lips and smiled without showing her teeth. The effect he found to be both a little sad and secretive.

He read from the page he'd been writing on.

"Voudriez-vous boire un verre d'eau avec moi?"

He held up his water pitcher and pointed to two glasses. She looked a little puzzled, and for a moment he hoped he hadn't mispronounced something and accidentally offended her.

"Would I like to have a glass of water with you? C'est ça. All right."

He beamed at his success. He wanted to tell her that he would like to offer something more than a glass of lukewarm water, but that was all he had. He had no idea how to explain all that to her, so they just drank their water in silence.

"I only know one more thing in French," he told her. "Je m'appele William Buchanan."

The Visit

The Buchanan kitchen probably hadn't been this disheveled in a decade. The table was covered with seed packages, pages ripped from the Dominion Seed House catalogue, and at least five versions of my diagrams showing garden layouts. In the middle of the room, I had a card table set up with potting soil, seed containers, water, and fertilizer. A trail of muddy footprints, all mine, ran between the back porch and my makeshift potting table. I fetched a tray from the porch and turned for the kitchen, when a sharp rap on the back door scared the daylights out of me. It was already dark. Too late for Nancy and little David to be calling. If Ray was dropping something off for William, he would have called ahead. Besides, he always used the front door. I blindered my eyes with my hands, trying to peer into the dark before opening the door.

"It's okay, Eleanor. It's just your neighborhood cop dropping by to check on your safety."

I opened the door to find Frank, in uniform, rubbing his gloved hands together in an effort to stay warm.

"Frank O'Donnell! Come in."

He entered and closed the door, keeping his hand on the doorknob.

"I'm just on my way home, and I wanted to see if you're all right," he said.

"I'm fine. Why wouldn't I be?"

He shrugged. "No reason. Your husband asked us to keep an eye on you. I finished shift, had some time to spare, and here I am."

"No more word from George Knowles?"

"Not a peep. Winter generally keeps the crooks at home."

"I wish I'd never written to that character. I was such a fool."

"Hey, everybody makes mistakes. You were just trying to be nice."

"I know, thanks." The snow on Frank's shoulders was evaporating, and I felt the conversation winding down. I didn't want that to happen.

"Do you have time for a coffee?" I asked him.

"Don't see why not."

"No one waiting for you at home?"

"Nope." He didn't offer any details. He came the rest of the way into the kitchen and set his policeman's forage cap on top of the seed catalogues. All the chairs were piled with gardening books or perennial cuttings, so he stayed on his feet.

"I see you're an optimist. You must think we're gonna see spring someday."

"Sure we will. Then before long, we'll all be griping about the heat."

I scooped coffee into the percolator, glad to be occupied. The truth was, I didn't know how to act with Frank O'Donnell in the house. I was acutely aware of having a man in the house when William was not. Funny, I had never had this sense when Ray dropped by with some files for William. I just had easy conversations with him. This guy, he just seemed to fill up the room differently.

That was when I felt my nipples grow taut, and when I turned from the counter, I kept my arms folded over my chest. I stayed close by the coffee pot, not ready yet to risk moving closer to him.

"Beautiful home you have here."

"Thank-you. It's very quiet."

"I imagine so. You need some little Buchanans to liven the place up."

"I agree." I left it at that and wondered if my disappointment came through.

"Ah well," he replied, "all in due time."

Suddenly the sound of every shift and creak in the house was amplified by the charge in the kitchen's atmosphere. The sigh of the percolator as it burbled to a finish and the splash of cream poured into the pitcher became a cacophony. I wanted to swallow, but I was afraid to, because it would sound loud and gulpy. I gripped the coffee mug tightly to prevent my hands from shaking when I handed it to him. It didn't work.

"I didn't mean to make you uncomfortable." He was barely audible and didn't look directly at me.

"It's just a bit of a touchy point." Speaking of which, I did a quick check of my sweater-covered bosom and crossed my arms again. "I thought by now we'd be expecting a baby. It just doesn't seem to be happening for us."

Frank developed a compelling interest in stirring his coffee.

"Sorry," I laughed, more shrilly than I meant to. "I shouldn't be telling you this stuff. Now I'm the one making you uncomfortable."

"Okay," he grinned.

I moved back to my folding table and busied myself with spooning the soil into the starting trays. I set my own coffee on the few free inches of surface area, close to the edge of the table.

"So tell me, what do you spend your time at? Bonspiels at the Cataraqui Club? Golf tournaments in the summer?"

"I do a little of that, I'm sorry to say. I kind of have to—for appearances, you know."

He stood ramrod straight, as if he was interrogating me. No leaning on the ladder-back chair or slouching against a doorjamb for him.

"You don't like that? Lotta women would give their right arm for that kind of life."

"What kind of life? Playing games with women twenty years older than me? I have nothing to talk to them about."

"Still doing your church work?"

"You're looking at it! These," I swept an arm across the table, "will all be planted in a garden we're putting in at the church. The kids are going to help me plant seedlings and pull weeds, and when we get flowers, we'll put them in vases and take them to shut-ins."

"You sure they can do all that?"

"With help, they can do a lot more than most people give them credit for."

"So you've really latched on to this work?"

"I have. We've even given ourselves a name—Friends of Retarded Children."

"Oh yeah? I just heard about them! The police foundation donated money to them."

"What? You're the first person I know who's heard of us! How'd that happen?"

"From Stan—you know, my partner? He has a daughter, crippled, retarded—the whole nine yards. Anyways, she used to be down in Orillia, but Frank wanted to bring her here. Trouble is, there's no place for kids like her around here, so she's staying with a woman over on Bagot Street."

"She could go to Smith's Falls; it's not that far away."

"Stan doesn't want her in a hospital any more. He says she was dying in that place."

"What's his daughter's name?"

He frowned trying to recall. "I can't think of it just now. Anyway, it's kind of funny because she had this friend with her in Orillia, a mongoloid girl, and the two of them don't want to be separated. So when Stan tries to take his daughter, the girls raise such a ruckus, he ends up having to bring them both to Kingston."

"Wait a sec. Is his daughter's name Annie?"

"Yeah, Annie, that's it. You know her?"

"She's in our group. I didn't know she'd been in Orillia. How long was she there?"

"Since she was a kid, I think. Frank doesn't talk about it much, but down there, they used to get their food, clothes, medicine, pretty well everything they needed."

"Everything except their families," I countered.

"Well, yeah. But now, Stan has to supply all that and pay the woman to look after her."

"I know exactly who you mean. May. She looks after Annie, and her friend is Betsy. And it's called Down syndrome now, not mongoloid."

"Oh, sorry. What causes that, anyway?"

"They have an extra chromosome, and it starts right at the beginning of life, with the very first division of the cells," Eleanor explained.

"So anyways, Stan's working at the bus station on weekends, just to cover the bills. I guess the other girl's parents cover her costs, but they don't see her much."

"The bus station! That's where I remember him from! Oh boy, now I'm really embarrassed."

"Embarrassed?" he asked. "Why?"

"It was my first day in Kingston." I could feel the blush high in my cheeks, and Frank looked me over as if I was as captivating as a new puppy. It was the same look I used to get from William.

"It's probably not all that interesting, just funny to me, you know, looking back on it."

"Tell me," he coaxed.

I wanted to tell him. Wanted to launch into the whole kooky story. Wanted him to stay, or at least not leave, not yet. I checked the clock.

Eight-forty. Late enough for this to feel clandestine, early enough to be respectable.

"It's a long story—sure you have time for this?"

"I'm off duty. Got all the time in the world."

Still I hesitated, uncertain.

"I came up the lane at the back. No one saw me."

"Oh, it's not that," I said.

"It's that." He laid the words out like a corpse, and I didn't disturb them.

We picked up our coffees at the same moment. He wrapped his fingers around the cup, ignoring the handle.

"Okay, but you better sit down, 'cause this could take a while."

He moved some clutter from chair to table and spun the chair backwards and straddled it. He settled in, arms crossed over the back, watching me like I was going to perform a magic act.

"I'd never been more than a hundred miles from home," I started, "and here I was, going past Toronto all the way to Kingston on my own. I didn't want people to think I was a country bumpkin on my first adventure."

"What people?" he asked.

"Anybody. The people on the bus or the ones at the bus station."

"So what'd you do?"

"I worked very hard to appear nonchalant. I'm telling you, the Toronto skyline took my breath away, but I only allowed myself to glance at it a couple of times. I even made a point of yawning, as if I'd seen it all a million times. The further east I went, the more I realized I was really far from home. I'd never seen walls of rock the way they are along the 401. In Faderton, everything is flat. Crops grow right up to edge of town; everything just looked so different.

It wasn't just that. I'd had a blow-up with my dad, and he made it clear that if I took this job, I was on my own. So I was scared to death about that too. Anyway, I didn't want to gape out the window, the way some girls might, so I closed my eyes and pretended to sleep, as if I made this trip every week and was bored with it."

"Did you talk to anybody on the bus?" he asked me.

"Are you kidding? I was too scared. Anyway, by the time the bus pulled into the depot on Bath Street it was after five o'clock. I had no idea what to do. I didn't know if I had to show my ticket again or how I was supposed to get my luggage. And," I wasn't sure if I should mention this next part, but I was on a storytelling roll, "I was desperate to find a bathroom."

Frank laughed at that, and it struck me how easy it was to talk to and laugh with him. This house hadn't heard a whole lot of laughter, and even this would be silenced if William happened to come home unexpectedly. The wind sizzled snow pellets against the window.

"So the first thing I had to do was find a place to stay. It was the first time in my life I hadn't known where I would lay my head that night. So I planned it all out—or I thought I did. I bought a newspaper and put a stash of nickels in my wallet so I could look through the advertisements and make calls from a payphone. Oh boy, I thought the world was my oyster, until I walked into the bus depot. That place stinks, by the way. It's a combination of sweat and fried onions. I spotted a newspaper stand right away, but no washroom. So I stuck to my plan and bought a copy of the *Whig-Standard*.

Then I had to find a pay phone, and that's when the first thread of my strategy started to unravel. The tables where I could spread out the classified section were a good forty feet from the telephones. Meanwhile, if I didn't get to a ladies' room soon, my sophisticated veneer was going to be destroyed. But what was I supposed to do with my luggage, purse, and now the newspaper I was carting around? I was wishing I'd struck up a conversation with one or two of the people on the bus. That way, I could ask them to watch my things while I dashed to the bathroom. But it was too late for that. To top it all off, I was wearing this stupid daffodil-colored sweater that had struck me as cute and perky that morning in Faderton. But in the bus depot, what you really need is beige and bulky."

Frank looked completely relaxed, something I wasn't, because I had this nagging sense that if William happened in, he would catch me with Frank. But there was nothing to catch: two friends talking. But he would say, "Appearances Eleanor. We have to be concerned about appearances."

"So did you find a place?" he asked.

"I found a prospect, anyway. My hands were so full, I had to push my suitcase with my toe toward the phone, and all of a sudden it flopped over on its side and made a sound like a gun shot. I grabbed for it and dropped my purse, and all my nickels spilled out, rolling in every direction around the depot."

"Is that when you met Stan?"

"I'm getting to that. I gathered up the money, and after some more fumbling around, I arranged to go to Mrs. M's—but there was no way I could keep going without using the bathroom.

"I was desperate, so I lugged my things over to the ticket counter and asked this portly man—"

"Stan," Frank interjected.

I smiled and held up a hand as if to say "wait."

"I asked this man for directions to the washroom. He didn't look up, just jerked his thumb in a general direction over his shoulder. Then, trying to make it look like an afterthought, I asked if it was okay to leave my stuff there for just one minute.

'Up to you,' he said.

But I wasn't sure he understood what I wanted. So I said, 'What I mean is, would you keep an eye on it while I go to the washroom?' Finally he looked at me. 'We have lockers for that you know.'

'Well, I'm just going to be a minute or two.

'A minute or two? What happened to one minute?'"

"I can just picture him," Frank shook his head.

"When I came back he asked, 'Where you from, sweetheart?' No one had ever called me sweetheart before, so of course I was all flustered. Anyway. I answered him. 'Faderton. It's near London.'

But he said, 'Not very near. Closer to Stratford, I think.

'It's my first time in Kingston, and—'

'If I were a betting man, I'd say it's the first time you've been anywhere.'

Ohhh, that made me mad, and I said, 'Well, if you were a betting man, you'd lose. Now could you tell me how I can get a taxi?'

That's when he stopped his tallying and folded his arms across his belly. I should have known right then to give up the show.

'How did you get a taxi when you needed one before?'

'I never needed one before.'

Stan went back to ticket counting again. 'Well, I don't know how these things are done in Faderton, but here, we just use that phone under the big yellow taxi sign, and that takes care of things.'

I looked around, and sure enough, less than fifteen feet away was the sign and phone.

I wanted to disappear into the floor. Instead, I just said thank-you and shuffled my things in the direction of the phone, before taking a good look at it. I was really hoping I wouldn't have to talk to him again—ever. So I just stood there. He must have eyes in the back of his head, because he kept his head down, counting and writing in a ledger, and he said to me, 'No, it doesn't have a dial. I guess you haven't seen one of those in your world travels either.'

Then he came out from behind the counter and picked up my stuff and carried it toward the door. Outside, a line of three cabs waited.

'You always take the first cab in the line. They arrange themselves to take turns getting a fare. It's polite, you see.' All I could do was nod.

Then he said, 'Want a word of advice, from an old guy?' I kept my eyes on his tie. 'I see a lot of young folks like you coming into town this time of year. We get the army boys, the intelligentsia at Queens, and lots of junior bureaucrats starting their first government jobs. The ones who get along best, from what I see anyway, are the ones who are just honest. If you don't know, ask. If you need help, say so.'

I managed to get into the cab, and the whole time I was thinking, what's the right word for what I'm feeling right now? Then it came to me—'mortified.' That's what I was."

"Stan wouldn't want you to feel that way. He was trying to help you."

"I know. Just goes to show, you don't know what's happening in someone else's life. Just to think he has Annie, the way she is, and he was trying to help me."

"He's quite a guy," Frank agreed. "Likes to follow the rule book a little too tight for me, but he's all right."

"He's protecting his job; he needs it with that girl to support."

"So what do like about working with, what do I call them, the people you help?"

"We call them kids because they're like children in adult bodies. I just feel like I'm doing something useful, making a difference in their lives."

"So what do you do for them?"

"Take them on picnics, play music for them-"

"So you can talk to them, but you can't talk to the other women at the golf club?"

"With the kids, I can just be myself. At the club, I worry that I'll say something that might offend someone, or worse yet, something that makes me look stupid. But the kids need me. I'm helping one of the girls, Betsy, to learn to read a little."

"Read?"

"Yep. And play the piano too. You should see how proud she is when she gets something right. She absolutely glows."

"I can see her teacher does too."

I couldn't stop planting seeds to cross my arms again, so I made up my mind to stay hunched over my work.

"Well, I am proud of her. Our kids have to work so hard for every little bit they learn, but once they've got it—boy, they hang on to it."

"They're lucky to have you, Eleanor."

"Thanks, but it's the other way around. I'd rather spend my day with them than slide a curling rock down the ice or traipse after a golf ball."

"A lot of people don't have time for anyone who's, you know, defective. You're an unusual woman."

"I don't know if I'm so unusual."

"I do know. I had a cousin—he wasn't right in the head," Frank tapped his temple to illustrate the point. "He was younger than me. He wasn't a bad little guy, just, different, ya know."

"Oh yeah, I know," I smiled.

"Anyways, he had that, what did you call it some kind of syndrome?"

"Down syndrome?"

"Yeah right. Anyways, he died when he was about ten. They don't live too long, them kids. Something about their hearts."

"I didn't know that. I hope Betsy's okay." I needed to change the subject. "I'm thinking about getting a puppy."

"A walking companion?"

"A companion of any sort, I guess."

"Good idea. It's not safe for a woman to be out walking alone as much as you are. There's a lot of tough characters work along the waterfront."

"How do you know how much walking I do?"

"Eleanor, do you honestly think I've forgotten about you? You must walk four or five miles a day. I've seen you on the other side of the Leslie Causeway, way over near Fort Henry. You're not exactly easy to miss."

I could feel the conversation drifting into dangerous territory. I set the gardening implements down and picked up my coffee. I looked at my hands locked around the mug. My fingers were laced so tightly together that my nail beds were white.

That was when Frank swung off the chair and stepped toward me in one smooth movement. He wrapped his broad hands over mine, and together we cradled the mug of cooling coffee. His gaze was steady, and though I was both startled and pleased, I didn't know how to react.

"At least I know I'm not imagining things," I finally said.

"Imagining things?"

"I wondered if you really did come by as a favor to William or if you wanted…"

I trailed off because even now, with the heat from our hands threatening spontaneous combustion right there in the kitchen, I couldn't bring myself to ask if it was me he wanted to see.

"Yes," he said, "I wanted. I still do."

I had never seriously considered that our flirtations would lead to adultery. I couldn't do that—could I? Was I already doing that?

I glanced up at the clock above the table. He couldn't have been here more than a few minutes, and the coffee in my cup was still warm, yet everything seemed different. The perky curtains over the sink, the oblong cover on the butter dish—the props of my everyday life appeared sharper to me now that my hands rested under his. I didn't unclench my fingers, but I didn't pull away from him either. It was as if my day-to-day belongings stood by like eyewitnesses. My world of this house, this kitchen, the seed catalogues, was shocked into the mute observation that the lady of the house was not who she seemed to be.

I looked up to see Frank studying me patiently. His expression told me nothing. No expectations, no admiration; it was simple surveillance. I wondered if he shared any of my inner turmoil.

"I want too," I finally said. "But I'm married. And not to you, I might add."

"So?"

"Doesn't that bother you?"

"Not a bit. I don't think about it that way."

"How do you think about it, then?"

He appeared to choose his words carefully.

"I think that life is a banquet. And most sons of bitches are starving to death. That's not original, but it pretty much sums things up for me."

He released my hands, but stayed close. Close enough so I could have touched him easily.

"So if you want something, you just take it?"

"No, that's what thieves do. I put thieves in jail, because stealing is wrong. But who says this is wrong? The church? Well, I stopped listening to what they had to say a long time ago."

"So you're a bit of a libertine. I always wondered when I'd get a chance to use that word."

"A what?"

"A person who thinks for himself. Has no regard for religious rules. So what have you got against God?"

He stalled his answer by wiping his knuckle under his nostrils. "Against God—nothing. But the church, that's a different story." He paused, but didn't need any encouragement to go on. "There's four boys in the family; I'm the youngest by quite a bit. The old man was rough on everybody, me especially, but he saved the worst for my mother."

"You mean he hit her?"

"Hit, slapped, pulled her hair. But he was a cop, so he knew enough to leave bruises where nobody would see them. Sneaky bastard."

I remembered William saying something about cops knowing just enough about the law to break it without getting caught.

"Couldn't your brothers stop him?"

"Coulda—but they wouldn't. Said she brought it on herself. Anyways, when I was about eight or nine, I went to the priest—asked him to help her. Help us. You know what he said? He said 'She made her bed; she'll have to lie in it.'"

"What did he mean by that?"

"At the time, I figured it meant she married a mean one, and she'd have to put up with it. Wasn't till I was older, I found out I had a different father than the rest of 'em. That explained a lot, but that's when I decided I don't need a priest to figure out right from wrong for me."

"But how do you figure it out?"

"I get a gut feeling. It's never let me down yet."

He took the cup from my hands and set it on the counter. I reached toward him, but stopped just short, his hands hovering over mine. I could feel the heat radiate off him.

"You can't tell me that you don't feel that," he said.

I couldn't resist raising my own hands to meet his. Wordlessly he positioned them, fingers extended, palms facing, but separated by a couple inches of pulsing space. Between us, the energy was palpable, like an invisible ball we rolled between ourselves. I watched in wonder as our splayed fingers mirrored each other, and I was surrounded by a vortex of energy that spun around the two of us. And still, we didn't physically touch each other.

"Of course I feel it." I became aware of my breathing, and I stifled a moan.

"We both feel it. So, no, I'm not stealing anything from anyone. I'm reaching out for what's on offer at the banquet."

We spoke in the low, whispery tones of lovers. Not for privacy; no one could possibly hear us. But our mood and the subject demanded it. His hands moved through the energy field to touch mine. Fingertip to fingertip, we paused. Our hands were like playing cards, tipped toward one another in a delicate balance, and I was as close to toppling as I had ever been.

Frank shifted his fingers to fit between mine. Whether it was his movement or whether I consciously retracted wasn't clear. But as his hands moved to strengthen his hold, I pulled my own away.

"I can't," I said.

He said nothing.

"I just can't. I'm sorry. I should never have let you in here."

"Eleanor," he said quietly. "I'm not pushing you to do anything you don't want to do. I just don't know why you're stopping."

"I feel guilty. I'm afraid someone will find out. Even if no one ever did, I'd still feel so guilty."

"I thought only Catholics felt guilt like that," he smiled.

"You're Catholic. Apparently you found a way to get around the guilt."

"I'm also a cop. It doesn't take long to see there are rules, and then there are people. I'll bend the rules in favor of people every time. People's hearts don't lie to them."

I watched him closely as he spoke and wondered if he was sincere or just practicing some Irish blarney. Ever since the night in Faderton when I had learned that my mother's life had been filled with artfully disguised resentment, I'd lost trust in people. I wanted to believe what I was seeing, but after that betrayal, I didn't know if I could. It didn't help that Frank had an ability to keep his face devoid of emotion while he talked. I simply couldn't read him.

"Before I got married, I kept waiting for you to ask me out. Why didn't you?"

"I had just started with the force and was still on probation. We're not supposed to date anyone we've met on the job. Stan would've been down my neck if I'd even tried it."

"How would he know?"

"Stan? You said yourself, he's got eyes in the back of his head. He finds out about everything. Nothing gets past that guy."

"Maybe that's why they paired him with you."

He remained maddeningly inexpressive, so I kept going.

"Frank, my heart, or at least some part of my body, is telling me one thing, but my brain is shouting out the seventh commandment."

"'Thou shalt not commit adultery.' I learned them all too. They're just words. This," he motioned in the space between us, "this is real."

"So is my guilt. Whether or not Stan or anyone else found out, it doesn't matter. I'd know."

He looked like he was listening to someone he arrested deliver an alibi he was neither accepting nor rejecting.

"You know, your face doesn't give much away. You'd make a great poker player," I said.

He picked up his cap and held it between his hands.

"You don't give much away yourself. You'd make a great Catholic."

It didn't sound like a compliment.

"I just can't."

He nodded curtly. "I understand. Really I do. I just hope the honorable member knows how lucky he is."

I stood with my head against the door long after his dark uniform disappeared into the night.

"I hope so too."

CHAPTER SIXTEEN
En Français

William cancelled the lessons with the French teacher, whom he had secretly started calling Madame Verb Tense.

"I learn far more by talking to you," he explained to Madelaine one evening.

"That's because we talk about real life," she said simply.

"Exactement," William agreed. Not to mention the value of a motivated student.

William didn't realize, or wouldn't admit, how much Madelaine inspired him, until he began rearranging his work habits to accommodate her cleaning schedule. Early in his term, he began taking the Thursday evening train back to Kingston. He discovered that if he took the last train of the day, it gave him three extra hours at the office, and one of those he reserved for French lessons with Madelaine.

Eleanor didn't even question him when he explained his later arrival time. *Well, why would she? It's not like I'm doing anything wrong.*

Coming home to Kingston made him feel like a fraud. Early on Friday mornings, he opened mail and fielded telephone calls from constituents eager for a word with the member of Parliament. People asked for his time with a deference he didn't feel he deserved.

"Our committee would be grateful if you could find time in your schedule...," a typical letter would begin.

People with solid backgrounds and old family names would call him and open the conversation with, "I'm not sure if you remember me, but..." William could tell their perception of him was far more elevated than his actual power in Ottawa.

Power. He snorted when he thought of it. It was all but imperceptible, as a member of the House. He was developing a reputation as a strong constituency man, but he still secretly wondered why some well-trained secretarial staff couldn't do that work and free him up for—for what? He had no interest in the open bar receptions that dominated so many politicians' lives. He had never mastered the art of small talk, which was undoubtedly a detriment, but anyway, that was Eleanor's strength.

"So how was the open house at the Legion the other night?" he asked, one Saturday morning at breakfast.

Her expression was blank. "How would I know?"

"Eleanor, I RSVP'd my regrets, but I said you would go. I told you about that invitation."

She appeared to be making an honest effort to recall the conversation.

"If you did, I forgot. Anyway, why would they want me there? I don't know anything about legions."

"Look, there's every indication we'll have another election next year."

"What? You just got elected a few months ago!"

"I know. But a minority government can topple any time, and when it does, we'll be fighting hard to get into power ourselves."

Eleanor rolled her eyes.

William decided to ignore that.

"So that's why it's important for me, or someone who represents me, to get out to these events." William could feel exasperation rising. "I wanted you there."

"When was it?"

"Thursday night."

He cut his reply short. He knew he could have been there himself if he hadn't lingered in Ottawa to meet with Madelaine. He held his breath, hoping Eleanor wouldn't follow that same line of logic, wishing he had dropped the argument two sentences earlier.

But Eleanor's mind was on a path of its own. "Well, I couldn't have gone, even if I did remember. I was at the church Thursday afternoon as usual, but Annie had a seizure, and I ended up taking her to the hospital for some tests. I didn't get home until almost nine."

"Do you realize there were probably two hundred voters at that event who expected some kind of representation from me?"

"And did any of those two hundred people need me more than Annie did that night?"

Her tone was arctic, and she clattered the breakfast dishes into the sink and slammed out of the house. William supposed she was off for one of her solitary walks along the waterfront.

Yet no matter how icy things might be between them now, he knew she would melt into eagerness in the bedroom. He would respond as expected, but he suspected that the intensity she brought to their lovemaking was not a yearning for him, but stemmed from her own near insatiable desire to conceive a baby. It had been close to a year now, and he had no idea why the obvious outcome of their lovemaking hadn't occurred. Fathering a child was turning out to be one more front where he wasn't producing impressive results. He checked his watch. Just thirty-six hours until he could leave for Ottawa and his room at the Lord Elgin Hotel.

The Lord Elgin suited men like William perfectly. The building was less ostentatious than many of the structures in the capital; in fact, people looking for the hotel often passed by without recognizing it. The rooms were on the small side, less wasteful in William's opinion. Best of all was its location, less than a twenty-minute walk to his office in the West Block, and for a man who cherished his daily walk to work, this point alone had been enough to draw him to the place.

Some of the veteran MPs shared apartments near Parliament Hill, but for William, raised as an only child, sharing was not one of his strong suits. Others, especially cabinet ministers, ensconced themselves at the Chateau Laurier, the grand dame of the Canadian Pacific Railway hotels. But the more modest Elgin was the setting that made William acutely aware of the exceptional honor he felt in being a representative in the young democracy of Canada. The Lord Elgin was often filled with budget conscious tours and school groups eager to see the seat of Canadian government. These were ordinary Canadians taking rare, maybe once-in-a-lifetime trips to see the place where William worked and lived every day of his fortunate life.

He would navigate his way around the tourists, alert to his uncommon privilege, even in the most junior position in

Parliament. That and the promise of seeing Madelaine each evening were more than enough to make his morning footsteps light as he walked the short distance from the hotel to Parliament Hill every day.

With every conversation, Madelaine's English was improving as much as his French. She asked him why he worked so late, when others were often gone hours earlier.

"People things, I guess," he answered. He picked up a handwritten letter that had been folded and refolded by the sender. "This is from a mother whose boy is in prison. He's a bit slow and probably should be getting tutored instead of doing prison time."

He picked up another file. "These people have a glitch with immigration. They're trying to sponsor a brother and his family to come to Canada from Portugal. I do what I can," he shrugged.

"Me, I think what you do is very important."

"Thank-you. Merci."

"These are real things for real people, hmmm? This matters in their homes, in their hearts," she touched her chest above her left breast.

He smiled kindly at her. He was impressed by her ability to say profound things with simple language.

"And you, mademoiselle, why are you in Ottawa?"

"Me? Oh, I'm a problem to my family." She lifted her hands, palms up, in resignation. "Most girls marry. By my age, they have children. I did not find a husband who suits me. I have not enough education or English, so—I clean in Ottawa."

"You're only twenty-eight."

"Still, I won't marry just to be married."

"You're very wise," he said.

"I don't know. Maybe naïve. I wait for love."

He paused, wishing he could think of a suitable response.

"I envy you," he blurted out.

"Envy?" She hesitated, as if trying to recall the meaning of the word. "Why?"

He leaned back and tossed his pen on the desk. "You can talk so freely. Everything you say comes from your heart."

"You could do the same."

"Uh-uh." He shook his head. "I can't, never could."

"Why not?"

He looked at her, across the desk from him, waiting for his answer. She, with the dust rag, the shapeless uniform of the cleaning staff, and the expectant look of someone who had asked a simple question and expected a response.

"I don't even know what's in my heart."

He tried to sound more detached than he felt. He asked himself why it mattered what she thought. This woman's social connections were so humble, they had yielded nothing more than a cleaning job. She was just a woman with spotty English and an incomplete education, from one of those oversized French Catholic families. She followed her heart, and look where she'd ended up. He followed his head, and it should have been obvious which path led to success. He sniffed in derision.

Then he saw something in her eyes that he didn't comprehend. Tenderness, caring, maybe pity, even. But one thing was certain: this enigma on the other side of the room, in fact on the other side in so many ways, viewed him as the unfortunate one. Unable to consult his heart, bound by duty and judgments, he was as confined as any inmate in the Kingston Penitentiary. He slumped in his chair, bone-weary from the weight of obligations he had never considered unloading. Now a simple question, posed by a complex woman, was unanswerable.

She was so wrong for him in every way; yet she created a seismic shift that he felt move up through his shoulders and out his body. For a moment, he actually thought the feeling might be from snow sliding off the roof above him. He cast around wildly in his mind. This sensation was unnamed, and yet something about it felt consoling, like coming home to a warm welcome on a cold night. But what was it?

"Love."

She said the word with unexpected authority. It was as if she answered the question posed by his very soul.

"That's what's in your heart," she said with certainty.

Then William, for the first time in thirty-three years, did something entirely out of character. He took a chance, a real chance. No calculating the risks, no cerebral measuring sticks held up to appraise his actions. Emotion overcame him, and he went against a lifetime of training and habit.

He got up from his desk and reached for Madelaine, the unadorned beauty who made him feel worthy, and he pulled her toward him. At any other time, he would have prepared. He would have been showered and shaved and would have waited until she dropped enough clues for him to be reasonably sure he wouldn't be rejected. He had no such assurances this time, except the boulder that had moved out from between his shoulder blades, and, feeling nearly weightless, he floated toward her and kissed her with a passion that literally made him weep.

She didn't ask why he cried. She knew—and she took his tears on her tongue. They were at home in each other. The act of making love on the couch in his office was almost immaterial. Their spirits braided in a way that was so complete that joining their bodies in full-out passion was little more than a formality.

Yet it was a formality they indulged in throughout the winter. William marveled at his ability to compartmentalize his life. He was even energized by the arrangement. Weeknights were for Madelaine, weekends for Kingston and Eleanor, and through it all, he worked unstintingly as the elected representative of the Kingston riding. He felt a peace and balance he couldn't remember experiencing before.

On winter evenings, Madelaine often lingered in his office. Their companionship was easy, sincere, and as comfortable as putting on a favorite sweater. She showed a genuine interest in his work. One night in March, she asked him a question.

"About the woman with the boy in prison—how's she doing?"

"We've arranged for a volunteer tutor for the boy; it should help."

"Maybe the mother needs tutoring too. Then when he gets out of jail, she could help him."

"What makes you think that?"

"Remember her letter, folded the way it was? It took her, I think, a long time to write that. She didn't write it all at one time."

William considered this for a minute.

"I'll see if we can get a tutor for her too."

He added it to his next day's to-do list.

As smitten as William was, he kept his wits about him and had no desire to bring scandal upon himself by having fellow MPs at the hotel see him with Madelaine. But he knew that they couldn't continue to risk discovery by using the office for their trysts. Madelaine's home with her aunt and uncle was out of the question, so he resolved the problem by renting a small furnished apartment near the ByWard Market. Madelaine moved, with excuses to her relatives, who, she reported to William, were glad to be relieved of responsibility for the family spinster.

DIVISIONS

William went through the election, the second in ten months. This time, when he knocked on doors, people recognized him. Even from his short time in office, he had a budding reputation, and the voters' reception was warmer than the previous year.

"So do you think we have it in the bag?" Ray asked the candidate, as they huddled over a late dinner.

"Not sure I'd say that, but the tide is turning. People want change. They're asking about the new divorce law. Everyone has an opinion on a design for the new flag."

"You think it's just here? University towns change before any place else." Ray's voice was cautionary.

"No, it's bigger than that. In Quebec, they're even talking about letting married women own land—how's that for progress?"

"Quebec women can't own land? That's incredible!"

"Not if they're married. That's what you get when the church runs the state."

After the election, which put William and the Liberals back in office with their own minority government, his first item of business was to hurry back to Ottawa to see Madelaine. He arrived at the tiny walk-up unannounced and let himself into the place. The apartment was warm and smelled of cinnamon and tea and, incongruously, fresh paint.

"I had a feeling you would be back soon," her voice sang out from the bedroom.

"So what do you think?" She appeared in a soft blue sweater that enhanced her eyes and made her blond hair come alive. Touching her became a sweet imperative for William.

"You are a sight for sore eyes," he said, wrapping her close to him, "That's what I think."

"Thank-you. But I don't mean me," she talked between kisses. "I mean the place."

He pulled his gaze away from her to look around.

The dull gray walls had been painted the color of soft butter. Drapes on the windows hid the blistering wood frames, and bright pillows were at the corners of the shabby furniture supplied by the landlord. An oval braided rug covered the drab tiles in the living room. In the corner, a rocking chair, with a knitting project on the seat cushion, occupied a previously empty space.

"What have you done with this place?"

"I sewed," she gestured to a sewing machine, "and I painted. You see, I have time when a certain man is away, and I wanted some color."

"You, my sweet Madelaine, are a woman of many talents."

"I'm glad you notice. Would you like your tea now? I just have to pour it," she said, moving into the kitchen-built-for-one.

Alone for the moment in the transformed living room, William felt shaken, a state that was beginning to feel familiar when he was in Madelaine's company.

He recognized what was happening. She was nesting. He was the one who had arranged for this place and paid for it with money so inconsequential that it changed nothing in his lifestyle. He'd found a cheerless flat with uneven floors and doors that didn't quite latch. He'd rented it for the convenience of having Madelaine close by, but not close enough to prompt any embarrassing questions from his colleagues. Now, she had turned the tables on him.

She had filled this space with love and an ease he'd never felt in the mitered right-angles on Kensington Street. His thorough ways, his keeping of accounts, his logic, none of those were needed in this tiny home—for that was what it had become. A meager apartment in the market district had been metamorphosed by this woman, and her generous touch moved William toward a precipice he had never before approached.

She returned with their tea, and they settled on the couch that was supported by three legs and a can of tomatoes. She nestled her head into the space just below his shoulder, and he cradled her there, savoring the serenity she brought to his life.

Outside, the wind whistled and groaned, and they could hear the sifting of icy snow as a late spring storm hit the window. It deepened the tranquility of the moment into something William felt was nearly sacred.

"I want this to last forever," she murmured.

"If we could bottle this feeling and sell it, we'd be richer than the Bronfmans," he said.

"Oh, no, this is not for sale. It's only for us." She stretched luxuriously.

It occurred to him that a year ago, he didn't even know her. Now the thought of being without her triggered a sense of loss so profound that it left a gap inside his chest. Losing Madelaine and the solace she provided would be unbearable.

He allowed himself a vision of how their lives might work as a couple. He fantasized about capitulating to the seduction of comfort and acceptance exuding from this unusual woman beside him. Madelaine, living with him in a new place, their old lives left behind. With her, he could move far from the competitiveness and grasping ways of political life. Away from the responsibilities of community leadership and rendering well-informed advice to people who wanted to secure ever higher ground for themselves. An image of a charming country home, perhaps at the edge of a lake, came to his mind. Here, with her, there would be no striving or jostling for position. They could have a dog, a collie maybe, and raise children in a home filled with books, maps, ideas and—now he recognized it—peace. They could enjoy the seasons and tend to a garden, to their family, and, best of all, to each other.

"What are you thinking about?" she asked.

"Just embracing the moment," he answered and began kissing her in a prelude to making love.

"Wait a minute," she interrupted. "I have to go to the bathroom."

While she was out of the room, he looked more closely at the rocker. Press-back oak, solid. William nodded, impressed with the quality.

"Where'd you get the chair?" he called down the hall to her.

"Secondhand shop. Three bucks. Not bad, eh?"

"Not bad at all."

He picked up the ivory-colored knitting project that was clearly a baby sweater.

"And who, in your prolific family, is expecting a baby this time?" he asked.

Madelaine reentered the room, looking full of anticipation.

"Oh," she said. "This time, it's me."

CHAPTER SEVENTEEN
Gardening

It was Saturday of the Victoria Day weekend in May, and I bounded out of bed, eager to get to the plant sale at my old school. I pulled on a pair of pedal pushers and a sleeveless top, and on my way out the door, topped it off with an oversized shirt of William's. I couldn't wait to see how the children fared at the sale today. The plant sale had been my idea from last year, but this was the first time many of the kids had taken seeds and cuttings and nurtured them into plants. The money raised from selling the plants was supposed to buy more books for the school.

After the sale, I planned to meet Nancy and little David, who was struggling valiantly to walk on his own. I found them by the bake table. Nancy's blond head was bent low, examining the butter tarts. I hurried over as quickly as a person toting a cardboard box full of plants could move. Nancy looked weary, but smiled when she saw me. She guided David's little hand into waving at me. Nancy peeked into the box I lugged to a nearby table.

"What's this? Your own personal reforestation project?" she asked, sitting down and rummaging through a bag before coming up with David's bottle.

"Nope. It's for the church. We're planting our new garden today."

"So that's why you're all gussied up. Isn't that an old shirt of William's?"

"It is, and I think it's perfect for working in the garden. I have a big straw hat in the car that completes the ensemble."

"Might as well wear it. They wouldn't let you on the golf course at the Cataraqui with it."

"That place." I turned my eyes heavenward.

"So what are you planting?" Nancy switched the subject.

"We are planning an eclectic mix." I put on a sophisticated accent, mocking my own choice of words.

"Eclectic? You and your ten-dollar words. I've told you my brain has turned to pablum ever since David and diapers came into my life."

"Eclectic—isn't that a great word? It means a collection from all over. Actually, it's not very original; sometimes it's called an English garden. It's plants with a mixture of heights, textures, colors; anything goes, really. There are no rules to it."

"No wonder you like it," Nancy teased.

"You don't weed it either—that's the best part."

"Sounds like our kind of garden, doesn't it, David?" Nancy had developed that motherly trick of asking and answering questions for her baby, pretending somehow that she was having a real conversation. She broke off a generous piece of cinnamon roll and popped it into her mouth.

"Can I hold him, Nancy?"

"Be my guest. Watch out for baby drool. He's getting more teeth."

I cradled David closely, and he squirmed uncomfortably. "He likes to sit up now and look around," Nancy offered. I tried to shift him around, but felt I might drop him at any moment, so I handed him back. "He's just making strange," she tried to assure me. Nancy automatically took up the ancient rocking motion innate to women and the babies they love. Where did she learn all this stuff?

"What's William think of this?" she asked. "Wearing his clothes, working over in Swamp Ward with the kids, planting a wild garden...He must be wondering what kind of a woman he married."

I grinned, and Nancy shifted David higher on her hip. "That's not all; I got a puppy too!"

"You what! Are you trying to give the man a heart attack?"

"That's the funny thing. He's hardly said a word about any of it. He seems so distracted lately."

"Ray says the same thing," Nancy said, taking the last bite of bun and looking purposefully at me. "What do you think is going on with that husband of yours?"

I reached out to play with the little navy boot on David's foot.

"I expect I'm part of the problem. Please don't take this the wrong way, because you know I love David. It's just that I want a baby so much, and William knows how frustrated I am. He's away most of the time, and when he is home lately, he doesn't want to—you know—do it, because he thinks I'm pressuring him to make a baby."

Nancy touched my hand. "I'm sorry. I knew it was important to you, but I didn't know you were this concerned."

"Has he said anything to Ray?"

"No. Ray was hoping you might know what's going on with him."

"I don't. He's so distant lately. I woke up the other night, and he was just standing at the bedroom window. I watched him for a long time; he thought I was sleeping. Finally I did fall back to sleep, and in the morning he just brushed me off when I asked about it."

"Have you two gone to a doctor?"

"No. It's kind of personal, and William isn't exactly the type to open up to a doctor about it."

"If it makes you feel any better," Nancy offered, "you can borrow David any time you want. He loves the attention."

I felt my eyes fill with tears and kept my gaze low while I traced the seams of the baby boot with my thumb. I could only manage to nod an answer to Nancy.

"I might just do that. I could use some attention myself, especially the male variety. Anyway, I'd better go and get these plants into the ground."

I gave Nancy, then David, one last hug.

"God, he smells good. Say hi to Ray."

The tulips in the church garden had finished blooming, and I dug up the bulbs and dumped them into a bushel basket. No more straight rows of identical red flowers like stalwart Canadian Mounties for me. Between the seedlings I had started last January and the profusion of greenery from the plant sale, there wouldn't be a scrap of space without something growing in it. I planned to reshape the squared-off beds into an arch and looped pattern that took up most of the yard. My garden sketch was pinned to the inside of the door on the shed that housed a couple of discarded pews, a few pipes from an ancient organ, and some aging garden tools. The diagram was showing signs of grubby finger marks and smudges from the times I had taken it down to explain it to Betsy, Annie, and the gang.

DIVISIONS

Mrs. Marsh and I were gathered with the group by the front steps of the church. Betsy pouted because May hadn't allowed her to wear a party dress, and Annie kept trying to rock her chair toward the church door.

Mrs. Marsh smiled, "She wants to go inside and sing."

"Well, that's what normally happens when I'm here, so she expects it. Betsy, why don't you take Annie for a walk along the sidewalk until we're finished digging?"

"'Kay," Betsy answered and grasped the handles of her friend's chair, happy to escape digging in favor of a promenade along the sidewalk.

Bobby and a couple of the men stayed with the project. Together they all toiled to mark the outline of the new garden. I showed them how to push the spade through the sod and pull up strips of grass, banging the dirt off the underside to save the scant topsoil for the garden. My back grew wet with sweat, and the muscles in my shoulders ached from the effort.

"Bobby, I couldn't do this without you," I told him.

He grinned, delighted to be noticed. After an hour or so, Mrs. Marsh brought out a pitcher of juice and a tray with glasses. Betsy wheeled Annie over to be first in line for refreshments.

"Betsy, do you think you should get a drink first? Everyone else has been working awfully hard," I teased.

"I work," Betsy said defensively.

The digging crew laughed.

"I work hard," Betsy insisted.

"Yes, Betsy, you've been looking after Annie—that's important," Mrs. Marsh agreed with her.

"And since we've all been working so hard, I have a surprise," I announced.

Bobby bounced on his toes, anticipation written all over his face. Annie squealed in her chair and pressed her hands together, her gesture a hybrid of applause and prayer.

I crossed the sparse lawn to my car and opened the back door. I pulled out a rectangular brown box and carried it cautiously over to the steps. Flaps were folded loosely over the top.

"A cake!" cried Betsy, before the lid was opened. "It's your birthday?" she asked.

"Nope, my birthday's in September."

"Mine too!" Betsy gasped with delight. "Fifteen. When yours?"

She had my attention, even though the contents of the box were shifting around precariously. "The fifteenth! Betsy, we have the same birthday."

"Me too," Bobby announced.

"Really? Bobby are you fibbing?"

"Maybe. What's in the box? A cake?"

The box threatened to fall from my grasp, and I realized once again the gift of Betsy, Bobby, and the rest of the kids. Birth dates were vague, and last year was forgotten, but they were with me, really with me, right here and now. Which, it occurred to me briefly, was a darn sight better deal than my clever husband had to offer. He could be in the same room, but as distant as Timbuktu.

"No. Better than a cake." I tried to prolong the suspense but was foiled by the adorable head of a black Labrador puppy poking out of the box.

"Puppy!" Betsy called out excitedly.

I set the dog down gently within a circle of admirers.

"Name?" Bobby asked.

"Inky," I replied. "Can anybody guess why I named him Inky?"

"Because he's stinky?" Betsy tried.

"No." I pretended to be insulted. "Whaddya mean? My dog isn't stinky."

Everyone laughed.

"I know. I tease." Betsy hugged me.

"Maybe because he leaks sometimes, like ink from a pen," Mrs. Marsh suggested.

"He does sometimes, that's true. But that's not why I called him that."

No other possibilities were offered, so I prompted them.

"When it's really, really dark outside, we sometimes say it's inky black. And Inky is a type of dog called a black Labrador Retriever."

The teacher in me recognized how my students' attention shifted from the garden to the puppy. Like so many simple pleasures they hadn't experienced, it seemed like none of them had been given the chance to care for a puppy.

"What he eat?" Bobby asked, trying to get the dog to bite a dandelion leaf.

"He gets special soft puppy food for now. In a few weeks, when he gets more teeth, he'll eat food that's harder," I explained.

The puppy squatted to pee, and one of the men clapped a hand over his mouth in horror. "That's bad." He shook his head as if Inky had committed an unforgivable transgression.

"It's okay if he's outside," I reassured him. "We have to teach him not to do it in the house."

"Annie wants to hold him," Betsy interpreted for Annie, who was grunting excitedly in her chair.

I knelt to show Betsy how to pick up the puppy securely, with one hand under Inky's belly. The door on the garden shed was caught by the wind, and slammed open unexpectedly.

"That's funny," Mrs. Marsh said. "I'm sure I latched that."

"That old shed's falling apart. Probably the latch rusted through. I'll go shut it."

"I go," Bobby piped up.

"Do you know what to do, Bob?"

"Close the door?"

"That's right. Close the door and hook the latch so it stays closed."

"I know."

I watched Bobby duck his head and trot toward the shed. I turned back to the group, who was still enthralled with Inky's antics.

"They love to help, don't they?" Mrs. Marsh commented.

"You know, I've never really thanked you for inviting me to help out with these guys," I told her. "They've helped me a lot more than I've helped them."

Mrs. Marsh nodded knowingly, "Funny how that works."

I wondered about my parents and their twice-yearly visits to underprivileged children. Why did they do it? It didn't seem to invigorate them the way it did me and Mrs. Marsh. Dad came home from those trips quiet and drawn, and my mother—every trip took an increasing toll on her. For days afterward, her movements would be slow and fluttery, as if she was moving through water. The trips had started to seem mysterious to me, but I was blocked when I tried to ask about them. It was private, they told me; the children's families didn't want them identified. I imagined them to be ashamed, embarrassed by their children and wanting them to stay hidden. I learned that to pursue my questions caused my mother to dissolve into tears, and she offered up the same answer regardless of the question. "Life is just a 'raw deal' for some people, Eleanor. Just a raw, dirty deal."

DIVISIONS

A question from Betsy jolted me back to reality.

"Where Inky sleep?"

"In this box," I pointed. "I give him a hot water bottle and hope it keeps him warm, as if he's sleeping with his brothers and sisters."

"Not the same," Betsy said sadly.

I put an arm around Betsy's broad shoulders. "You're right, Betsy. It's not the same."

Bobby came bounding back to the circle.

"Done," he announced. Then, putting his finger to his lips, he added "Shhhh."

"Shhhh? Why shhhh?" I asked.

"Man said."

"Did a man tell you to be quiet, Bobby? That must have been another day."

Bobby looked nervously toward the shed, with the door closed but the latch hanging loosely.

"Why didn't you latch the door? You said you knew how. Did you forget?"

"Not forget. Door close, but no latch. Man said."

"What man, Bobby? What are you talking about?" Mrs. Marsh asked.

"Him." He gestured toward the shed.

"Sometimes they have imaginary friends," Mrs. Marsh whispered.

"I'll go do it," and I was halfway to the shed before Mrs. Marsh could respond.

"No," Bobby called to me. "Don't look."

I kept walking and raised my hands as if to say, "Don't know what you're talking about." At the shed, I began to pull the latch, and then decided to check inside to see if anything there would make sense of Bobby's mutterings. The interior smelled of rotting wood and gasoline stored for the lawnmower. It was too dark to peer to the back corners, and just when I was satisfied that nothing was there to cause Bobby's concern, a ray of sunlight filtered through a crack, and I caught sight of a hand with dirty fingernails wrapped around a length of organ pipe. I forced myself to hold in a scream, not wanting to scare the group. Instinct told me to slam the door fast, to trap the intruder, but something even stronger kicked in when I thought of someone, anyone, spying on my vulnerable little group.

"What are you doing in here?" I growled, surprising myself at how brave I sounded.

The answer I got was to see the hand grip the pipe tighter and raise it into the gloom of the shed. The air whirled when the pipe came arcing through the shadows in a wide, vicious swipe. The metal whizzed by my head and landed hard on the shed's rear wall. The rotted boards fell away from the force, and the sinister character raised a boot through the slant of sunlight I depended on to see. The toe of the boot glinted, and with one kick, created a hole in the wall large enough for a man to escape through.

My insides surged. I wanted to protect Bobby, the rest of the group, and even Inky, more than I feared for myself. The sensation created a fury I hadn't known I possessed. The man in the shed was scrambling through the hole he'd created, and I burned with the need to know who this was. I didn't care if I stopped him, but I had to know who would lie in wait for my kids, spying, and who had actually talked to innocent Bobby. I considered reaching out to pull the man back, but with no light, I still wouldn't be able to see this invader. My best bet was to get around to the back of the shed, but he was flattened and scurrying through the opening like an escaping rat. Even now, I could see he was out as far as his thighs.

Rage directed my legs, and I propelled myself around the back of the shed with a speed that startled the man emerging from the wall. As he tried to pull himself out the ragged hole, he tripped and sprawled on the grass. I saw that he wasn't much bigger than me, and when the pipe fell from his hand and rolled beyond his reach, I became utterly fearless. I raced toward him and landed a kick to his ribs. But he was tough, and with a grunt, scrambled to his feet and ran hard. He had split-second timing, and he used it to grab a look at what I hoped was the most ferocious expression he had ever seen contort a woman's face. That fraction of time was enough. I got the glimpse I needed. That was when I saw an expression of abject terror on the face of George Knowles.

Touched

George's room smelled like sweat. Not workingman sweat, but the sharper kind, the kind that fear produces. He lifted up his shirt and stood on tiptoes, trying to see himself in the mirror above the sink. He wanted to get a look at his ribs where Eleanor's kick had landed. He touched the spot gingerly, knowing from experience that the welt would blossom into a bruise the color of dry rot. She might even have cracked one of his ribs. He smiled at the thought. He could imagine the doc taping him up, wrapping the adhesive around his midriff, asking how it happened.

"A woman," he'd answer with a wink, as if he was used to fending them off. He fingered the spot where the toe of her shoe must have driven into him. Right there; he flinched at his own touch. That's where she made contact.

He closed his eyes, as if recalling the gentler press of her fingers against his forearm that day at the KP. He drifted his hand over the place she had touched long ago. Her touch had infected him. He had felt love; it moved through the skin on his arm, into his blood, and had been circulating and multiplying virulently ever since. Seeing Eleanor, following her, knowing where she lived, hiding just to catch a glimpse of her—it was enough for him. She was afraid of him; he had seen that today. If she only knew he was the last person in the world she should be afraid of. Just yesterday, he had created an elaborate fantasy of her losing her puppy, and he would be the one to return it and earn her undying devotion. He couldn't let her see him, not yet.

Today had been a mistake. That kid, he heard her call him Bobby, had to go and tell on him. Now Eleanor would probably call the cops. But it didn't matter. He cupped his hand protectively over the injury as if he was trapping a butterfly. Nothing mattered, because she had touched him. At least, at last—she had touched him.

CHAPTER EIGHTEEN
Expectations

William stood at the bedroom window, looking out on Kensington Street but seeing something entirely different. His mind was—where it had been so often this summer—back in that mundane apartment with Madelaine. The shock of her announcement had not been as great to him as the realization that she had resolved matters about this baby before he even knew of its existence. Throughout the summer, the scene when she had told him about the baby replayed involuntarily, like a record needle skipping on an album.

Her French accent, with its unusual inflections that put the emphasis on the last part of a word, had always been irresistible in its charm. He heard ba-bee as she said it and knew that in other circumstances, he would have savored that pronunciation. He loved the way she stretched English words into long, soft sounds that ran together like pulled taffy. Entire sentences would be delivered with her voice making one low sweep across the words. Yet this time, her words were in opposition to the comfort he usually found in her voice. Normally, he loved to listen to her, even to watch her mouth as she spoke. Now those sweet lips delivered shrapnel that ricocheted around him and threatened his world.

"Actually, this time it's me," she'd said when he found that partially knitted baby outfit.

"What? What did you say?"

His mind worked so quickly that he was already sure he could dismiss the conversation, once she explained that she had made a mistake with translation.

"Me. You heard right. It's me who is expecting the baby."

He took in her blue eyes and the flush of color on her fair skin. He expected her to react with embarrassment, shame even, but he realized that she was not blushing—she was glowing.

Then it hit him. This painting and sewing and finding of bargains was not because she wanted to warm up their secret refuge. She was creating a home into which she could welcome a baby. These changes were fueled by mother love, not lust. William was at a distinct disadvantage, and unaccustomed as he was to playing catch-up, he had to try.

Madelaine's voice pulled at him.

"I know it's a shock to you, but me, I've had a few weeks to think about this," she said.

"Shock—yes, it is that."

William could feel a wave of nausea in his stomach and a sour taste in his mouth.

"What are we going to do?" he asked her. He pushed the hair off his forehead with a hand that felt icy cold.

"I have thought about that." She settled deeply into the couch and looked pleased with herself.

"I am growing a strong, healthy baby. Each day I take exercise, I don't drink any wine, and I even sing to the baby—in French, of course."

William was confused. She hadn't thought about this logically at all. He put his hands on her shoulders and shook her gently, as if trying to wake her from a dream.

"Madelaine. Is that your idea of thinking something through? What are we supposed to do with a baby? Do you understand me?"

Her eyes narrowed into a fierce expression he had never seen on her.

"Of course I understand. I'm not stupid!"

"I know you're not stupid. So why did you insist on using that ridiculous rhythm method for birth control? They've invented pills for that, you know!"

He knew, logically, that all his blustering was pointless now. Still, he felt compelled to pinpoint exactly what had gone wrong.

"Why do you even ask? You know the reason."

"Of course I know—it's the Catholic Church. But we were already violating the rules by being together, so why the hell couldn't you have broken just one more and used some birth control that actually works?"

"And where would I get these pills? I'm French, and I am Catholic. Who is there to teach us how to prevent babies? My mother? A woman with twelve children? Until I came to the city, I didn't even know it was possible."

William stopped. As usual, she went to the heart of the matter with precision. Her problem was the same that beset generations of women from her province. He sagged into a seat at the far end of the couch. With his fingers laced together, propping up his chin, he broached the next subject cautiously.

"But you do understand—we can't have this baby."

Madelaine gasped, and her hands flew reflexively to her abdomen to protect the life inside her.

"Mon 'estit' de batard!"

He didn't know exactly what she said, but the emotion behind it was abundantly clear.

"Well, what do you have in mind?" he snapped.

"Lots. I have lots in mind. I—not we—will have this baby. In January. Nobody tell me what to do with this baby while it's 'ere." She spread her fingers over her belly like a shield.

William noticed her English crumbling as she grew more emotional. He hoped she wouldn't lapse into French, because he'd never be able to keep up with her.

She continued, mercifully for him, in English.

"For once, I have something, and if only for a few months—I decide about the baby. Not my father, not the priest, not you, and never, never some doctor who would take this baby out of me. No. Never. So now it's my turn to ask you. Do *you* understand me?"

William felt like a student lawyer, so outgunned in a courtroom debate he could only blink silently in her direction.

"So, I will love it, grow it, and protect it. After that, I don't know. For now, yes, this is my plan."

William knew enough to keep his mouth shut. Up against this elemental force, any argument he could offer would be specious to the point of disgrace.

Yet he could also see that Madelaine's idea of a plan, compared to the strategy he could create, was like comparing finger painting to art by the Group of Seven. A baby would arrive in January, that much was clear and beyond his control. He would spend the next while figuring out how this would play itself out in a practical sense. Squarely back in familiar territory, William closed the shutters on the view of the serene country home and a future with Madelaine. He set his mind to sorting through how best to clean up the mess he'd made when, for a few months of his life, he'd let his heart rule his head.

He stood in the moonlight and listened to his wife's soft breathing. He could see her slender form and wondered for the thousandth time why such a healthy specimen couldn't conceive.

He rubbed the bridge of his nose and pondered the backwardness of the situation. Beside him, his wife, who was plagued daily by her desire for a child and the inability to have one. While in Ottawa, his what, lover, mistress, girlfriend? True love, perhaps? So unprepared, so unsupported—and so pregnant. It gave him an uncomfortably close understanding of the phrase "cruel irony."

For a few seductive moments, he wondered if he should consider it to be a sign. The ease with which Madelaine had become pregnant, the way everything about her made him feel lighter, less burdened, and natural. Had he made a mistake marrying Eleanor? Maybe she was too young. She was forever resisting his requests and questioning things. And those retarded people. She actually had one of them coming to the house for piano lessons. He supposed someone had to help them, but he secretly wondered if her attraction to them was the lack of challenge they offered. They wouldn't notice or care if one of her Faderton-inspired comments happened to slip out.

As he wrestled with his thoughts, his Protestant upbringing, the source of so much of his work ethic, exhorted him to make the best of the situation. He couldn't change the past. He would have to find the proverbial silver lining and focus on that and on nothing else, to resolve the problem of Madelaine's pregnancy.

At least he knew he could father children. He'd been afraid he might have been divinely ordained to be childless because he wouldn't be a good father. Now he knew that was not the case, and knowing that gave him the courage to go ahead with the scheme he'd been brooding over all summer.

By September, he had a solid plan. Stubbornly, Madelaine kept her own sights firmly set on her decision to care for herself and her baby, as well as—and for as long as—she possibly could. When he presented his plan, he persuaded her to admit that it was the best they could do under difficult circumstances. In the end, she submitted to his scheme more than actually agreeing to it. He knew it was his job to make it work.

CHAPTER NINETEEN
The Plan

When William came home for the Christmas recess, Eleanor met him at the door with a list.

"Here are all the people who want you to attend something or other during the holidays," she said.

He glanced at the full page with a tired smile.

"I see you've booked in a Mrs. Buchanan for a few hours on Christmas Day."

"I thought it might be my only chance to see you."

"Oh no, you'll probably be sick of my face around here by the time I go back to the Hill."

"Not a chance." She tried to kiss him quickly, but he held her close so she couldn't escape. "I even got you an early Christmas present, so we'll have something to do together."

"You did?"

"I did." She pointed toward an unwrapped box under the tree. "My Dad and I used to play checkers every day during the holidays."

"Checkers? Ever tried chess? I can teach you."

Her shoulders sagged, and the corner of her mouth told him she wasn't pleased. He dashed to her good side.

"I got you something too." He pulled a package, elegantly wrapped, from his briefcase.

Eleanor opened it like a happy child. "A silk scarf, and look, it has my initials on it!"

"It's called a monogram."

"Great, I'll wear my monogrammed scarf while we're playing chess, so I can lose in style."

"We can play chess and checkers." He put everything he had into sounding conciliatory and pulled her close. "I have something to talk to you about," he said. She gave him a look he found full of suspicion. *Don't get paranoid*, he coached himself silently. It was a technique he had learned to use before going into a trial. *Lay the trail so they'll follow you where you want to take them.*

"Something big," he added, to inject the right degree of anticipation.

"Okay." She brightened.

"Can't tell you right now, though; I have a meeting with Ray. He's taking Nancy and David to Florida for Christmas. Leaving tonight," he said, glancing at his watch. "We'll talk this afternoon—during checkers."

"Sounds mysterious, but I guess I can wait until then."

"Jump, jump, and sorry, my dear—jump." Eleanor pushed back from the checkerboard and reached high in the air in an exaggerated stretch and yawn. "That's three for me, and let me think, oh, none for you. Betchya didn't know you married such a good checkers player."

DIVISIONS

William looked appreciatively at her slim form and her lissome movement. His mind instantly made the comparison to Madelaine's newly rounded shape and languid pace.

"I am truly blessed. But now," he reached for the velvet bag containing the chess pieces, "we play my game."

William set the back row of players, taking the white pieces for himself. Rook, knight, bishop, queen, king, bishop, knight, rook. He repeated the order on Eleanor's side of the board.

"What do you call those little castle ones again?" she asked.

"Rooks, though some people do call them castles."

"They remind me of the East Ditch Tower over at Fort Henry."

"Ah yes, your resting spot."

"It's not my resting spot; it's my thinking spot."

"So have you been thinking about what I said this morning Aren't you curious about what I want to talk to you about?" he asked.

"Oh yeah, I was wrapping presents for Annie and Betsy before you got here, and I forgot all about that."

William swallowed a peevish response and put eight black pawns in front of Eleanor's players, moving his hand methodically between the bag and board. He placed a row of white pawns on the board and contemplated his opening.

"What's this? You're not going to spot me a couple? I'm just a beginner."

"After you whupped me three straight in checkers?"

"I sure did, didn't I? I guess my only hope is to distract you. So what's the big thing you want to talk about?"

He looked at his wife, took a deep breath, and made an aggressive first ply.

"I found out about a baby we might adopt."

"Adopt? We've never even talked about adopting a baby!"

He didn't expect to get blocked so early. "Maybe we should talk about it. We don't seem to be having much luck the old-fashioned way," he tried to sound reasonable.

Eleanor pushed back from the wooden table, folded her arms under her breasts, and said, "Go on."

He did a mental headcount of the points and counterpoints he had ready. Satisfied that all were in position, he jumped, bold and knight-like, into the fray.

"There's a girl. She's seventeen, lives in Ottawa—"

"—and she's going to have a baby." Eleanor finished the sentence for him.

He nodded deeply, letting her supply the filler to minimize the number of lies he'd have to tell.

"She's from a well-connected family. Naturally this needs to be handled discreetly."

"So how did you find out about her?"

"Her uncle. He's a deputy minister. He knows I'm active for people here, and he wondered if I knew anyone who might want to adopt." Lies number one, two, and three.

"What did you tell him?"

William felt like he was leading a fish into a net. But he remained focused on the work at hand.

"I told him I'd make some tactful inquiries over the holidays. I didn't say anything about us." At last, a truthful sentence.

"Aren't there agencies, you know, like Children's Aid, who could do this?"

"They usually want to put the kids in foster care first. The girl's family wants adoption right away. That way, the baby goes to a family that really wants it, not just to somebody looking for a handout from the government."

Eleanor nodded as if she was buying the story so far.

"What do you know about the baby's father?"

"I'm told he's bright, has a good education, from a solid family, but…" William lifted his shoulders in resignation, as if to say, "You know how these things are."

"So why doesn't he marry her?"

"Well, that's another problem. It seems he already has a wife."

She studied the chandelier for a moment. "Let's hope morality isn't inherited."

William sacrificed that one.

"Is the mother healthy? Is she eating well?"

He thought of the bags of produce he'd carted to Madelaine each day. He pictured the dinners they'd shared where she refused even a sip of wine, choosing instead an extra helping of vegetables. He was proud of the small part he'd played in providing for the child already.

"Healthy, yes, apparently."

"When in January is she due?"

"Early. The first week or so."

"Why'd they leave it so late?"

Another question he'd expected.

"She didn't tell anyone. She was probably scared."

"That doesn't give us much time to get used to the idea."

"I know, but we've wanted to have a baby for a couple of years now, so in a way, we are used to the idea."

The tempo of the exchange halted. The chess pieces remained untouched between them, and Eleanor moved to the window, looking outside, saying nothing. William knew how to use silence. Inky, nails clicking on the hardwood, moved to her side, and she reached a hand down to scratch his ears. Then she said, "That's the point. We wanted to *have* a baby. One of our own."

It was a blunder, and he'd left himself wide open. Fish can be slippery, and she wriggled directly to the lone gap he'd left in the argument for adoption.

"It might be hard for you to understand, because you're a man," she turned toward him. "But I want to experience being pregnant; I want to breastfeed a baby that's ours. I want to go through it all from morning sickness to delivery."

William was pinned. If he tried to move, he jeopardized a future for the baby and the fruition of the tactics he'd spent months developing. He let her take the next turn.

"What happens if we don't take the baby?" she asked.

"Probably Children's Aid will take over."

"So you mean, if you and I don't take this baby, it'll go to Children's Aid?"

"Unless they can find someone else to adopt privately. The family wants the baby to go to people in similar circumstances, which shouldn't be too hard to find, with the uncle's connections."

He tried to sound casual, as if there were plenty of others who would take this baby if they didn't want it. *Create a demand — basic rule of economics. One baby on the supply side and lots of families wanting it.*

She pulled the dog leash from the drawer and put on her coat. "C'mon, Ink, let's go for a walk. We've got some thinking to do."

"Want some company?"

"No, thanks. I think better when it's just me and Inky."

When they were gone, he went to the den and pulled a notebook from his briefcase. He sat at the desk and sketched a flow chart. At the top he placed a capital "E" for Eleanor. A left pointing arrow for no, and a right arrow for yes. On the right side of the page were a number of entries in William's strong block printing:

DIVISIONS

CONVERT DRESSING ROOM TO NURSERY

ARRANGE CHRISTENING AT SYDENHAM UNITED CHURCH

PREPARE STIPEND DEPOSITS FOR M.

It was the left side of the page that concerned him. If Eleanor said no to the adoption, this side would become complicated. Madelaine would not be able to return to her family, especially with the baby. When he remembered her explanation, he felt disgust and revulsion.

"My father, he would beat me. That's for sure. And the baby—the baby would not be safe."

He lightly penciled "C.A.," short-form for Children's Aid. It was an imponderable prospect. He recalled a conversation he had overheard between two young women in an Ottawa coffee shop. One, a hard-looking blonde with dark roots, spoke with a brassy voice, too loud for the location. She was a revealer, spilling personal information that embarrassed him. Her voice knifed through his efforts to tune her out.

"I went to thirteen schools before I finally dropped out. The best family I was ever with could only keep me for five months. After that, whenever I went to a new place, I never even unpacked my clothes."

William compared that to his own life, where he still lived in his childhood home.

She continued, unable to edit herself. "The men, they were the worst. They'd come into my room at night, and, you know, do things." The blond's friend hushed her at that point in the saga. The storyteller took a long pull on her cigarette and exhaled a dagger of smoke into the air.

William stayed long enough to hear her sum up by saying, "Anyhow, I'd smother my kids with a pillow before I'd put them in a foster home."

William put a pen stroke through the left side entry. He supposed decency demanded that he feel guilty about manipulating his unsuspecting wife. But he didn't. Pragmatic, that's what he was. The life he had felt kicking through Madelaine's extended belly had the right to every resource he could muster to protect it.

He'd anticipated a quick win against Eleanor, and now it was, at best, a draw. It was a position he couldn't improve until she was ready to resume the match, and he had no idea when that would be. He set down his pen and wandered through the house. A photograph he hadn't seen before was framed and on top of the piano. It showed Eleanor, between two girls, one in a wheelchair and the other pudgy, with bangs cut severely short. Who were these people, and when had the picture been taken? There was so much about her he didn't know. She'd changed since, well, since when? He could see she'd become headstrong. Working with the defectives at the church, getting a dog—all without discussing any of it with him. Madelaine would have talked it over with him, asked for his opinion, and listened to him. He stopped himself. Madelaine was not part of the long-term plan. He'd have to stop thinking about her soon. The adoption would be complete sometime in January. He had a few weeks before he'd have to cut himself off completely from the life blood that was Madelaine.

William waited through the holidays to see what Eleanor would decide. On the afternoon of Christmas Eve, he came home to find Eleanor, listless, slouched in a chair, staring at the flames in the fireplace with no evidence of dinner started.

"Feeling all right?" he asked.

"Nope, but at least I know what I am. I am torn asunder," she announced sadly. "I looked it up in my *Roget's*."

"That's probably good. It means you're thinking it through." He was cautious, not daring to push her too hard in the direction he needed her to take.

"Feel like going out to the club for dinner?" he tried to sound offhand.

"Nah," she shrugged. "You'll never believe what I did today," she told him in a flat voice.

"Volunteered to score the spring golf tournament?"

That produced a weak smile on the face he still found so compelling.

"Right, and after that, we're going to a skating party in hell. No, almost as weird, though. I called my mom."

"Your mom? Why?" He inflected just enough confrontation to sound disapproving. He didn't want this to get complicated. Alone, he could shepherd her along the path he'd devised. With her getting help, he couldn't be sure which way she'd decide.

"I need someone to talk to about the baby. Nancy's in Florida. I wish Mrs. M was alive; she'd know what I should do. She used to say I was looking for something. Something I'd have to find for myself, by myself, and in my own time."

"So what is it you're looking for?" William deliberately kept his voice gentle, open.

"Something that would prove I'm worth all this."

"All this what?" God, women could be so maddening.

"This life. I wasn't born into this, and I didn't earn my way over to this side of Princess Street. Now someone else is even having a baby for me. Sometimes I feel like I'm an actress in a play; the house, the car, your job—they're all props."

"So what did your mom say?" William was anxious to guide her back to where he needed her to go. She lifted her face to look toward him. She'd been crying. He was sickened by how many tears had been shed over this mess.

Eleanor gathered her hair into her hand and brought it round to the side of her face. *God, she's beautiful. Even sad, she's beautiful.*

"You want to know what she said?" She didn't give him time to answer. "She said, 'Maybe you should wait until this baby's born, to be sure it's not crippled or something, before you agree to take it.' Why would she say that?"

"I have no idea. But it does bring up a point we haven't discussed." When he had set up this match a few days earlier, this was a piece he had been willing to sacrifice. "Some people don't feel up to the job of raising a handicapped child."

"Don't you think I know that? The kids at the church for instance. Most of them got dumped by their families before they were three years old. They've been at Orillia, Smith Falls, Cedar Springs," she counted off the provincial institutions on her fingers. "Oh yeah, then some of them were sent to a couple of private hellholes in between."

"I'm sure their families thought they were doing the best thing for them."

"I'm sure they did, but I can tell you, those families lost something. Something that can never be replaced."

"I didn't know you felt so strongly about this."

"I feel strongly about a lot of things, the more I learn about how this province treats retarded people."

"So about the baby...our baby," he said nudging her back toward his chosen conversational fold.

She wheeled back on him, defiance in her voice. "If we decide to take this baby, then we take it. No going back. If it's not a so-called normal child—it's still ours, and we'll be grateful for it."

William was speechless. He'd come face to face with the powerful force of motherhood in Madelaine, and he'd learned his lesson. Even the prospect of going from a woman to a mother brought out an intensity of emotion he had simply never seen in his two loves. Protectiveness he understood. Providing for his child—that he looked forward to doing. But this was raw emotion, and it terrified him, because he of all people was aware of its force. He had been the grateful recipient of the generous passions of both women. But he was fooling himself to think he had even begun to tap the vein of ardor that ran through them. Both of them hid reserves of emotion that would only be unearthed by their children. That was probably why they call it the "mother lode," he thought. Still, it sounded like she was leaning in the direction of taking the baby, and William wouldn't risk so much as another syllable for fear of shifting that delicate balance.

"Of course, I agree. I agree absolutely."

On New Year's Day, William and Eleanor went to church, and when they emerged to the steps of Sydenham United, they discovered a rare day in a typically overcast Kingston winter. White clouds superimposed on an impossibly blue sky and inflated to perfect proportions looked to be in danger of impaling themselves on the church spire. The air was lung-searingly cold. Eleanor turned her mink-trimmed coat collar up to cover her ears. The member of Parliament and his pretty brunette wife walked the distance from the church back to Kensington Street, cutting through the campus of Queen's University.

"I've decided about the baby," Eleanor announced unexpectedly.

"Good." William's heart pounded in direct opposition to his noncommittal response.

"If we go ahead with this, it will be with some conditions."

"That sounds like something I'd say." He traded his King James Bible from his right hand to his left.

"Yeah, well, you're a bad influence." She sniffed from the cold.

He took her teasing as a positive sign, but couldn't be sure until he heard the words.

"So, what's the verdict?"

"I want to keep trying for one of our own."

He flinched in the same way he'd seen clients do when the word "guilty" was pronounced by a jury foreman. "All right," he said.

Bile rose burning his throat, and he concentrated on putting one foot in front of the other. The only sound was the dry squawk of bitterly cold snow being mashed by their boots. *What would become of the baby? What would he tell Madelaine?*

"I mean, people do that all the time right?" Eleanor continued.

"Do what?"

"Raise one child and try for a second or third one."

"You mean you do want to adopt?" He scarcely breathed, waiting for her reply.

"On the condition that we keep on trying for one of our own—yes."

A less disciplined man than William would have leapt into the air, pumping his fist in victory. William settled for putting his right arm around his wife's shoulders.

"Fine by me. What are your other conditions?" He would have agreed to raise the child in a wolf den in exchange for a yes.

"We take this baby regardless of physical or mental condition. We all hope for a healthy child, but this is not a catalogue order we can just cancel if we don't like the goods."

DIVISIONS

William nodded. "You've changed, you know. That group from the church has done that to you."

"They've done that *for* me. And it wouldn't hurt you to spend some time with that fine little band of human beings. You'd be changed by them too. You'd see the world differently—guaranteed."

"I think it's a noble condition, and I agree, hoping it's a bridge we won't have to cross. Any more?"

They turned on to their own street now. A warm house, and maybe an afternoon nap, were within reach.

"Just one. If we do this adoption, it's final. I don't want the mother changing her mind or coming back in a year or two, saying she can handle the baby now."

"I couldn't agree more."

"So although it's not exactly the way I planned for this dream to come true, I guess I'm going to be a mommy."

"And an excellent one at that," he added proudly.

Yet William felt a surge of despondency for Madelaine, who by virtue of luck, timing, and circumstance, would face the heartbreak of losing her firstborn. He supposed it to be the price fatherhood would exact from him. For every joy he and Eleanor would get from the child, Madelaine would be deprived. He wondered if he'd ever be free from that sentence. Meanwhile, Eleanor would be a good mother; she just wasn't invested in the child yet. *Well, how could she be? She thinks she's getting the consolation prize.*

Until

William returned to Ottawa filled with resolve. He had set a chain of events in motion and had moved past the point of no return. He went immediately to see Madelaine, and when he entered the apartment, a lamp cast a soft light about the cozy room. A white wicker bassinet was placed near the rocking chair, and in the chair itself was Madelaine, a vision of contentment with an infant asleep at her breast.

The new mother held a finger to her lips to signal him to be quiet. He crouched by the chair, not daring to touch either occupant of the rocker. He tried to get a look at the baby's face, but the infant was nestled deep into the mother.

"When…?" he asked.

"New Year's Day." Madelaine spoke just above a whisper.

"And…?"

"A girl. She's healthy. Seven pounds, seven, how do you say, hounces?"

"And you?"

"I'm fine." She looked past him, down the hall to the bedroom. He turned to follow her gaze and saw a woman in her twenties regarding him warily. "It's my sister, Marie-Josée. She was with me and will stay until," she faltered, "until later."

William nodded thanks toward the girl and stood to take off his coat.

"Don't," Madelaine commanded. "I want you to go. I know what I have to do, but for now, please—leave us with each other."

"For how long?"

"Two weeks."

He was dismissed. Bewildered, he stood for a moment before offering his help. "Do you need anything? Is there anything I can do?"

She shook her head.

He stepped into the kitchen, so diminutive his mother would have said it wasn't big enough to change your mind in. He emptied his wallet, leaving the cash under the sugar bowl. He pivoted to leave and lost his balance when he nearly collided with the silent sister, who was still watching him.

"If you need anything…" He let the sentence drop and left the apartment.

CHAPTER TWENTY
Restless

Betsy moved quietly through her morning routine, finishing by raising the roller blind on her bedroom window. Movement on the sidewalk caught her eye. Two girls, clutching books to their chests, passed by, chatting to one another. Betsy followed them with her eyes. After that, a boy on his own ambled by, kicking at the snow in his path. Close behind him, a woman held hands with a little girl who carried a book and chattered without stop to the woman.

May, wearing a pink quilted robe cinched at the waist, came into the room.

"What are you looking at, Bets?"

"Kids. They go with books. Where they go?"

"School. They're going to school, Betsy."

"What do?"

"They learn things, like reading and writing and adding and subtracting."

Betsy turned from the window and without another word, made for the front door.

"Bye, May."

"Bye? Where do you think you're going?"

The door was open now, and May had to hurry to catch up to Betsy's stocky backside. Betsy moved quickly, as if she could sense May's approach from behind, and pulled the door shut.

"Betsy. Stop!" May commanded from the top step. Betsy paused, but didn't turn around. She trotted on a few more steps, and May knew that if she didn't come up with a distraction, she would have to chase after her and risk a tantrum of major proportions. May pulled a trump card, in fact her only card, from thin air, and she prayed it would be enough to convince Betsy to come back inside.

"You have sing-along today at the church. You don't want to miss that, do you?"

If it didn't work, May knew that she was no physical match for the girl, who already had a full head of steam up, powered by her obstinate determination to go to school. Betsy took two more steps before May's words found their mark.

"Sing-along?"

"You betcha! Eleanor will be there to play the piano."

Betsy paused, considering her options.

"Bobby will be there."

Betsy didn't move.

May needed something more persuasive if she was going to get Betsy to acquiesce without a confrontation.

"I sure hope you're going to help me push Annie. I can't do it without you."

Betsy turned back as if pulled by the weight of her obligation. "Okay. Eleanor be sad if Annie and Betsy don't sing along."

"She sure would." May drew Betsy back inside the house, but she knew she had secured a temporary victory, at best.

CHAPTER TWENTY-ONE
Michelle

On January twenty-first, William sat in the backseat of a taxi cab with his right arm steadying the basket beside him. He instructed the driver to pull into the Lord Elgin Hotel, where Eleanor waited in his room. He looked up at the copper roof topping the hotel's limestone facade, twelve stories above him. He forced himself to shut out the horror of what he had been through this morning. He could still hear Madelaine's inconsolable sobbing. He steeled himself against feeling emotion, because if he didn't, his plan would unravel. He resolved to make the love he and Madelaine shared a bittersweet memory. For now, and forever, he would dedicate himself to being a father to this baby and a husband to his wife. It was both a duty and an honor, he told himself. It would begin in the next few moments, when he launched himself over the first crucial hurdle of introducing Eleanor to their daughter.

He looked again at the sorry little bag Madelaine had packed so carefully with diapers and clothes for the baby. It was an aging

TWA flight bag, the kind given to economy class passengers. It probably belonged to someone in her family. William imagined Madelaine packing her own things in it, her heart filled with optimism when she left her home in Montebello for the job on Parliament Hill. The bag with the vinyl corners worn through was like a symbol to William of how limited this baby's life would be without him. He pictured the small room at the top of the stairs on Kensington Street, transformed now into a proper nursery. There, the baby had a room painted a delicate pink, a white crib, toys, pink dresses, bonnets and best of all, a mother and father who could love and raise her.

Gingerly, he lifted the baby and basket out of the car and immediately set it back. He winced at the frigid wind at his back and dreaded bringing the baby from the warm cab into the biting gusts. The driver waited while William pulled two soft blankets from the TWA bag. The smell of Madelaine wafted up from them, and William's knees nearly buckled under him. Yet he gritted his teeth, determined not to be swayed from this mission. He tucked the blanket securely around the infant, who slept with the pursed open-mouth perfection of a newborn. He covered her completely, first with the pink blanket, then with the white. The icy Ottawa air wouldn't touch her, not today. Again he lifted the carrier and shifted it to his right hand and reached for the pathetic TWA bag. Nothing about this felt familiar.

"Conspicuous as a whore in church," he muttered as he crossed the hotel lobby. There wasn't a peep from the basket.

William suddenly stopped, stock still with horror.

What if I've killed her?

He tore the blankets off the baby in an instant, and he was greeted with a pair of the most trusting blue eyes he had ever seen. He ignored the stunned expressions of the front desk staff and, weak with relief, stumbled into the stairwell. He set the basket down gently and sat beside the precious cargo with his back against the cement wall for support. He fought to get his breathing under control.

His gaze was riveted to his baby girl. "Don't look at me with all that trust. I'm a lawyer, you know, and a politician; I don't deserve it."

He coached his heart into calmness by talking himself through the ordeal. *Picture Eleanor.* He had trouble conjuring the image. He tried to focus on her dark beauty and wide white smile, but the vision of Madelaine, her fair skin blotchy from sorrow, her face convulsed in pain, imposed itself over everything. *Close the door,* he commanded himself. He summoned an image of the Kingston Penitentiary door. Thick as a railroad tie and twenty feet tall. He placed Madelaine on the other side of that door and swung it shut. He drove home the point by picturing himself securing a deadbolt thick as his wrist, barricading Madelaine out of his world. His throat relaxed enough for him to speak aloud to his daughter. "C'mon sweetheart, let's get you out of here."

He looked again at the carrier and saw it the way Eleanor would look at it. It was not new. It was probably something Madelaine had found in her haunts around secondhand shops. It didn't look like the kind of carrier a teenage mother from a well-to-do home would choose. The lawyer in William saw it as inconsistent with the story. It had to go. So did the TWA bag.

William mounted the steps carrying an infant, two blankets, and a couple of cloth diapers tucked into the bundle. The telltale carrier and bag were stowed deep under the stairs of the Lord Elgin stairway. Outside the hotel room door, he paused, gathered the disheveled blankets around his baby girl. He flexed his jaw open and shut a couple of times and cocked his head left and right, to drop some tension from his shoulders. He knew how to smooth concern off his brow with two deep inhalations, which he released slowly into the fourth floor hallway of the Lord Elgin hotel. He couldn't risk dropping the baby while fumbling for the room key, so he knocked. Eleanor whipped the door open in an instant.

"Oh my God..." Tears sprang to her eyes.

"Ready to meet our daughter?" his practiced smile was in place.

Eleanor hovered while William lowered the infant to the bed like he was placing a Ming vase.

"My God, she's beautiful," Eleanor breathed.

"Isn't she just?" He concentrated on producing facial expressions appropriate for a new father.

Eleanor reached to pick up the infant. Just as her hands grazed the blankets, she paused.

"Are you sure?" she asked.

"Sure about what?"

"Sure she's ours? They won't take her away? She's really and truly ours?"

"She's ours. It's legal, it's binding, and it's final. This is our daughter," he declared.

"Oh, little darling," Eleanor cooed and lifted the baby. She brushed her cheek against the child's velvet soft head and breathed deeply.

"She smells like a baby. How is it that all babies smell so good and the same?" she asked through her tears.

"I understand they don't always smell so great," William smiled.

"Oh, our baby won't ever smell to us—will you, little one? We've got to decide on a name. We can't just call her 'Baby.'"

William hesitated. "Well, there's just one condition I had to agree to in order to finalize things this morning," he said.

"What was that?" Eleanor looked wary.

"It was the mother's only proviso. We have to agree to call her Michelle. Can you live with that?"

"Michelle," Eleanor tested it out. "She looks like she could be a Michelle," she conceded. "But I'd like her middle name to be Elizabeth—like my sister."

William nodded. "I like the sound of that."

"Michelle. It's a beautiful name. But you didn't tell me the mother is French."

William froze. "Oh." He forced a chuckle out of his throat. "This is Ottawa; there's lots of frogs around here." He hated himself for saying "frog." To call Madelaine that was a betrayal more harsh than any curse he could have formed. It was a word from his youth, and in his normally clear state of mind, he would have edited it from his mind. But he was not himself, and the boyhood word that denigrated the French Quebecois revealed more about him than he wanted to admit.

William and Eleanor spent a glorious twenty minutes with Michelle before she began to cry. She started with tiny squawks that they quelled by jostling her gently as they took turns walking in the narrow space between the dresser and the foot of the bed. Within minutes, the sounds had escalated to the sharp, piercing noises nature provides babies with to assure their survival. Impossible to calm now, the baby was passed back and forth between her new parents, but William, already frazzled from the morning's events, found this auditory assault more than he had bargained for and handed the child resolutely back to Eleanor.

"Did the doctor tell you what we're supposed to feed her?" she asked above the caterwauling.

"Doctor?" William looked confused and edgy from the crying. "Oh yes, I wrote it all down here."

He removed a carefully folded paper from inside his suit jacket. The information on the paper had been communicated in considerable detail by Madelaine, not a doctor. William had been careful to record it in his own handwriting, so Eleanor's suspicions wouldn't be aroused.

He read the instructions aloud. "It says here, Carnation Milk, diluted. Four ounces at a time—warmed."

"So where is it?"

"What?"

"The milk, for God's sake! She must be crying because she's hungry. We need milk and bottles and more diapers."

By this time, Eleanor cradled the baby, who was turning her head hungrily in the direction of Eleanor's breast. The cherubic face had transformed into a red ball of fury, and the cries were increasing in volume.

"William, was the mother breastfeeding?" Eleanor looked truly stricken.

"How...how the hell should I know?"

But he did know. He remembered Madelaine's utter enchantment when she nestled into that secondhand rocking chair and held the baby to her breast. She had told him this morning, the baby had fed almost exclusively from her until the last couple of days when Madelaine began giving her a little Carnation milk in a bottle. William wished he'd paid closer attention to what she had told him. Now he was worried that other guests in the hotel would be disturbed.

"Well, I thought they'd send all the baby stuff." Eleanor's words brought him back to reality.

"This is it," he gestured toward the few items on the bed.

"You better go get something for her, because I can't take much more of this screaming," Eleanor said.

Michelle's mouth was wide open, and her tiny pink tongue and gums were in full view as she kept up her demands. The new parents looked at each other and, even over the most distressing sound known to humans, they smiled. They smiled at each other, at their baby girl, and at the new and awkward situation they were in.

"So we're off to a rocky start," Eleanor shrugged. "Sorry, little one," she spoke lovingly into the baby's ear, "your mommy and daddy need some training."

William reached his arms around his wife and daughter for an embrace of heartfelt love for them both. This baby was just what Eleanor needed, and he was beyond relief with her warm reaction to the child.

"I love you so much," he said to Eleanor.

She turned to him, surprise on her face. "I love you, and I'll love you more when you get back here with some milk and bottles for this baby."

When he returned, he was greeted with blessed silence, and Eleanor held up a hand, warning him to come in quietly. She sat on the edge of the bed with the baby face-up beside her. Eleanor gently jiggled the mattress with her hands on either side of Michelle. The reward was an infant with heavy eyelids and a tummy that rose and fell in short little bursts as she drifted into sleep.

"You're a natural, El," he whispered.

"A natural disaster maybe," she whispered back. "I think we should take her home after she has her bottle. Much more crying like that, and they might kick you out of the hotel."

Motherhood

"So where's the newest Liberal in the riding?" Ray called out when he and Nancy and little David came to visit.

"Can't you hear her?" William asked. Nancy handed me a brightly wrapped baby gift, and we went through the usual "good lungs" quips, but Michelle's prolonged wailing sent the males, including Inky, scurrying to the den.

Nancy tried every mom trick she knew. She rubbed Michelle's back, laid her tummy-down across her knees, and tried to distract her with lullabies.

"I don't know. I guess you've got yourself a colicky one," she said, handing Michelle back to me. "It usually wears off in three months."

"Three months?" I thought I might start crying too.

"Don't worry about it. I can help you out. Drop her off when you need a break."

"If I did that, you'd be raising her. Honestly, Nancy, I'm not sure I'm cut out for this."

"Hey, you're doing fine. Don't forget the rest of us had nine months to get trained for motherhood."

I shot a look at the door of the den—still closed. "Is it possible for the baby to miss her real mother? I mean, do you think they know, even at this age?"

Nancy wrapped her arms around me and my ever-whimpering baby. "Eleanor, you are her real mother. A teenage girl couldn't raise a cranky baby like this, especially without a father around. You just call if you need help. I might as well tell you now, I'm pregnant again, so I'll be around for the next twenty years or so."

On our first Sunday afternoon together, Michelle agreed to a temporary truce, but she waited until I was sitting in a ladder-back chair at the kitchen table. Together in the least comfortable chair in the house, she rested her head grudgingly on my shoulder to sleep. Cried out, her tiny body shuddered against me as she caved in to exhaustion. I wanted to shift to a more comfortable spot, but that would risk Michelle's wrath, and it wasn't worth it.

Upstairs, William was getting ready to go back to Ottawa. I could hear him opening the latches on his luggage, the rustle of paper from the dry cleaners as he packed his shirts. Then he whistled. It was just a short, airy trill, but it made me feel that I was being locked in the tower while he was skipping away to freedom.

I wanted to run upstairs and beg him not to leave me alone with her. But I didn't dare move, because that would disturb Michelle, and the toll she would extract for any uncondoned movement would be at least two hours of screaming. I was a captive, and my cell mate was upstairs, whistling his way toward early release. There wasn't a single thing that felt right about this. I glared at him with accusing eyes when he came into the kitchen.

"Don't tell me you're leaving now."

William gripped the handle of his suitcase tighter and looked toward the door as if it was an apparition that might disappear. "I have to, El. Parliament is sitting tomorrow. I'll be back Thursday—early, I promise."

"Don't leave me, William. I can't do this, not alone." I hated the way I sounded. Panicked and whiny, so much like my mother. I knew it wouldn't please him, so I tried to gather myself long enough to make sense to him.

"Is there something wrong with me or the baby? Why can't I handle this? Do you think the baby hates me?" I asked, hoping he'd know.

"No, I don't think the baby hates you. She's just getting used to us, I guess."

"But she won't eat. She hates that milk. When I manage to get some into her, she throws it all up, about ten minutes later. I have one clean outfit left in the drawer for her."

"She looks fine now. See how she's settled right down? She'll adjust; you'll see." He reached into the closet and came back with his coat and gloves. I wanted to fling myself at his legs to keep him from leaving. I had to keep him talking.

"But how do other people do it? I haven't slept more than two hours at a stretch since we got her. Poor Inky, I haven't walked him all week. How do people do it with four or five kids?"

"Or twelve? That's where friends or grandmothers come in."

"Thank God for Nancy, because grandmother isn't much help." I huffed. "I called my mother. She was at her usual best. She said she hoped we'd be able to manage a trip to see them in the spring. I wish Mrs. M was here. She'd help me."

"Well, we can't choose our families," William tried to console me, but he was taking nervous glances at his watch. I couldn't stand seeing him walk out, when I wanted to do exactly the same thing. Suddenly it occurred to me.

"You could take a later train."

"What?"

"Why can't you take the nine-fifteen? What's the big rush to get back to Ottawa?" I said it with a sharpness that came from too little sleep and a nagging sense of betrayal.

"No rush, I guess. Uh, sure, I can go later, if that's what you want." He set down the suitcase with a clatter that caused Michelle to startle.

"That's what I want." That's what I told him, but what I wanted was to get on the train myself. Any victory I might have gained by coercing him to stay was short-lived, because the baby was fully awake, and the reprieve was over. I handed her to him, holding her at arm's length as if she was something odious.

"I really wanted to take Michelle to the church group on Thursday. I thought everyone there would just love a baby. I don't think I'd better do it, though; her crying will upset all the kids."

"You might have to take a break from them for a while. They'll understand."

"Take a break from them? I don't want a break—not from them."

"Well, someone else is counting on you now," he signaled with his chin to indicate the baby, recharged and ready to lay on some punishment.

"I'm going out. I haven't had a bath or washed my hair in two days, but I am going out with Inky."

He shot a longing look at his suitcase, and when I snapped Inky's leash to the collar, I could hear his voice over the renewed wailing.

"It'll turn out all right Eleanor. Everything will be all right."

"Try to say that like you believe it."

Alone Together

Alone with Michelle, William paced the length of the center hall, rubbing her back, patting her backside, and crooning into her ear. The baby reacted with agitated whelps that threatened to spill over into full blown protests at any moment. He remembered how Madelaine would place his hand on her belly as they lay in bed and talked the easy endless prattle of two lovers feasting on getting to know each other. Madelaine swore the baby calmed when he was in the room, but he wasn't sure if it was true or if it was her sweet nature that wanted to assure him.

"Baby girl, I'm afraid you have cried more in the past two days than you did in three whole weeks with your mama. You look like her, you know." He cradled the baby in his arms and made eye contact with her. Incredibly, she quieted and reached a hand toward his face.

He carried her to the mirror in the front hall. He held her so he could see himself beside her. "Let's see, do you look like your old man at all?"

He studied the visages in front of him. "I think I can see a little Buchanan nose there," he touched her nose gently and ran a finger along her chin. "And that chin, that's been in the family for generations."

Michelle blinked and focused on her father's hand and drew it toward her mouth. "Now it's time we had our first father-daughter chat. I know you miss your mommy, and she misses you." His nose began to sting, and he heard his own voice catch. "But you have a new mommy now, and you have to be patient. She didn't have eleven brothers and sisters to practice on, you know."

He walked her to the top of the stairs to the nursery that still smelled of wallpaper paste. "See all this? See the horsey?" He touched the rocking horse that she would be ready to climb aboard in a couple of years. "And look, here's your teddy bear." He nosed the toy into her soft belly, hoping for a reaction. He was greeted by a pair of solemn eyes that refused appeasement.

"Not buying it, eh? So you don't care about your room, and you hate your milk. I guess screaming all day and night should be enough to get the message across."

The baby grew heavy in his arms, and like a man shouldering a burden, he sat down in the new rocking chair. The back and forth of the rocker was uneven and jerky, as though the weight of the occupants had settled unnaturally.

DIVISIONS

"We're both missing the same thing, baby girl. It takes every bit of strength I have to get me through the day without her, so how can I expect you to do it?"

He stroked the top of her head, velvet and vulnerable at the spot where the fontanel hadn't yet grown together. Eleanor would be back from her outing soon, and he knew he risked everything by even speaking aloud, but he needed to form the words and have them disappear just as quickly. No one but Michelle would hear what he had to say on the subject, but his need to voice his thoughts was as urgent as anything he'd ever felt.

"The only one hurting worse than us is your mama. She's back in Ottawa, and I know she's miserable without her baby. Then again, your mommy here is having a tough time too. Michelle, I'm sorry." He saw, rather than felt, his own tears splash onto the satin binding of her blanket. He tipped his head back against the chair and released the crushing weight of his decisions. He could see it was the baby and the women he loved who were taking the brunt of them.

A howl, long and keening, erupted from his throat, and he clawed at his mouth to smother it. But like a steam billow, it was impossible to rein it in until its pressure was spent.

Outside, Inky bayed in response. By the time Eleanor and the dog were in the house, William's eyes were wiped and his emotions mustered.

"Everything okay in here?" Eleanor asked when she poked her head into the nursery. "I thought I heard something funny."

"Fine, everything's fine. Michelle's just whimpering a little." He handed the child over to Eleanor, whose resigned expression told him to make good his escape.

He checked his watch with a flick of his wrist. "It's close to nine. I really have to run."

The response to that was silence from Eleanor, and just as he latched the front door, a cry from Michelle propelled him out the door and toward Ottawa. He wanted to slow the process and wished for time, more than he could get on a two-hour train ride. He needed to identify the lesser of two evils. He had resolved to stay away from Madelaine, yet he ached like an addict with the need to see her. She was the only person he could talk to about Michelle. He needed the relief of Madelaine, not just her voice and her body, but to be able to talk out loud about the unspeakable secret of Michelle. Yet if he went, she would demand to know every detail about Michelle, and he would tell her the truth. He would have to report the nonstop crying, the fretfulness, and the tough sledding he and Eleanor had with the baby. He couldn't lie, not to Madelaine. For one thing, she would be able to tell, but more than that, he lacked the capacity to lie to the woman he loved. You had no trouble with Eleanor, he reminded himself. True, he mused. So what the hell do you make of that?

CHAPTER TWENTY-TWO
Division Street

I look like five miles of bad road.

I splashed cold water on my face and examined myself in the mirror to see if I had changed as much on the outside as I had inside. Looking back at me were eyes rimmed with red. Dark half circles, like scuff marks on a curb, stretched from my lower lashes down my cheeks. My hair was greasy, and just to get a full and accurate picture, I stepped onto the bathroom scales. I had lost six pounds in the two weeks since adopting Michelle. So it was confirmed; I looked as bad as I felt—great.

It was almost 9:00 a.m., and the baby was asleep. I was limp with relief, but I knew she'd punish me later for the indulgence. Babies were supposed to be kept to a schedule. They were to awake at sunrise and go down for nice, orderly morning and afternoon naps. The baby books said those naps were important for the mothers to rest too or to get some chores done around the house. Clearly, Michelle had not read the books. Maybe she was waiting for a French edition.

I couldn't remember the last time I had slept through an entire night. Could it really have been only two weeks ago? Now I woke up with my shoulders hunched up, as though sleep was a furlough between skirmishes.

Coffee. It was my newly developed vice, and just when I had taken the first cherished sip of the day, the telephone interrupted me.

"Mrs. Buchanan." I immediately recognized Frank's rumbling tone. It invoked a pleasurable response, immediately attended by its doppelganger, guilt. Still, the prospect of a conversation with him was like sugar in my coffee.

"Frank."

"I wanted to give you some news about our friend, Georgie."

"Arrghh, will I ever be free of that albatross?"

"There you go, using those fancy words again. I'm just a dumb cop, remember? I can't keep up to you society dames."

"Oh, you can't play that dumb cop routine with me. Besides, I'm just a humble country girl at heart."

"Well, country girl, I called to warn you that George Knowles is back out on the streets of Kingston, as of this morning."

"I didn't know he was back in."

"Yeah, he was picked up a while ago for a drunk and disorderly. You might just want to be, you know, a bit more careful."

My pulse beat a staccato rhythm. What if he comes here? He might hurt Michelle. The thought turned my coffee cup to lead.

"Maybe he's learned his lesson."

"Always the school teacher, aren'tchya?"

"I guess…"

"It's what I like about you. Well, I like lots of things about you, but you do have this innocent way that I don't get to see much of in my line of work."

DIVISIONS

I wrapped my robe more tightly across my chest, dreading what I had to do next.

"Frank, I'm glad you like me. But we can't go on having these little talks. No more visits either."

"Why not?" His tone was cajoling, not defiant.

Michelle was awake now, and I could hear her rev up for the day-long assault she had planned for me. *I've got to get out of here before I lose my mind.*

"Is that a baby crying?" Frank asked.

"Yes, that's what I'm trying to tell you. I—we adopted a little girl and…" I couldn't go on.

"Tell you what," he said. "I'm off early today. At least come over to my place for a chat—or whatever."

"I shouldn't."

"Why not?"

"It wouldn't look right."

"See, that's the difference between your side of Princess and mine. Over here, nobody's looking."

Michelle's cries pushed like a tailwind. God, I wanted to get out of here. Frank spoke again.

"How about this afternoon? Three o'clock?"

I struggled to shut out Michelle's cries and concentrate on what Frank was saying. He gave me an address and directions to park at the back of a building on Division Street. I had a tough time focusing on his words, because his voice wrapped me like a warm blanket on a cold night. Then there was the third voice. The one that belonged to my Pentecostal conscience, lecturing me about secretly meeting a man who was not my husband. After talking to Frank, I called Nancy right away to see if she'd take Michelle for the afternoon. It was the third time I'd left her in two weeks. Each time felt like a morsel of freedom had been meted out, and I was starving for more.

The day dragged by, except for two incidents of panic when I picked up the phone to call Frank to cancel our rendezvous. The first time, I hung up after one ring, and the second time, Michelle vomited on the receiver before I finished dialing.

I showered, fixed my hair, and picked an outfit demure enough not to arouse Nancy's curiosity, but a cut above what I'd wear to volunteer at the church. My scarlet sweater struck me as appropriate.

At five to three, I pulled into the rutted parking lot of a three-story Victorian conversion. A curtain opened in a second floor window, and Frank's dark form filled the space. Snow swirled around the wooden steps that led to the back doors of the upper floors. The stairs were so thick with ice and snow that I had to hold the rail as I climbed.

The second story landing was crowded by a kitchen chair and a tin garbage can, its lid frozen in place. By pushing hard on the door, Frank plowed a semi-circle and created just enough space for me to squeeze through into the kitchen.

I hadn't seen him for a year, since the night I had been planting seeds in the kitchen, but the spark was just as ready as if it had been yesterday. We didn't speak—just looked into each other's eyes—and he placed his strong hands on either side of my face. He ran his thumbs gently down my cheeks and paused at my earlobes.

"Beautiful earrings," he said.

"They're from France."

"Well, la-tee-da."

I laughed and realized with a shiver how long it had been since I'd heard the sound of my own laughter. The kettle on the stove whistled.

"I'm making us some tea," Frank said.

"I can't stay."

"I know. Just long enough for a cup of tea."

I took off my navy wool coat and pulled the silk scarf into the sleeve. I didn't want my initials to show. Revealing them would make it feel as though I had left a calling card face up on the table. While Frank rummaged through the cabinets, I wandered into the living room and looked down on Division Street. Snowplows hadn't yet made it to this side of town, and snow lay in deep ruts where cars had passed.

The house had seen better days. The living room, originally a bedroom, creaked as I walked, and it reminded me of our house in Faderton. What would my mother think? Leaving my baby on a winter afternoon to meet a man? My mother would say nothing. She'd sigh and shake her head. I wondered, not for the first time, how I could possibly be the daughter of such an ineffectual woman. I placed my coat over the back of the chesterfield and sat down. There was a spindly coffee table, bare except for a package of Black Cat cigarettes.

Frank brought mugs of hot tea, and we sat half-turned toward each other on the couch. He wore a flannel shirt, the kind farmers from around Faderton wore into town. At such close range, I could see that his morning shave was regrowing into coarse stubble. I wanted to touch him but was careful to keep both hands on the mug of tea. He must have been thinking the same thing, but unlike me, he reached and gently twirled a lock of my hair around his finger.

"So how are you?" he asked.

"Fine."

"You are?" He sounded skeptical.

"Well, maybe not fine, exactly."

"Not fine, exactly," he repeated. "Then how are you? Exactly."

"Tired, overwhelmed, confused—typical new mother, I guess."

I leaned into his hand and closed my eyes. Tears squeezed out and rolled down my cheeks, and Frank wordlessly set our mugs on the table and pulled me toward him. He felt as thick as a bear. His chest and body sheltered me, and I sobbed and clung to him like a worn-out child, exhausted and finally able to rest. He stroked my hair, held me, and didn't once try to shush me or ask what was wrong.

He slid onto the floor, easing me down so I could have the couch to myself. I lay face down and buried my face in my arms and wept. Kneeling beside me, he rubbed my back and neck until my sobbing diminished into little hiccups and shudders. I turned on my side to face him, but I kept my eyes closed as I spoke.

"I must look ridiculous. I'm afraid to open my eyes now."

"You look delicious to me, and you don't have to be afraid."

I raised my eyelids just in time to see him lowering his head, and his kiss was full and soft on my lips.

"*You're playing with fire,*" warned the Pentecostal voice. I pictured candlelight. "*Good,*" I answered the voice, "*I like fire.*" I deliberately fanned the flame by returning Frank's kiss. He pulled me toward him, and I could feel the heat radiate around us. Then the blaze between us caught with ferocity, and I was drawn to it like a pyromaniac. Drawn, because I had carried burdens into that apartment, and I was ready to fling them all into the flames.

The first thing in was Michelle's constant bawling and life-sucking insatiability. After that, I chucked the frustration of my own infertility. Into the fire I dumped all the accommodations I'd made to William and his exacting demands. Then I loaded up the Pentecostal chidings, the guilt, and the judgment, and cast them in to be destroyed.

DIVISIONS

I felt wild and free and refused to think about what lay beyond this room and what would come after this unfettered afternoon. I was on a roll now, casting about for dead weight to unload. I found more. I flung in an armload of frustration over too little time with my kids from the church. I added my newly discovered inadequacies as a mother and watched them all burn in my mind's eye. With so much going up in smoke, it was easy to hold my own marriage over the flames until it caught and flared in that bonfire I had set in the Division Street apartment.

But there was one more thing. Everything to this point was nothing more than kindling compared to what I still had to contribute. And it had to go in before I could be free like the ashes and smoke that floated above my fire. I had stored it away deeply, and if I was ever going to haul it out, it might as well be now. I kept my eyes averted from it, even as I lugged it to the fire. My mother's resentment. The pain I'd caused my family by simply existing. It was as if I was begrudged the space I took up on the planet. It was the impediment that had started multiplying the moment I was born. It had disabled me as surely as Betsy's extra chromosome had hindered her. I poured it over the fire like an accelerant.

Of course, this was my fire. It existed only for me, and Frank had no way of knowing it was the fuel that drove me to him. When I responded to him with deep moans and an almost feral attack, he hesitated, as if he was unsure whether I was fighting him off or pulling him in. But I made it clear.

I tumbled off the couch to the floor beside him, voracious and untamed. We ignored the discomfort of the hardwood floor and tore at each other's clothes. His eagerness to get to my body had only one equal—my own rapaciousness to get him there.

Life is a banquet, and most sons of bitches are starvin' to death. That's what he told me. I've been one of them, and I didn't even know it.

Frank looked at me like a man who knew what he was about to partake of, and he intended to savor every morsel. He smiled in amusement at my signals that said I also intended to gorge myself at this particular banquet. I moved about his naked body, with my lips and tongue, frantic to feed on him as if he embodied some essential nutrients that I lacked.

"Slow down, slow down," he told me, chuckling.

He guided me into position where he could enjoy the spectacle of my body. His touch was light and sweeping, like a chef brushing a pastry. And it drove me nearly mad with desire.

"I can't wait; I have to now," I pleaded.

"Well, help yourself then," he offered playfully.

Instantly I pushed him to his back. I kissed and nipped my way down his chest and reached my splayed fingers down his belly. I traveled past his hip bones and backed my way down the banquet table. I bowed my head and gave thanks.

Frank's hands went to my face. He tensed up, as if he was nervous that in my frenzy I might hurt him. To answer that, I moved up, rolled onto my back and pulled at him to follow. Frank followed my lead, and got to the part of the repast that has been attracting men and women since they first shared an apple. Frank was burly and careful to hold back the full force of his body. But I was famished, not for the act, but for the abandonment of it all. I raised my hips again and again.

Tucked into the feast as he was, I was relieved to read his expression that showed he could pace himself in a way that was beyond me right now. I gave over to gluttony and relied on him to provide whatever manners might be displayed at this banquet.

DIVISIONS

I grimaced, tightened, and rose to climax in a fury of release so stunning that Frank locked into me, not moving. When my gasping and rasping for breath subsided, I pushed him off me with a finality that told him that, for this course at least, I was sated.

When I could speak again I said, "I hope your neighbors don't mind a little racket. I wouldn't want them calling the police." I laughed giddily at my own joke. My hair lay in tangled strands on my face, and Frank smoothed it back and narrowed his eyes, all without saying a word.

He went to the bedroom and came back with some blankets for us to spread under ourselves. I reached up and pulled my silk scarf from the sleeve of my coat. I fluttered the fabric across Frank's body, teasing and tickling with it. He lay beneath me, and with hunger staved off for the moment, I now controlled his access to the buffet he couldn't resist. Making love to William had taught me how to accommodate a discriminating man, and I brought that to the Division Street hardwood. I understood that the scarf, like a sauce, could be overused, ruining the experience, so I dished it up in a perfect portion. His hungry attention to my breasts reminded me of Michelle when she gulped hungrily at her bottle.

No. I won't think of her. This is just for us.

When we finished, there was a calmness between us—the first I had felt after weeks and months of distant foreplay, a wait too long to be so easily quenched. The aroma and taste of our bodies were like appetizers that called us back to one another. And when he pulled me toward him, I didn't feel anything but relief from the weights that I had cast into the fire of our passion.

He transported me. There was, for this moment, nothing needing my attention but us and our desire. For these few hours, at least, I was no one's wife, daughter, mother, friend, accompanist, or teacher. I was a woman, alone with a man who wanted me without conditions. He held me as though I were a precious chalice that held a secret elixir. It was as if this potion, once swallowed, would connect us to each other in a way we would both know and conceal in a bond made safe by what we had done this clandestine afternoon. At least, that was how it felt to me.

Frank, apparently feeling less languid and romantic, stood, stretched like a satisfied cat and pulled on his pants. Shirtless he picked up our empty mugs.

"More tea, Mrs. Buchanan?"

I winced. "Don't call me that."

He answered by hoisting the mugs and nodding in their direction.

"No tea thanks. I have to get going," I said, pulling the blanket up to my chin.

Frank padded back from the kitchen and settled onto the couch.

"So what do you think the Honorable William Buchanan would say if he knew you were here with me?" he asked me.

My stomach churned. "Don't spoil this, Frank."

"Spoil it? That doesn't spoil it—it's the icing on a delicious cake." He reached out to caress my hair, but I pulled away.

Frank eyed me from his place on the couch.

"He wouldn't like it, would he?"

"Frank, this is just something that happened. It's not about him."

"Eleanor, this is not just something that happened. It's something that's gonna keep happening. You may not think so now, but believe me, you'll get to thinking about this when you're alone, and you're alone a lot. You'll be back because you've got an appetite for this. Ever done it on the living room floor on Kensington Street?" he goaded me.

My mind dashed to the primly drawn blinds and the ironed sheets in our bedroom.

"Naw, I didn't think so." He laughed lustily.

"Frank, what do you want? Where are you expecting this to go?"

"I want you."

"You want me to leave William for you?" My voice betrayed the shock that was registering.

Frank lifted a shoulder indifferently. "Not necessarily. I think we could make this kind of thing work just fine."

"Is it me you want, Frank, or do you just want to take something away from William?"

"It's you I want." Then he added with chilling candidness, "You bein' Buchanan's wife just makes it a bonus."

"What have you got against my husband?"

Frank reached for one of the Black Cats and took his time lighting it. He inhaled deeply, leaned back, and opened his mouth to let the smoke drift into the room.

"You haven't figured it out?"

I looked around for my sweater, hoping to pull it on. Suddenly I felt exposed in front of Frank.

"Figured what out?" I tried to reach casually for my clothes.

"I don't like thieves. I put 'em in jail every chance I get. A certain class of them, anyway."

"What's that got to do with William? He's not a thief."

Frank flicked the lighter open and shut with his thumb. Rasp, click, rasp, click. It irritated me.

"You sure about that?" he asked, as if he knew something I didn't.

"What are you saying? Why would William have to steal anything?" I turned aside and slid on my underwear and skirt fast. I needed to be dressed for this conversation.

"Why would William, sweet William, have to steal anything?" he mimicked my voice. "After all, he has everything a guy could ever need right? Unless, of course, that's what he stole in the first place."

I sensed that Frank was warming to his own voice, and I reached past him to get my coat. He wrapped his fingers around my wrist; it didn't hurt, but his grip was tight.

"What's that supposed to mean?" I asked.

"Remember the scuffle over at Mrs. M's that day?"

I couldn't answer. It was as if he had stuffed the scarf into my mouth, and it was all I could do to breathe.

"It's amazing what you can get a couple of assholes to do for a bottle of Jack Daniels."

The clicks and groans of the floorboards were the only sounds to fill the space around us. I felt like he was handing me puzzle pieces, one at a time, and with each one, the image became more appalling. The boozy attackers, brandishing the black labeled bottle of Jack Daniels like a trophy. Mrs. M's face. Gasping for breath, looking to me to help her back into the house. Then Frank, arriving at the last moment, timed to look like a hero, but not early enough to actually catch anyone.

"George Knowles sent those guys." But even as the words wavered out of my mouth, I knew it wasn't true. If I needed any confirmation, I could look to Frank's face, back into cop mode now, deliberately expressionless. "You. You set that up? Set it up to look like George did it."

No answer.

"But he had nothing to do with it, did he? Did he!"

He picked the scarf from the floor and smoothed it repeatedly, admitting to nothing.

"Answer me! What would you have gained by having me beaten up?"

"C'mon, you're exaggerating. They didn't beat you up."

"What would you call it then?"

He tilted his head from side to side as if trying to figure out exactly what and how much to tell me.

"It was just...," he started and stopped. "Just meant to make you nervous."

The monstrousness of it all made my stomach lurch.

"Make me nervous? You killed Mrs. M!"

"Now, that wasn't supposed to happen. But I didn't kill her. The size of the old gal—if it wasn't that, it woulda been something else pretty soon."

Snapshots of Mrs. M came to me. Stitching the red bows for the Christmas concert, holding me after Mr. Wallace bawled me out, waiting for me with a hot meal, eager to hear about the kids at school. All that kindness gone, and without knowing it, I was the cause of it. Sick didn't begin to describe how I felt.

"Why?" It was a whisper. "Why would you do that?"

He answered as though he was talking about someone he barely knew. "I thought you might see the wisdom of hooking up with me. Especially if I played the gentleman, driving you to school, eventually taking you out on proper dates. A cop and a teacher, that's a pretty good match don't you think?"

"Why the hell didn't you just ask me to go out like a normal person?"

"I told you already. I wasn't supposed to associate with people I met through work. If Stan ever found out, and he would, he'd write me up. So if I wanted to see you, I just had to manufacture some situations."

"Some situations? What do you mean, 'some'?"

Frank pulled the scarf taut between his hands and moved toward me, close enough that I could smell the smoke on his breath.

"I," he paused, as though hand-picking his words, "created opportunities to meet up with the Buchanans. We don't exactly travel in the same circles, you know."

"You mean when our house was broken into?"

He shrugged. This was a game for him, dropping clues, with me trailing behind, trying to piece them together. I wanted to escape, but more urgently, I needed to know what he intended to do, and I wanted my scarf back so there'd be no evidence for him to use against me. I glanced at the kitchen clock; Nancy was expecting me.

Think it through. He hired the attackers; he created situations…

"George didn't do anything, did he?"

"He was the one you caught in the shed at the church, wasn't he?"

"Watching, hiding—that's George's way. No, it was you all along. You tore up my wedding dress and blamed him for it. And you're the one who called my father. You son of a bitch. My father had a heart attack over that call." The panic in my voice betrayed the horror that was rising inside me. How could I have been so stupid? After my father's heart attack, Mrs. M's death, and the break-in, every time, it had been Frank I turned to for solace and protection. It all became clear, like a slowly emerging sunrise, and I realized that I was in a disaster of my own creation.

I wrapped my arms around my chest and began to rock slowly back and forth. My burdens were like the bush in the Bible; they had burned, yet were not consumed. They had rematerialized and settled on me like a yoke. The price for a few hours of sweet abandon was going to be steep; Frank would see to that.

One last piece of logic begged an answer. "So, let me get this straight. Stan would write you up for seeing me outside of work, but he wouldn't do anything about you vandalizing our house, setting me up to be attacked, or making calls to my father?"

Already close, he leaned forward, tentative now. "There was one big difference," he answered. "If Stan had caught me, I always had Georgie Knowles to blame. I made sure of that before I did anything stupid."

My fingernails went to his neck and clawed four lines of blood from his earlobes to collar bone. He became inanimate, his hands still at either end of the scarf. Slowly, as if moving through water, he lifted the scarf and touched it to his wounds. He smeared the white silk with his blood and held it inches from my face. His mood shifted, and I felt sure I'd just taken some bait he'd set for me.

"Do you recognize this?" he asked, in an unexpectedly gentle voice. I was revolted, and I turned my head.

"Look at it," he commanded. "It's blood—Buchanan blood. Same stuff that flows through your thieving husband."

He looked at me as if he'd just delivered the punch line to an elaborate joke, but whatever reaction he was expecting, I failed to provide it. My mind wasn't taking things in as fast as it needed to, and he balled up the scarf and threw it into a far corner.

"Jesus, for a teacher, you're pretty damn thick. We're half-brothers. Me and that prick husband of yours—we got the same father."

That said, he wheeled away, picked up his shirt, and rammed his arms into the sleeves as though he could see that this was ending badly and he wanted to get it over with.

"What are you talking about—the same father?"

"Yeah, William's old man, a lawyer, my mother, his secretary." He formed a circle with one hand and poked the finger of his other through it in a crude gesture, to make his point. "Anyway, my father figured it out, held it against me for all his miserable life, and Buchanan denied everything. I wasn't anybody's son. And when Buchanan and his wife died—sweet William, their only child, inherited everything."

"Does William know about this?"

He shrugged. "My mother took me there one night when I was about sixteen. My mother drank too much; she was probably in the bag, and I remember there was some kind of a row—right there on your front porch. Not long after that came the car accident, then my mother suicided six months later."

"So you haven't even talked to him about it."

Frank shook his head. "I got no proof. That day at the prison, I saw him looking at you, and bingo, I knew there was something he wanted and didn't have. So the way I figure it, he took something of mine, and today I took something of his."

"So this isn't about me at all." It was all I could manage. "This is about getting even."

I was right back in Faderton again, listening outside my mother's bedroom door. For her, I was resentment; for Frank, I was revenge. Every comfort I took from them was a betrayal, and I wondered if there was anyone in the world who was real. I couldn't believe the man I had just made love with had about-faced into this malice-filled character. But this time, I wasn't going to slink out like a wounded dog. My mother's words had followed me like stones pelting a stray mongrel. This time, I'd stand up for myself.

"Frank—what are you saying? If I don't have sex with you again, you're going to tell my husband? Because I'll go straight home and tell him myself. I lived north of Princess before, and I can do it again. But understand this—you can't blackmail me."

"Blackmail you? I was hoping you'd want to keep seeing me as much as I want to 'see you.'"

"I have seen you—for what you really are. And no, Frank—it's over."

"You sure about that? You wouldn't want any more situations to crop up, now would you?"

"What's that supposed to mean?"

"Well, there's your little friends at the church or your precious mutt. You wouldn't want anything to happen to them, would you?"

My heart turned to ice.

"You're despicable."

"There you go, using those big words again."

"Okay, how about these? Scum, liar, filth. Can you understand those?"

Frank took two quick steps toward me and pushed me to the wall, his forearm just below my chin. "Yeah, well, after today I can think of a few words to describe you too."

A banging on the front door pulled him off me.

"Hey Frankie, open up. It's me, Stan."

"Get out," he hissed and gestured toward the back door.

My gaze shifted to the door, and I considered calling out to Stan, telling him everything. But I couldn't be sure Frank would get into any real trouble, and I wasn't exactly blameless after this afternoon. All I could think about was the threat he had made against the kids at the church and against Inky. How could I have been so stupid, not to see what he was really like?

I ran as fast as the icy steps would allow. Stan's cruiser was parked beside the Buick, conspicuous among the aging heaps in the lot. I recognized it as Stan's silent way of telling me he knew I was there. I sat still, trying to come to grips with the betrayals of the afternoon. I twisted the rearview mirror to check myself and was instantly sorry. I looked even worse than I had this morning. Just when I thought nothing else could possibly go wrong this afternoon, I noticed one more thing. One of my sapphire earrings was missing.

CHAPTER TWENTY-THREE
Melting

Like the ice in the Rideau Canal, William's resolve to stay away from Madelaine had softened, and by April, it had drained completely away. William would have found it easier to stop the seasons from changing than to resist Madelaine, and he barely noticed the open water of the canal as he hurried over to her apartment. He arrived with a paper grocery bag of produce for her, but he knew that her health and smile could not be restored with a few apples and imported Florida oranges. He let himself into the apartment and found her as he had so many times since he had taken Michelle from her in January. She was curled on the couch, under a blanket, still wearing her cleaner's smock and rocking herself gently back and forth. Going back to work had not improved anything for her. She was faded and thin.

"How was work?" he asked without enthusiasm.

"It was work." Her voice barely reached him.

He breathed in the sickly sweet smell of overripe produce. He made space on the kitchen counter for the fruit and noticed an identical bag from his earlier visit left unopened where he'd set it. He considered sitting on the edge of the couch beside Madelaine, but they were cautious of each other now. Lovemaking—that was nothing more than a memory from before Michelle's birth. He pulled the rocker from the corner and sat in it.

"How are you doing?" he asked her quietly.

"I'm not. I'm not doing. I'm done."

"What do you mean?"

"I can't go on. I've tried to get over this, get past it, whatever you call it. It's not working, William. I need my baby."

What she needs, he thought, is something to eat. Her cheeks were hollow.

William took on the persuasive voice he used on judges and juries. "Look here, the baby is being well cared for. We want what's best for her, don't we? I still think this is best."

"You think. You think. Well, I feel. Part of my body is missing. Not an arm. Not a leg. I could go on without them. No. It's my heart. My lungs." She pounded her palms against her chest as she spoke. "I can't live without dose."

William felt a queasiness in the pit of his stomach. He had headed off talk like this before, but this time she was building up steam. He could tell because her English pronunciation suffered when she was agitated. "These" and "those" became "dese" and "dose." Her sentences became short and simple. Still, she could make her point terrifyingly clear.

"Madelaine—we agreed. You said yourself you couldn't raise the baby. Your family wouldn't accept this from you. They wouldn't accept her."

"I know it's what I said. But my sister, you met her, she'll help me. My mother, she knows about the baby, she understands. People, they are becoming more open now."

"But your father, you said he might—"

"He wouldn't dare, not with my brothers around. Anyway, if I have to give up one or the other, I give up my family. I can survive without them. But without Michelle, no, it's not possible."

He recognized that the argument had veered from logical to emotional. He could—if he had to—mount a strong emotional counterpoint to Madelaine's earnest pleas.

"But Madelaine—what would it do to her to take her back now? She's established with us. She knows us. She even reaches out to pat Inky when he passes her."

"I notice you didn't say anything about love. Yes, she's established. She's an infant; it's still easy for her to adjust."

"She's not an easy baby. I've told you that."

"She needs me; that's why she cries. I dream about her every night. I go to her, in my sleep. She wants me."

"You're talking nonsense," William snapped.

"Yes, you would see it that way."

Her voice took on a defiant tone. She uncurled herself from the couch and folded the blanket, expertly matching the corners. She plumped the pillows she'd been resting on. Her hands darted along the table, picking up cups, plates, and a week's accumulation of litter. William stayed silent, but every instinct he had, legal and otherwise, told him that an abrupt shift was taking place. But he had no way of knowing how to prepare for the storm cresting the horizon. He was surprised when it arrived as a steady breeze, cool and level, delivered by Madelaine from behind her crossed arms and from a face that had grown wiser in the last few weeks.

"When you go home on the weekends, what do you do?" she asked.

"I meet with constituents, catch up on mail—"

"I mean at home," she interrupted.

"I've had Michelle a lot. I spend hours rocking her. I even sing to her, poor kid. It seems that if I don't, she cries."

"You," Madelaine emphasized the word, "spend hours with her. What about your wife?"

"She's ready for a break. She goes out. She walks the dog or meets her friend," he answered. "You've never wanted to talk about my home life. Are you sure you want to do this?"

"She's not happy, William—your wife. Do you want to know why?"

Whether he wanted to or not, she was about to tell him. He felt like a patient waiting for a grim diagnosis.

"She is stuck with a baby she doesn't love. She doesn't feel this baby—in her heart. Women, we can't love just because it's a clever solution to a problem. We must feel it. If we are pretending—the baby knows."

"The baby can't possibly know," he said dismissively.

She looked at him through eyes narrowed to slits. "You think you're so smart. You are the one with two homes, one there and one here, and you have no peace in either one."

William ran a hand through his hair and turned his head aside, without taking his gaze away from this woman whose simple words melted complications like April sun on a snow bank.

"This plan, it was reasonable. But it came from the head, not the heart. When the heart is not happy, the home can't be."

He cleared his throat and dropped his head into his hands. "What about my heart?" he asked, his head still lowered. "What am I supposed to do without Michelle? I love her. I look at that little face, and her eyes filled with trust, and she makes me feel like a king. I could honestly kill anyone who would harm her. I don't think I can go on without her."

"Then don't."

They both knew what she meant, and William's head snapped up to assess how serious she was. The set of her mouth told him what he needed to know. Without any effort, the vision he thought he had dismissed returned. He could see himself, with Madelaine and Michelle, snuggled deep into a warm bed on a snowy morning. A mother and father, equally smitten by their baby, content to simply be together in a circle of love that felt as natural as breathing.

He ventured further into the fantasy. Not yet forty, he was plenty young enough to start a new life, and at thirty, Madelaine was mature enough to know what she wanted and needed to be happy. He could afford the arrangement too. He could sell his law practice and the office on Johnston Street. He thought of the home on Kensington Street, and his daydream ground to a halt. His parents' home, left to their only child and now, of course, not just his, but Eleanor's home too. What would become of her without him? He shuddered to think of Mrs. McMullen's shabby boarding house where she had lived when they met. And her parents, they wouldn't know how to help her. She could go back to teaching, but he was the one who had insisted she give it up when she married him.

Divorce. William knew it was becoming more common; it was 1964, after all. Still, the sole reason a couple could be granted a divorce was adultery. To seek a divorce would be tantamount to publicly announcing his actions, and it was a brand that would not heal over quickly.

He had been so sure that the solution was to raise Michelle with Eleanor, but he could see how his decision was literally killing Madelaine. But how could he do it? How could he leave Eleanor, take Michelle, and make a home with Madelaine without destroying everything he'd worked for? Everything his parents had worked for.

"If you're wondering how to get what you want, without losing what you already have, the answer is, you can't."

"Are you a mind reader?" he asked, awestruck by her accuracy.

"I don't need to be. I've seen enough to know that's how you are." She didn't say the words kindly.

He felt confused. The conversation reversed as abruptly as a wind shear.

"It's how you all are."

"'How you all are?' What's that supposed to mean?"

"English. Protestant. Man." She spat the words at him, as if each one was a curse. "You want to screw the French maid, but go to church with your wife on Sunday. The Montebello was full of your kind."

"You don't know what you're talking about," he shook his head in a tight little movement. "What I was doing was thinking about how I could make it work for us to have a home together—with Michelle—and still be fair to the people I'm responsible to."

"No," she shook her head sadly. "You were thinking of how you could protect your property and what you own and still keep us. Your mind goes there because it doesn't know there is any other place to go. It's what I thought, but I had to see for myself before I really believe it. You and I—we're too different. I need to go back to my people."

He realized too late that he had trapped himself. Betrayed by the very instincts he'd honed for a lifetime, he didn't know how to stop using them.

"I risked everything for our daughter," he stormed. "My marriage, my home, my job."

"You risked nothing. Your clever mind, your lies, they work for you like always. You still have everything, and our daughter. You get to be the proud papa, family man, big member of Parliament."

"Madelaine, be reasonable—"

"No. I won't. This is not a matter of reason. This is passion. Keep your precious respectability. Marriage, house, job, keep it. I only want one thing. My baby. Give her back." Madelaine said the words levelly, without expression and not even a trace of hysteria. "Because if you don't—I will die. Look at me," she held up an emaciated arm, "I'm already dying."

"I can't just give her back. It'll take some time."

"Time for what? For you to think up more lies to tell your wife? Excuses you can make at the country club? No. Bring back my baby. I'll wait one day, twenty-four hours and no more."

William Buchanan was unaccustomed to rejection and ultimatums. To be given both, from the woman he'd dreamed of escaping with, left him floundering. He countered with defiance.

"And if I don't, what are you going to do about it?"

"Just watch me."

Strategy

Madelaine was desperate, which made her dangerous. William covered the distance back to the Lord Elgin in long, determined strides. He was certain that if she would just be patient and wait for him to maneuver into position, they would all get most, if not all, of what they wanted. But he heard her words still ringing in his head, "I only want one thing. My baby."

He ignored the hotel entrance, and with his hands jammed deep into his pockets and his head bowed, he circled the block three times. He tried to predict what Madelaine would do if he didn't meet her demand to return Michelle within twenty-four hours. Would she show up during Parliament, heckling him from the gallery? Not her style. Would she hire a lawyer and try to find a legal way out of the adoption contract? No, she'd dismiss it immediately as too expensive. Besides, her form of logic would ask why she, the mother, would need a lawyer to get her own baby back. She might go to the press. He could just imagine the front page of the *Whig-Standard* running a picture of him with Madelaine and the baby. He shook the image from his mind.

Finally, when he had spent enough energy for the hotel room to hold him, he went inside, and as easily as donning a comfortable sweater, William slipped into planning mode. Just as he had done thousands of times in his life, he took a fountain pen, pulled a clean sheet of Lord Elgin letterhead from the hotel desk drawer, and marked the date in the upper right-hand corner and began to make a list.

Along the left margin, he set a column of Roman numerals, prepared to enumerate each point of his strategy. He began mentally ticking off the items: offer a generous divorce settlement to Eleanor, resign his seat with sixty days' notice to the riding, begin searching for a home—perhaps in the Gatineaus—for the three of them. But this was more than a legal communication he was preparing, and he kept hearing Madelaine's accent break in on his thoughts.

"This isn't a matter of reason; this is passion."

He looked at the page in front of him and knew she would see it for what it was. A bid for time. "Time for what? More lies to your wife?"

Madelaine didn't have any more time. He hadn't seen her without clothes for months, and he'd been shocked when she had pushed up the sleeve of her cleaning uniform to display her scrawny arm. She was dying, right in front of his eyes, and here he was, doing what he always did. Covering his own ass.

He got up from the desk and rinsed his face at the bathroom sink. In the mirror, he paused and looked into his own eyes. *You gutless wonder. You've hung your women out to dry for what you've done, and you've let your baby girl suffer, all for the sake of appearances.*

Madelaine's words were coming louder and faster at him. "English. Protestant. Man." He was the history buff. He knew that Madelaine had, in three words, summed up the forces that had kept her down and had elevated him. The English had beaten the French on the Plains of Abraham, and two hundred years later, they still tried to keep them down. Protestants had sniffed haughtily for years at the overbreeding Catholics, gripped in the powerful fists of the parish priests. Man. William knew enough about history and the law to know that men had specifically drafted laws to exclude women and ensure the protection of rights like voting or land ownership accrued to men.

He moved back to the desk, took up his pen and ruler and in proper legal fashion, drew a line across the top of the page, diagonally across his words and along the bottom.

Jesus, Buchanan, you can't even tear things up like a normal person—it all has to be according to the rules. Then he lifted the paper in his fingers and tore it to shreds, and in one angry sweep, scattered the pieces across the floor. Then he did what only Madelaine could inspire him to do, and even then, not often enough—he acted without thinking. He let the words pour out of his heart, down his arm, and into his pen without filtering anything through his overactive brain.

Dearest Madelaine:

> I've been a coward and an ass. I should have owned up to my actions months ago when you first told me about Michelle. I have created a web of lies, all designed to make safe my reputation. What's worse, I tried to say I did it to protect you, Eleanor, and the baby, when my motives were purely self-preservation.

By doing that, I have ruined three lives. Your heart has been broken by losing Michelle, Eleanor is crushed because she can't make the baby happy, and our sweet child wants only one person in the entire world—you.

I have demanded from the three of you something I have nothing of myself—courage. As I write this, I realize that I have lived most of my life fearfully. Afraid of what others will think of me. I have lived in dread of being seen as incompetent. Ironically, this characteristic has made me an enormous failure in everything that really matters.

I will return Michelle to you, Madelaine, but I must have more than twenty-four hours to accomplish this. There are legalities and Eleanor to consider. As usual, I am being cautious, but these are the habits of my lifetime, and ones I confess I am too timid to break.

I have asked far too much of you already, and now I ask for one more thing I don't deserve. Forgiveness. If you are able to give me that, I promise I will spend the rest of my life being the man and father you and Michelle so assuredly deserve.

William

The next morning, William paused at the front desk on his way out of the hotel.

"Any messages?" He hoped, irrationally, that Madelaine may have tried to reach him. At his insistence, she had never once called him at the hotel.

"Just your mail, Mr. Buchanan." The clerk passed a handful of envelopes across a marble slab dulled by years of check-ins by legions of tourists.

William slid the mail into his briefcase; he could read it on the train this afternoon. For now, he had his own letter to deliver.

Letters

Madelaine turned to stone when she heard his familiar tread on the stairs. She held her breath, waiting to see what he would do. When the envelope protruded from under the door, Madelaine saw, for the first time, her own name written in the square block lettering of William's hand. It looked boxy and reined in to her. In her mind's eye, she could imagine him, waiting on the stairs, checking his watch before leaving. She timed her exhalation to match the sound of protest from the door hinges at the bottom of the stairs.

Her comprehension of written English was better than her ability to write or speak it. She took in the contents of the letter easily, and refolded it in the precise creases William had created. She reached into the pocket of her cleaning smock, a garment she would soon be liberated from, and pulled out her rosary and pressed the crucifix to her lips.

"Merci, Seigneur." She placed the letter and crucifix together in the pocket. "And thank-you too, William Buchanan, for giving me exactly what I need."

William stepped back into the chill of Ottawa's spring weather and resolved to come back to the apartment in three hours. Leaving that letter for Madelaine had gone against a lifetime of prudence. He understood for the first time why criminals confess to things the police have no hope of proving. There was a lightness about confessing. He realized that guilt, heavy as wet clay, had been pulling at him for as long as he could remember. Writing the letter to Madelaine felt like a first step in living lighter, and if she was willing, like a new start with a clean slate.

At noon, he shrugged on his overcoat and prepared to put his life's path in the hands of a woman on the cleaning staff. He was ready, eager even, to agree to any conditions she might suggest. Raise Michelle Catholic? No problem. Give up politics? Gladly. Learn to speak French? He was halfway there. He hurried to her apartment and took the stairs two at a time. He had his key with him, but chose to knock and wait like a suitor. The hallway and stairs were swept clean, and there was a faint smell of lemon. Madelaine—she dusted. *Probably the first person to do that since Confederation.*

He knocked again, harder. There were no sounds of stirring from the other side of the door. He popped open the flimsy lock with his key. The apartment was immaculate. The worn furniture was precisely where it had been the day he rented the place. The refrigerator was unplugged, with an open box of baking soda inside. The closet shelves bare except for the lining of scented paper. Sun streamed through living room windows. The old bathtub was scoured, and the bathroom smelled of chlorine bleach. She was gone.

William felt like something was being pulled out of his chest, and he put a hand up to stop it. His fast steps echoed in the stark rooms, then slowed as he took in the shabbiness of it all. Not just the condition of the rooms, but their arrangement. He had provided a seedy, convenient place, and she had accepted it with gratitude and an imagination that had transformed it into a refuge he liked better than the Lord Elgin Hotel. She had done so much more than her fair share, and he had rewarded that by taking her baby away. Shame pushed him to his knees in front of the rust-stained toilet, and he was still heaving long after there was nothing to throw up.

Finally, when he was able to stand, he paced through the apartment and focused on Madelaine. It was as if she was easier for him to see, to really see, when she was not with him. If she had been here, he would have been distracted by the sway of her blond hair when she shook it free from her headband. It was her absence that gave him clarity.

When he sat down, he sank deeply into the dilapidated couch. Madelaine was a mother now. She loved him, he was sure of that, but she didn't need him. It was the baby she needed. He should have seen it, but he hadn't, and now it might be too late. When she had turned those miserable rooms into a haven with her sewing machine and bargain basement fabrics, she hadn't sought his opinion. Most of all, when Michelle was conceived, she had followed her heart and not his logic. He had scoffed at her when she'd said, "I go to her in my sleep." He no longer doubted it. Madelaine and her child, they had a bond, one he was certain she wouldn't, probably couldn't, break. He'd come to tell her that he wanted to be part of the circle of love with her and Michelle. Now that he was finally prepared to lose all that had been precious to him, he feared that he had arrived with that news too late.

So where was she now? One thing he knew for certain, when Madelaine loved someone, it was in full measure. She would risk anything and use everything to get her baby. He knew because, even though he didn't deserve it, she had enveloped him with that kind of love. That was the magic of Madelaine. And he had let it slip away. He folded his arms across his knees, lowered his head, and wept the wounded sobs of the bereft.

When William boarded the train to Kingston, his stomach muscles still ached from the heaving in Madelaine's bathroom. He settled in the window seat, first resisting and then giving in to the urge to rest his head against the cool glass beside him. It would look undignified, but for once, he didn't care. He caught his own reflection and pulled the blind to hide his haggard image. He closed his eyes, resting, hoping to summon enough energy to continue inhaling and exhaling. Madelaine was gone. The thought shot through his midsection like a deadbolt.

There was no relief for William's misery. He couldn't sleep and had no inclination to talk to his fellow passengers. He decided to busy himself and reached for the mail he'd stowed earlier in the day. The usual invitations to cocktail parties and the press-the-flesh gatherings he loathed spilled out of the envelopes. He shifted them all to the bottom of the pile and came to one envelope, plain white, bearing nothing more than his address. When he opened it, an earring slid into his hand. It was one of his mother's sapphires. Eleanor hadn't said anything about losing an earring. Probably didn't want him to know.

He checked the envelope for a note—and pulled out a small paper, typewritten:

I found this under my pillow. Your wife might be looking for it.

CHAPTER TWENTY-FOUR
Unfit

Betsy, Annie, and some of the others were already at the church when I arrived. Halfway through the first song, we heard the door to the vestibule open, followed by slow, heavy footfalls. It meant that Bobby had arrived.

Betsy brought her watch close to her face and puzzled over it a moment. "Bobby late. Again."

He didn't come into the Sunday School room right away. I could hear muffled voices arguing.

"Boots on." I heard Bobby insist.

"Bobby, you should change into your shoes."

"No, leave boots on."

The second voice caught my attention. I listened hard, but could only catch the odd word.

"Bob, look—shoes—inside—muddy."

Bobby's voice grew louder and more insistent. "Eddy, no shoes."

"I'll go check," I whispered to Mrs. Marsh and the group, when I hurried out to investigate. When I opened the door, I saw

Bobby, one boot on and the other clutched in his arms, resisting the efforts of Edwin Wallace, who knelt in front of him, trying to wedge Bobby's foot into a lace up shoe.

"Mr. Wallace!"

Beet red wouldn't quite describe the depth of color that flushed up the neck and face of Edwin Wallace.

"What are you doing here?" he demanded.

"Ellie-nor. This Ellie-nor. Kiss? Hug?" Bobby held his one free arm toward me for an embrace.

"I play piano for the group on Thursdays," I explained while giving Bobby a quick squeeze around his shoulders, avoiding the muddy boot clasped to his chest.

Then it occurred to me, "You're Bobby's brother!"

Mr. Wallace, on his feet now, was trying to regain his composure by wiping the dust from his knees and smoothing down the clothes that hung on his bony frame. "Guilty as charged. Tell me, Miss Cole, how long have you been working in this capacity?"

He kept his attitude snippy, as if he was embarrassed to be seen here, especially in the undignified pose of trying to pry Bobby out of his boots.

"I don't really work here; I volunteer. And it's Buchanan now, not Cole."

A slight nod and a slow blink formed the response from Mr. Wallace. He's the only person in the world who could make a blink seem condescending.

"So Bobby's the reason you disappeared so often."

"So often?" Mr. Wallace was defensive. Bobby stood by, quietly witnessing the exchange. I turned to him.

"Bobby, those boots really are too muddy to wear inside." I reached for the one he still hugged close. "See?" I showed him the dirty streaks on his jacket. "Why don't you just wear your socks indoors? That's what everyone else is doing."

Bobby shot a "So there" look at his brother and jogged into the main room to meet his buddies.

Mr. Wallace seemed to regain some superiority with Bobby gone.

"How did you get involved here?" he talked to me as though it was a job interview.

"I used to come to this church before I was married. Mrs. Marsh needed someone to play the piano, so she asked me."

"Simple as that." Mr. Wallace's tone was flat and difficult to read.

"Pretty simple, yep. Now, I'd really better get back in there."

"Did anyone bother asking why you weren't gainfully employed, or was it simple because you're now a society matron?"

"*What?*" The sting of his insults from my time at Limestone came flooding back. The barbs about my education, the priggishness over the music at the concert, the way he implied that my presence was a danger to the children—I despised him for all of it. Then the final straw—being fired, for something William did—rekindled the smoldering fury about how I'd been treated by Edwin Wallace.

"Mr. Wallace, I do this because I love it. I love these kids, just like I loved the grade two class at Limestone. If you can't accept that, then I guess that's your problem."

"My problem?"

"Yes, because I don't work for you anymore. I volunteer here, Thursday afternoons and every other chance I get."

"Manage to fit it in between golf and curling seasons do you? Must be tough."

"What exactly do you have against me, Mr. Wallace?"

"I have very little against you personally. It's your type I have trouble with."

"My type?"

"Girls like you just seem to waltz into whatever they want. You lose your job? 'So what—I'm married to a rich guy so I'll just volunteer with the hopeless mental deficients.' Well, not if I have anything to do with it you won't. I didn't want you around my students, and I don't want your kind around my brother either!"

Every sinew in my body went on high alert. Frank O'Donnell was an enemy now, and I didn't need any more of those. But I couldn't resist reminding Mr. Wallace that his control of me was nonexistent.

"Well, you don't really have any say in the matter, do you?"

"The hell, I don't! I've lived here all my life. I may not have fit in with the Swamp Ward boys, and having a brother like Bobby didn't exactly elevate my standing. But I hung in there, stayed in school longer than any of them, and now I'm teaching their children. What I say may not reach the exalted elevation of Kensington Street, but on this side of Princess, people listen to Edwin Wallace."

Mrs. Marsh chose that moment to poke her head out the door, anxious to do-good her way into the conversation.

"Ahhh, Marjorie. We were just wrapping up; I wonder if I could speak with you a moment?"

"Well, only if Eleanor can keep an eye on things in there. I think they're ready for more singing."

Mrs. Marsh didn't make eye contact with me for the rest of the afternoon. When everyone was gone, Mrs. Marsh, a handkerchief wadded between her hands, hovered near me like a mosquito.

"Eleanor, I'm afraid there's something I have to..." She trailed off in a tremble.

"Edwin Wallace doesn't want me here with Bobby," I stated the obvious.

"Not just Bobby. He, Edwin, said—oh Eleanor, I'm so sorry about this..." She breathed deeply, a movement that hoisted her matronly chest into an attitude of momentary bravado, "He said you're unfit to work with our little group."

"Unfit?"

"That's what he said. Oh, I'm so sorry to be the one to say these things to you, dear. But it was something about...you know how he uses those words...something about criminals back when he knew you."

"Criminals? Me?"

"Consorting, that was it, consorting with criminals." She was like someone on a game show who surprised herself by coming up with the right answer.

"So because Edwin Wallace says something—that's it? People just automatically do what he says? That's..." I was thinking ridiculous, but wanted to use something stronger, "...ludicrous. Don't I get to say anything to defend myself?"

Mrs. Marsh started blubbering in earnest. "I tried to talk to him. But you know how he is."

"I know exactly how he is." I relented, knowing it would have been impossible for this harmless woman to hold her own against Edwin's flint. "It's okay, Mrs. Marsh," I tried to soothe her.

The older woman's lilac dress quivered, but between hiccups and shudders she choked out, "Bobby's the only one with family to look out for him. All the others," she shrugged her stooped shoulders, "they've all been farmed out. So Edwin's say-so goes a long way."

So that's it for me.

I felt like a light had been switched off. I gathered my music listlessly and went home and stroked the thick fur on Inky's neck while I steeped a pot of tea. I still had a few minutes before Nancy dropped Michelle off.

"At least you still like me, Ink. No matter what happens, I can rely on you. I don't know what I'd do if anything ever happened to you."

I palmed his silky ears and realized with supreme sadness how true and tragic my words were. I loved my parents, but we had failed each other. And William. Did I love him? I told him I did. And dutifully, he had lobbed back an "I love you too." But did he? I thought of the new Beatles song "She Loves You," and cynically added a sarcastic, "Yeah, yeah, yeah."

And when I compared my love for Inky with what I felt for Michelle—I was appalled. I had watched Nancy fawn and coo over David, and I knew the real thing when I saw it. But when I tried kissing and snuggling with Michelle, I felt like a cheap imitation of Nancy. I knew what I was supposed to do, but my heart wasn't in it. Instead, I had learned to tune out Michelle's cries while I chose music for the church group. I arranged the pieces by theme, then matched the decorations I put up each week. Then I would get lost in planning a craft activity, with adaptations for Annie. Before I knew it, an afternoon had passed, with Michelle fussing the entire time. I still couldn't understand why an infant would rather scream herself into exhaustion than be comforted by the only person in the house.

Was there something wrong with me? I was messing everything up. First I had thought I was going to help George. What a joke that turned out to be. Then I thought I could be a good teacher. Apparently I was not. And as a wife? I was always doing something to show I was too uneducated, not sophisticated enough. I couldn't have my own baby and didn't know how to get through to the one we adopted. Then there was Frank O'Donnell—God only knew where he'd turn up next and what he'd want. How could I have been so stupid? Now, it turned out, I couldn't even hold on to a volunteer job. They were desperate for help, and I couldn't give away my time.

I should have been in tears, totting up my deficiencies. But I was dry-eyed at the kitchen table, empty as the teacup in front of me, shocked at how thoroughly I had failed in every endeavor I had undertaken since leaving Faderton.

I ran my fingers along Inky's smooth coat until they were coated with the oily residue of a Labrador retriever. I heard a noise coming from the porch, which I took to be Nancy with Michelle. David would be in the car, and Nancy's pregnancy was beginning to show, a condition that suited her beautifully.

But it wasn't Nancy's glowing visage I found on the porch—far from it. I spotted a battered valise before I saw the woman who went with it. I was sure from the hesitant look above the gaunt cheeks that I was face-to-face with a Fuller Brush sales woman, her suitcase full of scouring powders and scrub brushes. I pushed open the screen door.

"Mrs. William Buchanan?" The woman spoke with a French accent.

"Yes." Her hands were chapped and she wasn't wearing gloves despite the cold day. I felt sorry for her and had already decided I would give her a sympathy sale. If she only knew, I was the one in need of sympathy.

"I need talk to you."

I judged her to be a little older than me, and I felt a pang of self-consciousness about the reversal of our situations. She pulled an envelope from her pocket, probably a list of instructions in French. The woman's pale hair was pulled back into the plainest of styles, and under her eyes, she had circles the color of ripe bruises, as if she hadn't slept in weeks.

"Certainly; would you like to come in?"

The woman looked surprised and returned the envelope to her pocket. She tried to peer around me and into the house, as if she was expecting to see something or someone. Maybe she was new to the job; certainly she didn't look like a person who would take to selling. Her eyes dropped to take in Michelle's empty buggy on the porch.

"The baby. Where is she?"

I didn't answer immediately. "She? How do you know it's a girl?" I asked.

"I know. Believe me when I say I know."

Behind me, Inky let out a low warning growl. I was sorry that I'd already invited her in. She looked weak and harmless, physically, but the solidness of her response made me edgy. She stepped into the vestibule and looked around, as if she was appraising the place. Her gaze swept from the fireplace to the carpets to the chandelier, and she nodded as if what she saw was at once predictable and disappointing. I decided not to let her get beyond the front hall. I didn't invite her to remove her coat, as I knew the heat would soon drive her out.

"You said you wanted to talk to me." I worked hard to keep my voice level.

"Yes. I need to talk, to tell you somet'ing you will not like, I think."

At that moment, Nancy wheeled into the driveway and sounded the horn. Instinctively, I didn't want Nancy to know about the strange woman in the house.

"Stay here," I commanded the stranger and dashed out to the car. It would look like I was sparing Nancy the effort of the trip to the door, and she didn't object to staying put while I gathered up Michelle and blew a kiss to David.

"How'd it go at the church?" Nancy asked.

I was jolted back to the memory of the sickening encounter with Edwin Wallace. "Long story," I answered quickly, uncomfortable with the strange woman alone in the house. "I'll call you with the details after the kids are asleep."

I bounded up the steps, Michelle in my arms, curious to hear what the exhausted looking woman in the vestibule had to tell me. She hadn't moved from the spot I'd left her in, nor had she unbuttoned her coat. When I crossed the threshold with the baby, only then did she move. Her arms reached out as though expecting me to hand the baby over.

"Mon Dieu," she said.

She took one step toward us. "Michelle!" she cried out, as though she was reaching for an apparition, and before I could decipher how she knew the baby's name, I had to figure out what I was going to do with the woman who had fainted at my feet.

CHAPTER TWENTY-FIVE
Explanations

With Michelle on my hip, I knelt beside the woman and touched her neck. There was a pulse, thank goodness. I knew she wasn't dead, but beyond that, I was clueless. I placed Michelle in her playpen in the living room and hurried back to the form splayed across the front hall floor. I undid the buttons on her coat, guilty because it had been my idea to get her to leave from being overheated. Now it looked like my plan had worked too well, and the heat had caused her to faint.

I opened the lapels of her coat and saw sharp collarbones above her neckline. A fine gold necklace with a filigreed "M" lay on her chest. "M." I remembered the paper I had found after Christmas, a list William had started and then stopped. On the to-do side, he'd written "Stipend for M."

The spot where I knelt started to feel spongy beneath my weight. Under me, the mahogany floorboards felt like lake ice that had softened and threatened to break up at any moment. I steadied myself against the hall table.

After a moment I eased the woman's arms from the sleeves and discovered that her coat was at least two sizes bigger than the form it covered. Either she had bought it too big, or she had lost a lot of weight recently. I decided that the latter was true, and that might explain the fainting too. And there was something else.

She wore a fine-knit sweater, pale blue except for large blotches dark and wet on her front. Dark ovals started at the breasts and extended to her waist. She was breastfeeding! But where was her baby?

Michelle started to whimper in the next room. I looked in her direction and back to the woman on the hardwood. And I watched as Michelle's sounds roused the woman from unconsciousness and as the dark stains grew, as her breasts reacted to the cries of a baby. Beneath me, the floor solidified again, and I knew two things for certain. This was Michelle's mother, and William had lied to me about a teenage mother in Rockcliffe. This woman had to be closer to thirty. But why would he lie? It didn't take a genius to figure that one out.

Groggily, she shook herself awake, and I helped her up. She was weeping now, and we understood without exchanging a word that we both knew what this was about. She half-staggered toward the divan at the window end of the living room, and I was relieved when she set herself into it without falling again. Beside this mysterious "M," I placed Michelle on the seat cushion and zipped open her bunting bag. As effortlessly as if we were long-time friends, the woman lifted the baby, and I slid the outfit off Michelle. Like always, Michelle's crying started to escalate, until the woman cradled her into her upper body and my inconsolable baby nestled like molten chocolate into the mold of her mother.

The woman's tears coursed down her cheeks and on to Michelle, in a christening ceremony more real than any created by church doctrine. Then the baby with whom I'd been locked in battle for three months shuddered a sigh of abandon and relinquished herself to the solace of that body. I'd seen all I needed to. I spoke with a strength I didn't know I had.

"Michelle is your baby."

She nodded.

"And my husband, William—he's the father, isn't he?"

Again she nodded.

Michelle was squirming in the woman's lap, her open mouth taking wide swipes toward the blue sweater. Without a word, the woman slipped her sweater up and expertly unhooked a latch and turned Michelle's hungry mouth toward her. Michelle gulped the milk she'd been craving with loud, grateful sounds.

"How do you still have milk?"

"I pumped," she replied simply.

There was only one thing I could do. "Would you like some tea?" I asked.

"Please, with honey, if possible."

I started from the room, feeling like a violinist on the Titanic.

By the time William came in the door, I knew everything about them. Madelaine (we finally introduced ourselves over tea) had showed me the letter and told me everything: how they had met, the apartment in the ByWard Market, the baby, and the plan to have us raise her. I listened to the story while Michelle slept peacefully in Madelaine's arms. As the story unfolded, especially the deception around Michelle's birth, I felt the same whirling sensation that always followed a moment when what I'd seen and what I knew, or thought I knew, were two different things. It was the same vortex I had been in outside my mother's room when she had talked to Linda Silver. It had felt like this when George Knowles turned out to be a creep and again in Frank's apartment, when he turned on me. Something inside me was missing. That thing that told you that what you were seeing or hearing wasn't the whole story. I didn't know if it was called judgment or intuition, but I didn't have it. And the story Madelaine confessed to as we sat together was more evidence of the same. I should have suspected that something was up with William. Coming home on the later train, his taciturn manner last summer, then suddenly at Christmas—a baby! Why had I just accepted what I was told without question?

William came into the house quietly. I heard him open and close the closet door, and he came straight to the living room and showed not a trace of surprise to find his wife, mistress, and child sitting together, a pot of tea on the table. The expression on his face was one I had never seen on him, and I groped for just the right word to capture it. Resigned. Beaten. Yes, but there was a trace of something else. Relief. As if he could finally rest after carrying a burden.

"I see you've met," he began.

We both nodded in his direction.

"So what have you decided?" he asked.

"Madelaine wants to take Michelle back," I answered.

"Back? Back where?" His voice wasn't unkind.

"To my people," Madelaine answered simply, "in Montebello. First with my sister. Then to a place of my own; my brothers will help build it. They will do this for us."

"That won't be necessary." William's voice surprised me with its firmness. "My offer stands. What I wrote in the letter, I stand by that." William's back straightened, practiced, familiar, ready to be in charge again.

I felt like I was floating above the group and watching this unfold in someone else's life. My husband wanted to leave and begin a new life that, except for financial details, wouldn't include me. Wasn't I supposed to be upset?

Madelaine shifted the baby against her and straightened as if steel fortified her back. "No thank-you. I told you before, I want only my baby. I have her. Now I can live."

With her accent, I couldn't tell if she'd said leave or live. But I guessed that both were accurate, and she stood up, holding Michelle closely.

"Madelaine—we can work this—"

"It is finished," she stopped him. Without any hesitation, as if having Michelle in her arms infused the woman with spirit, she moved toward the door.

I passed her the bag that Nancy had taken on their outing this morning. She took it without a word. The door was open, and I could see two dark, broad-shouldered men who looked like brothers waiting beside a panel truck. Madelaine strode out the door, and in the space of a few seconds, mother and baby had settled into the passenger's seat. William looked stricken with loss as he watched the truck disappear from view.

"Eleanor, I'm sorry." His voice was a whisper, and he didn't have the courage to look at me.

"I am too." I couldn't let all this fall on him. I had an apology of my own over Frank O'Donnell. "There's something I have to tell you."

He shrugged as if to say it didn't matter. "I know." He pulled something from his pocket and dangled it for me to see—the sapphire earring. William dismantled the crib, while I emptied everything from the dresser and closet into boxes. We moved the furniture into the hall, almost all of it done without exchanging a word. It wasn't a silence of tension or anger, but what the losing hockey team must feel like after the Stanley Cup finals. When the room was completely empty, we surveyed it together. I checked my watch. The whole thing had taken less than an hour. The pink flowered wallpaper was the only remaining evidence that a little girl had occupied this room.

"Do we have any paint?" William asked.

"There's half a gallon of beige in the basement."

He was almost to the bottom of the stairs when I called after him. "Bring two brushes."

We spent the evening painting over the decorator's work that was only a few months old. The sweep of the brushes was the only sound at first, until William finally spoke. "Don't you want to ask me any questions?"

"Eventually. First I want to explain about the earring."

The stories we told each other were unvarnished in their honesty. By the time the paint can was empty, we sat wearily in the middle of the room, our confessions complete. "It's times like this when I wish I smoked," I told him.

He smiled and reached for my hand. "I think we both have enough vices to deal with."

"There's one last thing. Frank told me the two of you were half brothers. Is that true?"

"Half brothers?"

"He said his mother was your father's secretary and that they had a thing together, and he was their child."

"O'Donnell. There was a Hattie O'Donnell who worked for my dad when I was a kid. Never knew what happened to her, though."

"He said there was some kind of argument a few months before your parents' accident. His mother brought him here, but your father denied it all."

"Does he have any proof?"

DIVISIONS

"No."

William got that calculating look on his face. The one that showed up when he talked about investing or tax advantages. Then he unpuckered his forehead as if the theme of the day had caught up with him. "O'Donnell may be right."

"I didn't know anything about a visit here, but one morning I could hear through the vents, my mother was yelling at my dad. The only time I ever heard her do that. I never did know what she was so mad about, but I remember my father saying Hattie O'Donnell was nothing but a trampy Irish souse. And my mother, the most prudish woman you could imagine, said Hattie should learn to keep her mouth and her legs closed."

"But why were they mad at her, when your father was just as much to blame?"

"My father? Just as much to blame? My mother would be spinning like an auger in her grave to hear a Buchanan suggest that we should be blamed for anything—ever."

"Then I guess I'd better give back the other sapphire earring, because if that's how she was, I don't want to wear her jewelry."

"Well, that is how she was, so we might as well forgive her." He paused meaningfully and added, "And each other."

"That might take a little longer."

CHAPTER TWENTY-SIX
The Fort

Frank O'Donnell swung his car through the campus and down Kensington Street, slowing as he passed Buchanan's stalwart house. The blinds in the master bedroom hadn't moved in more than a month. He took that to mean that William hadn't been around lately. He should know; he passed the place at least twice a day. Finally, one morning in May, his patience was rewarded when he spied the bounce of Eleanor's dark hair as she walked south toward the lake. Another couple of slow passes, staying behind her so she wouldn't see him. She turned toward the Leslie Causeway, and a slow smile spread across the young constable's face.

Headed to the fort. He'd seen her take that trek before, followed her without her knowing. She'd stride along like a woman possessed, right through the gates of Fort Henry, past the bulwarks, and would turn off into what appeared from the road to be just a path in the long grass. But Frank had been around Kingston long enough to know that a set of stone stairs led down to a clearing by the east ditch tower. It was unique because it was completely hidden from the road above and the boaters on the lake. Yet, anyone who secreted themselves there had a clear view of the lake over to Cedar Island and could hear the noises from the road clearly. One could see, but not be seen, hear, but not be heard, which made it popular with skinny dippers and teenagers looking for a make out place. He had seen her head into that clearing more than once on a weekday morning, and today he intended to intercept her there.

The steps ended at the edge of Lake Ontario. In summer, the drop to the lake was about four feet, but at this time of year, with the right breeze, the chilled water would wash right up on the slate clearing.

He parked a distance from the spot and walked quietly along the edge of the roadway, letting the spongy grass silence the sound of his steps. He had to play this right. He had gone too far the last time. He wanted to approach her quietly. Didn't want to scare her. He was already imagining that she might see him and melt into his embrace. It had happened once, hadn't it? Why had he been such a fool? He had come on way too strong. He'd frightened her. He wanted a second chance. She had to be getting lonesome by now.

She sat facing the water, looking out over Cedar Island, her dark hair fluttering toward the dog. Inky bristled and barked at the sight of Frank. Eleanor jumped to her feet, and Frank spoke before she said anything.

"Eleanor, I just want to talk to you." He held up his hands in surrender.

She looked around wildly, as if searching for an escape. He stood on the steps above her. Behind her was the lake, and to her right, hewn blocks of limestone, welded together by earth and stone and roots. Beyond the wall was a thirty-foot drop to the rocky ditch bottom. Moving left was her only option, but it was tall with grass and weeds, and the ground was steep. So escape wasn't an option, and Frank hoped she wouldn't want to.

"I just want to talk to you," he repeated.

"Get lost."

"Eleanor, c'mon."

"Do you honestly think I'm going to have a conversation with you, Frank? Are you out of your mind?"

"Don't think so." He moved down a step, edging up on her as if he was approaching a wild horse. "I hear you've had a spot of trouble over at your house."

"Yeah—that ought to please you."

"It makes what you and me done seem pretty simple, doesn't it?"

"What we *did*," she corrected his grammar, "was a mistake."

He moved down another two steps and squatted, absentmindedly pulling at the spring grass that poked through the fissures in the rock. The dog resumed his low growl and leaned his broad chest forward just enough to keep Frank's attention.

"That dog won't attack me, will she?"

"He," she emphasized her point, "will do whatever I tell him to do. The only male I ever found who'd do that."

Frank laughed.

"See? That's why I like you—you go through all this trouble with your husband and the baby, and you still manage to crack a joke."

"Don't even try, Frank. After what you threatened, I have no intention of listening to you."

Inky stood up and moved a front paw to a spot in front of Eleanor. His black face was intelligent and easy to read. He placed himself between Eleanor and Frank before the cop could take another step closer. It was a standoff.

The three of them remained like that long enough for the water to wash up on the lowest ledge in four separate waves. Inky relaxed his guard from menacing to alert. He showed a penetrating instinct that could outlast any human who might try to get past him and to his mistress.

Frank noticed that Eleanor's face had become more angular, less afraid than before. It would mean everything to him to get her to open up to him again. Maybe if he played his cards right, carefully this time, she'd hook up with him. They could date, and who knows, with her marriage to Buchanan over, she could be with him—the one she should have gone for in the first place. But he'd have to be a lot more careful this time.

"I should never have said what I did. It's just that I wanted you so bad. I'm sorry." He moved closer to the edge of the step, not ready to risk a move that might set the dog on him.

Eleanor stood with her arms folded. She was shaking her head before he finished his last sentence.

"Frank—you threatened to hurt the kids at the church and my dog. The fact that you even have those thoughts in your head, whether you act on them or not, makes me sick."

"I said I'm sorry." He edged his foot silently down toward the limestone tread, and Inky responded by rocking forward on his haunches. Frank held a hand palm out toward Inky. Eleanor acted like she didn't notice.

"C'mon, Ellie, I made a mistake. I'm human. Haven't you made a couple yourself?"

"Yeah—you. You were the biggest mistake of my lifetime."

Frank let the insult slide. He let the cicadas and the lapping water fill the space for him. The dog's tail lowered. Eleanor's brows were pulled together, forming parallel lines on her forehead, and her mouth was pursed in disgust as if she looked at him and saw something revolting, but something she could step around if she had to.

A rustle in the long grass distracted them all. Inky let out a sharp bark.

"Probably a groundhog," Frank speculated.

"My day for rodents."

The rustling stopped. Maybe the creature had reached its burrow or hunkered down for safety. Either way, Inky's attention was riveted on the point where the grass had resumed swaying in unison with the tall weeds around it. The black flanges of his nostrils quivered, and a thousand years of breeding overtook him, and he plunged into the grass to corner his prey.

Frank used the break to follow his own instincts. He descended the last three steps that separated Eleanor from him with a casualness calculated not to alarm Eleanor. He should have controlled his Irish yap the last time they spoke, but he'd been so filled with the triumph of making love with her that he'd said too much. His threats had scared her; she'd taken them seriously, and why wouldn't she? He was from a coarse tumble of boys. She was an only child. She took everything seriously. He had blown it, big time, and he wanted a second chance. If only he could get her to trust him again.

"Ink!" she called sharply. "Inky—you get back here."

Frank pulled a dog treat from his pocket, put a ring finger and thumb to his lips and whistled. Inky paused, twenty or thirty feet into the underbrush, his intelligent face weighing the options. Go for the unknown or return for the treat. He bounded back for a certain reward, which he took from the tips of Frank's outstretched fingers.

"Some guard dog." He ruffled the velvet nap on Inky's head.

Eleanor, indignant, grabbed Inky's collar and pulled him away from Frank. "Why should he be a guard dog? I didn't need any protecting until you came along. He's family. About the only one I have, too."

"It doesn't have to be that way."

"What?"

"I came here, followed you here actually, to tell you I'm sorry about the mess with your family. But not really sorry. Things ended bad between us—and that was my fault. About the dog being your only family—it doesn't have to be that way."

Eleanor stood with her back toward the stone wall that flanked the staircase. Purplish flowers hung from flowing tendrils that had pushed their way through impossible crevices. She held Inky's leash tight with one hand and plucked one of the blooms from its stem with her other.

"It does for me. See, I have trouble seeing through people. Inky is real—simple, but real. No ulterior motives with him."

Frank placed a hand high on the stone wall and leaned toward her by increments. He could smell her hair, and it lifted him back to Division Street, and his knees nearly gave way with the prospect of getting her back.

He wanted to keep her talking. "It could be different between us. I'm a simple guy."

"You? A simple guy?"

Frank swung his other hand up to the rock wall, so his palms were planted to the sides of Eleanor's face. He angled toward her, aching for a kiss that would signal that they were all right. He was determined to reignite what he'd doused with his words back in his apartment. His mind was racing ahead, thinking, if she went for him, right here and now, should they lie in the grass or find a flat part on the rock wall and just grind against it? Either way, he had to be at work in less than an hour, so he'd better make it fast.

Eleanor pulled her head back and sideways as much as she could for someone pinned against limestone.

"Get off me!" she screamed.

"What the hell?" Frank was sincerely puzzled. "You won't even kiss me?"

"Get off!" She pushed him. "Do I have to spell it out for you? You are not a simple guy. You lie, bribe, and bully your way through life. You're the reason Mrs. M is dead. You threatened to hurt the kids at the church. You want me to kiss you? I can't stand you. You make me puke."

Inky, free now, ran partway up the steps and barked a warning. Frank pulled back, enough to focus his dark eyes on the face that had beguiled him from the moment he had met her. She used the sudden maneuvering room to bring her knee up hard into his groin. He clapped his right hand reflexively to his crotch and doubled over at the waist. With his free hand, he grabbed at her and came up clutching her dark hair.

She brought a sharp elbow up, and connected with his nose hard enough that Frank tasted blood. "I'm not going to hurt you, for chrissakes," he bellowed.

She hadn't done any real damage, and he knew she probably couldn't, but the dog—where the hell was the dog?

As if in answer, Inky, fangs bared, came sailing through the air, his wispy-haired underside exposed and ready to slam Frank to the ground. But Frank had been a brawler since he took up walking, and he dropped to one knee and kicked deep into Inky's soft belly. The dog cleared Frank's head and landed with a thud, skidding on the slippery ledge at the bottom of the stairs.

"Inky!" Eleanor screamed and scrambled down the stairs to her last friend on the planet. Frank stayed on his knees and spit strings of saliva and blood into the long grass.

Jesus, now you've really done it. Probably killed her dog.

A figure charged out of the waist high grass, interrupting Frank's recrimination. The cop's head jerked up and back when the kick from a cowboy boot was placed deftly under his beefy chin. He felt his teeth jar together, and his incisors drove clean through his tongue, and a fury beyond his ability to control it exploded out of him.

George Knowles didn't stand a chance after his well-placed punt. His boots, slippery on the damp grass, couldn't have been more wrong for squaring off against Frank. Frank's hands, strong and thick-fingered, were around George's neck, squeezing as if forcing the life out of him was fair payback for the indignity he'd brought to the cop's jaw. Frank spluttered and horked blood into George's face, aware that he probably looked every bit the madman Eleanor thought he was. He knew she was watching him, but he couldn't stop himself. Enraged and out of control, Frank held George off the ground with his strong fingers wrapped tight around the smaller man's neck.

From the edge of the water he heard Eleanor screaming at him.

"Stop! Frank, let him go! You're going to kill him!"

She was telling the truth. A glimmer of hope ignited in Frank. *She doesn't want me to get into trouble.* Frank loosened his hold on George's throat just enough for the kid to draw a loud and labored breath.

"What do you care?" Frank sneered. Testing to see if she'd give him the response he felt it essential to have.

"About you? Nothing."

DIVISIONS

Frank allowed one conciliatory breath, and George used it against him. With one hand clutching at his own throat, the other reached into the pocket of his sagging jeans. His fingers found what he wanted, and the sunlight glinted a warning to Frank just as a switchblade flicked toward him.

The graze George inflicted on Frank's thick forearm was barely enough to raise blood, but it, and the finality of Eleanor's words, sent Frank over the edge of reason. He grabbed George's thin wrist and bent it so the knife was pointed back at George's middle. Then he pushed his thick midsection into George, driving the blade deeper, without ever touching it himself. He switched to bashing George's thin shoulders against the rocks, watching the undulations pass through George's body. First his head, then legs, then feet, snapping against the wall like a sheet in a stiff breeze. Frank hadn't planned it, but he knew he had to finish it.

Let her see. She thinks I'm scum? I make her want to puke? This ought to help her—let her puke her guts out! And the rage of losing a chance at life with Eleanor, caused by his own temper, powered through those thick arms and demanded payment from George, because somebody had to pay, and as wild as he was, even Frank knew he'd never strike out at Eleanor.

Maybe that was what made him stop, finally. He dragged George down the steps, past Eleanor and the dog, George's silver tipped boots scraping equal signs on each tread down to the water's edge. He dumped George's body into the lake that was warming up to welcome a summer's worth of cottagers and kids doing cannonballs off docks. Frank stood, panting, his back to Eleanor and the damn dog. He didn't want to turn around. Didn't want to see what he had so irretrievably destroyed.

Behind him, Inky whimpered, and even before he turned to look, he knew Eleanor was cradling the dog's head, comforting him with the body and love Frank so wanted for himself. A dog. A goddam dog got more than he did! Frank put his hands on his knees and got his breath back. His right hand was streaked red with George's blood, and he wiped it in the long grass.

It had gone all wrong. He'd wanted to show her he was the lover she needed, the safe place where she could be herself. But that hadn't turned out. First the dog, then George Knowles had gotten between them. Knowles had looked like he was coming in on a white horse to save her. Frank should have known better. But he had lost control and overreacted—now there would be trouble. She was the kind of person who wouldn't keep quiet about this. She was a school teacher, for God's sake. He turned to look at her. He opened his mouth to speak, but that brought a fresh cascade of blood pouring out his lips. Eleanor, mute and huddled close to Inky, watched him with terrified eyes.

He'd never win her now. But he had bigger worries than getting the girl. There wasn't a snowball's chance in hell that Frank O'Donnell was going to pay for what he'd done to a slug like Knowles. The only bars he intended to be looking at had girls like Shelagh, the barmaid, behind them. He left Eleanor with one last look of contempt and dashed up the stone steps and out of sight.

CHAPTER TWENTY-SEVEN

Trust

Inky tried to keep up with me as we clambered up the bank and toward the road. I had to lift him from behind so he could make the last couple of stairs. There wasn't a chance he'd be able to make the trek all the way home. He winced as he took the first few steps, and with his back arched, he moved as if walking on broken glass. He dropped his hind end and tried to hitch himself along with his front paws. He didn't manage more than a few feet before he stopped.

I crumpled to the ground beside him. George was dead. I lay beside Inky, sick with fury directed toward Frank. I felt disgusted with myself for getting involved with him and aching for the pain that Inky felt. It was too late to help George. He'd been dead before Frank had thrown him into the water. Still, I had to tell someone. Inky stirred as if sensing I was going to leave him. His eyes pleaded for help. I felt his heart pounding through his powerful chest, and it skipped a beat. I pulled back to look at him, and he must have felt it too because everything on his beautiful face said, "What's happening to me?" The only question I had for myself was, "How could I have let this happen? To George, to Inky."

I pressed into him again. His fur was luxurious, but beneath it, his heart fluttered, and his breathing came in shallow, panicky huffs. My own heart responded with steady, strong thumps, the results of miles of walking. That was when it occurred to me. Every step I'd taken in the past year had been with Inky by my side. His heart was just as strong as mine. Not much had gone right since I had come to Kingston, but Inky was the one thing I could point to and say, "See. I can do something right." I had grown a strong and loving dog—and I was not going to let him go without a fight.

I got to my feet and stooped to lift Inky, but he was heavy, and I half-carried him into the shade. "I'll be back as soon as I can, boy. I'm going for help, and you are going to be fine."

Inky's response was a fast flaring and contracting of nostrils, as he concentrated on breathing. I kissed his forehead and started running for the fort. I hadn't gone one hundred yards before I realized that there was something different about me. I wasn't confused. I didn't have to think anything through. My mind was as assured as my strides. I could almost see myself as if I was outside my body. See myself running, sure-footed and strong. I saw someone resolute in her bearing and manner. This was not the frightened girl who had cowered away from Frank. This couldn't be the same person who had wanted to pull Frank off George but had been too terrified to move. I was looking at someone who, in only a few minutes, had grown into adulthood, and I knew with the same certainty that there would be no going back.

Inky could die. I didn't want to lose anyone else. My parents, William, Michelle, Frank, Mrs. M—one way or another, I'd lost them all, and I was certain that I did not want to lose one more time. I had to be strong, and I was. All the time I'd been wondering who to trust and who to believe. Running to get help for Inky showed me exactly who I could trust. It was me.

Because this was the long weekend in May, the grounds around the fort were filled with tourists. It wouldn't take long to find a ride, and as soon as I did, I'd take Inky—where? The veterinarian's office would be closed. Shouldn't I be going to the police first to let them know about George? Frank was escaping, and Inky was dying. I kept up my pace, hauling air, and forced myself to concentrate on finding help. I looked up to see a police car cruising toward me. I halted, terrified that it might be Frank back to shut me up. Without Inky, I was vulnerable. But it was Stan's face, filled with concern, that I saw. He took one look at me and sized things up perfectly.

"You're in trouble, which means Frank has to be around here somewhere."

An hour ago, I would have collapsed into a welter of tears and excuses. The newly minted adult in me didn't do that, and for the second time, I stood back and watched myself.

"He killed George Knowles, Stan."

Stan nodded.

"He might have killed Inky too. I was just running to get help."

"Get in the car." He used a jacket to brush off the passenger seat for me and adjusted the air vents. "Comfortable?" he asked.

"I'm okay."

Stan looked like he wanted to say something more but didn't trust himself. He nodded and gave me a reassuring smile.

He spoke into the microphone, alerting the police to look out for Frank O'Donnell and calling for units to come to the East

Ditch tower. I pointed to Inky, lying on the grass, his dark coat almost hidden in the shadows. He gave a weak yelp when we lifted him onto the back seat.

"Where should we take him?" I asked Stan.

"The vet?"

I shook my head. "Long weekend. They're closed 'til Tuesday."

As if he understood, Inky let out another plaintive sound. Stan reached back to pat him. "Don't you worry, boy, we'll find you some help. Now what about Knowles—where's he?"

"Dead. And Frank threw him into the water."

"How long ago?"

I hesitated. *A lifetime ago. I was just a kid when it happened.* "Ten or fifteen minutes," I answered.

Another cruiser and then another crested the hill and Stan got out of the car to talk to the other cops. I reached to the back seat and stroked Inky's ears, but I stayed quiet, not wanting to make any promises I might not be able to keep.

Stan slid into the driver's seat and put the car into gear in one movement. "I'm taking you two over to May's. If anybody knows what to do for the dog, it'll be May."

"What if she's not there?"

"She's there."

"What d'ya know about dogs?" Stan asked May as he set Inky gingerly on a worn blanket spread on the chesterfield.

"Not enough to help this guy. What happened to him?"

"He got…" I didn't want to upset Betsy, who was bent over Inky, burying her face in his soft fur. "He's had a blow to his belly."

May's response was an understanding nod, as if I'd explained everything perfectly.

"I've got to get back. You okay with this?" Stan asked May.

"Handled."

It was as if the two of them had a shorthand between them. Whatever it was, I trusted it. Before the cruiser pulled away, May had come to a decision.

"We need some help, and I know exactly who I'm going to call." Whoever it was, she knew the number without looking it up. She checked her watch and paced as far as the cord on the wall phone would let her go.

"Hello, it's May Wilson calling, and we need your help over here. No, nothing like that. It's about a dog. My friend's dog has been hurt and..." she listened a moment. "The vet's closed. Long weekend." Another pause. "I would appreciate it."

May didn't sound like her regular self, talking to whoever it was.

"About ten minutes?" She gave me a wink that said, *It'll be all right*.

"Thanks, Edwin. We'll see you then."

Edwin? Mr. Wallace? He'd ask questions, and my answers would be nothing but proof for Edwin Wallace that trouble seemed to be linked to me like thunder follows lightning. But for once, I didn't give a damn.

"Ellynor, Ellynor!" Bobby burst through the door ahead of his brother. He wrapped me in a hug that was as sincere and love-filled as any I could remember. Edwin carried what looked like a doctor's case. He greeted me with distinctly less enthusiasm than Bobby showed.

"This is your dog?" he asked, folding his long legs and kneeling beside the couch.

"This Inky," Bobby declared excitedly.

"What happened?"

I glanced toward May. She started to answer for me, but I, the adult me, responded. "He's had a blow to his belly. Below his ribcage."

Edwin began running his hands over Inky's head and down his ears and along his jaw.

"Did he fall?" He asked the room without taking his eyes off the dog.

It was my first encounter with Edwin Wallace where I didn't really care about his judgment; I just wanted him to help my dog.

"He was kicked. As a result, he took a bad fall."

Edwin reached into his bag and pulled out a muzzle. He guided Inky's face toward it.

"He won't bite!" I spoke to him sharply.

Edwin didn't answer me, but I could see the color move up his neck. He kept stroking Inky gently and eased the muzzle slowly over the dog's mouth and nose. When he spoke, it was to the dog.

"Of course you wouldn't bite, not normally, would you, fella?" Inky's look of desperation eased, and he sagged as if giving himself over to Edwin's care.

"But this isn't normal for you. You'd have every right to go after anyone within biting distance after what's been done to you. Eh, Inky? So we're going to keep you and me and everybody in the room safe with this nasty old muzzle." Edwin talked as naturally as a mother to her child, and much more nicely than he'd ever talked to me or to anyone else at Limestone Elementary.

Almost as if the rest of us had disappeared, Edwin slid his hands the length of each of Inky's legs. Working around the muzzle, he nudged back the skin along the mouth. He retrieved a flashlight from the bag and tenderly pulled the eyelids up and down, shining the light into Inky's eyes.

"Bobby, could you give me a hand with this blanket?"

Bobby was at his brother's side in a heartbeat.

Edwin explained carefully. "Remember, Bob, how to move an injured animal?"

"Slow. Gentle."

"That's right." Edwin's long bony hand hadn't left Inky's fur since he started examining him. "You've helped me do this at the shelter, Bob; this is just the same. We're not going to move Inky; we're going to move the blanket Inky is on. I want to get a look at his belly. Ready?"

"Ready."

Bobby and Edwin eased the blanket toward the edge of the couch, and Inky growled and pawed at the muzzle. "Easy, Ink," Edwin spoke calmly. "Bobby and I are trying to help you, but you have to let us have a peek."

Edwin was a natural at this. It obviously came easier to him than talking to people. When they had Inky turned to examine him, Edwin's fingers moved efficiently. He came to a spot that made Inky yelp and try to scramble off the couch, but Edwin soothed and quieted him back into position. He paused by Inky's flank to separate the hair. He reached into the bag, came up with some gauze and ointment, and cleaned a small cut and applied the salve. All the while, he chatted calmly to Inky, assuring him he'd have the muzzle off as quickly as he could and apologizing for the smell of the ointment.

Then without hesitating another moment, Edwin unfolded his gangly frame, slipped off the muzzle, and tossed it into his bag. He turned to face me, and when he did, transformed back into the Edwin Wallace I had always known.

"Your animal has a small abrasion near his hindquarters, extensive bruising on his underside, and worst of all, a fractured rib. He must have sustained one hell of a blow to break a rib in such a young, strong canine."

"Will he be all right?"

"Probably. Depends on whether you can keep him away from the kind of people who kick dogs." He snapped shut the case. "Let him rest, and take him to the vet on Tuesday, just to be sure." He motioned to Bobby. "C'mon, Bob, time for us to go."

"Edwin..." May spoke quietly.

"No thank-yous required, May."

"I'm not thanking you."

"You should."

"There's something you should do too, and you know what it is."

Edwin made a face as if he'd swallowed some of the foul-smelling ointment he'd put on Inky. I looked from him to May. Her arms were folded across her chest, and she cocked an eyebrow in my direction. Edwin pinched the bridge of his nose like someone trying to hold back a nosebleed.

"Eleanor, Mrs. Buchanan," he edited himself. "May and several other women in the community have made it clear that your services as an accompanist are sorely missed over at the church. I...I'm..."

Was he actually going to apologize?

"I'm not going to stand in your way if you decide to resume that little job."

Little job? Was that how he thought of it?

"In fact, the group has been asked to take part in an outdoor Dominion Day concert on July first, and your musical leadership is needed."

"You need me to play for the concert?"

DIVISIONS

"We need someone. Bobby and the others are familiar with your style, so you are the logical choice."

The old me would have gushed in gratitude. Instead I said, "Thank-you for helping my dog. As for the concert, I'll talk it over with May."

He nodded and shot May a look that asked "Satisfied?" and judging from her thin smile, I believed she was.

CHAPTER TWENTY-EIGHT
Dominion Day

"We'll run this piece one more time, and then we'll go home," I promised.

"Okay!" Betsy's face was filled with her usual unmasked happiness when she was given one more song to sing.

We launched into "This Land is Your Land." We had ten singers, one for each province. Just as we wound down the final bars of the song, the door to the church basement banged noisily.

"Thought I might find you here!" It was Nancy, holding little David on one hip and swinging a picnic basket with the other. "We brought treats!"

Betsy and Bobby were at Nancy's side in an instant. "We'll help," Bobby offered. And they did. Helped themselves to the muffins inside, then reluctantly passed the basket to the rest of the choir who had completely abandoned their formation.

"Not only did I bring food, but I arrive with great news," Nancy said.

"From William?"

"No, Ray still hasn't heard a thing from him. Anyway, this is way better. What's your biggest problem in life right now?"

"With Frank O'Donnell vanished, George Knowles dead, and William hiding out in Ottawa, my biggest problem is getting costumes for the concert."

"Wrong," Nancy used the muffin to trace an "x" in the air. "You have costumes."

"We do?"

"I am making the costumes." She pulled a coiled measuring tape from her pocket. "That's why I'm here. Came to measure everybody."

Tears filled my eyes. "Nancy, are you sure? It's a lot of work, and so much will have to be made specially. Like Annie's—she needs special fasteners for her clothes."

"Sweetie, what you're doing is incredible. I figured if, after everything you've been through, you can get up a choir, then the least I can do is help. You inspired me."

"Let's hope David has long naps so you can sew. We need the costumes in less than two weeks."

With a hand at each end, Nancy snapped the measuring tape taut. "Let me at 'em."

When the measuring up was finished and everyone had been sent home, I stepped outside and pulled shut the door to the church basement. When I looked up, William stood waiting for me. He looked pale, and there were pouches under his eyes.

"Can't keep you away from this place, eh?" He seemed self-conscious.

"No one's been trying to lately."

I moved toward the Buick and piled the music books into the back seat. "I suppose you'll want your car back."

"Nope. I think you need it more than I do."

"The house?"

"No, I don't need that either."

"So what do you want?" I asked showing my impatience. "Inky's waiting at home—he needs to be let out."

"Inky—right. Why is it you're happiest when you tend to helpless creatures? Is mixing with my kind of people too intimidating, so you go where it's easier?"

"I go where I'm appreciated."

"I did appreciate you. I gave you a beautiful home and a car to drive. You could have spent every day at the club, if you'd wanted to."

"That's the point; I didn't want to. I didn't know that when I married you. You appreciated me for what I could do for you. But when I wanted to work with the kids, that wasn't good enough for you."

"Because I wanted something better for you. Eleanor, these people, I realize someone has to help them, but I hear you're planning a concert, a public concert on Dominion Day, no less. Don't you think you're being cruel, putting them on parade like that? People will make fun of them; you'll see. Most people aren't as accepting as you are."

"No, I don't think I'm being cruel. Cruel is separating babies from their families and raising them like cattle in institutions. And why? Because they're different, they're not as able as others. And yes, some people will be mean and ignorant, I know that."

"Then why put yourself through it? You don't have to; it's not like they're family."

"They're the closest thing I've ever had to a real family. We love each other, we help each other, we drive each other a little crazy. In the end, we need each other."

"I needed you, Eleanor."

"No. What you need, what we all need, is to find what's in our hearts and follow it."

"What's that supposed to mean?"

"Something different for everyone. Mrs. M told me that, and I'm just beginning to get it now. She said 'You've got to find it for yourself and by yourself.'"

"What's 'it?'"

"Whatever makes you tick. And for me, it's these kids."

"So what do you think makes me tick?" he asked.

I shrugged. "What would you do even if you weren't getting paid for it?"

"Well, it wasn't the law, and it sure as hell isn't politics."

"William, can you remember a time, even one time, when we went out and you didn't explain something about Kingston's history to me? You knew about Bellevue House or the story behind Fort Henry or Sir John A. McDonald."

His old smile, the safe one, appeared on his face. "Did I bore you?" he asked.

"Not at all—but doesn't that give you a clue about what 'it' is for you?"

He pulled a folded paper from his pocket. "Read it."

"The University of Auckland? Where's that?"

"New Zealand. They want a professor of Canadian history. I'll be leaving in August."

"Now this," I pointed to the letter, "sounds like it was made for the William Buchanan I know." I leaned against the car and tried to imagine my life as a single woman. Couldn't do it—not yet, anyway. "So that's what you came to tell me?"

"That's part one," he answered in typical William style.

"I suppose you want a divorce."

"Not especially. You?"

DIVISIONS

It felt bold and adult to talk like this. The first time I felt like his equal. He waited for my response.

"Not yet. I think there's still hope for us." He blinked as if my answer surprised and maybe even pleased him. "So if it's not about divorce, what's part two?"

"I've been asked to be Master of Ceremonies at the Dominion Day concert. Do you have any problem with that?"

A smile tugged at my mouth. "We'll set some tongues wagging. Can you handle it?"

"Pretty soon I'm going to be on the other side of the planet. It's you I'm concerned about."

"The infamous Buchanans on the same stage. We might draw a crowd—let's do it."

I opened the car door.

"There's a part three," William added.

"There is?"

"It's about Frank. He's been arrested."

"Where'd they find him?"

"He was picked up for fighting in a pool hall in Toronto. Almost makes you think he wanted to get caught. Anyway, he confessed everything, so he's going to be a guest of the Queen for a good many years."

"Good. That's exactly where he should be."

"But you may want to sell the house before he's out. I tend to think he was telling the truth about my father."

"So?"

"So I was thinking, we should give him his share of the Buchanan inheritance. If and when you sell, we could split the money, a third for you, a third for me, and a third for Frank. What do you think?"

"I think you're out of your mind. After what he did to George Knowles and Inky?"

"I considered that. So I think it would be only fair to donate his third to the Kingston Humane Society or maybe one of those literacy groups at the KP. Imagine Frank getting a thank-you card for his generous donation. What do you think?"

"I love it. It would be worth selling the house just to do it to him."

I got into the car and put it in gear. I stopped to roll down the window. "You want to come over for a while?"

He gave me a stern look that made me instantly regret the invitation. "And get the whole neighborhood talking?" He walked around to the passenger's side and slid in. "You bet I do."

Sisters

"Welcome, ladies and gentlemen, to the ninety-fifth birthday of our great nation, Canada." William's voice was amplified so he could be heard by the crowd at the waterfront. "The greetings that I bring from the prime minister are being repeated in every community center, park, or school gymnasium across the land. What most of those places won't have is the gift of song from a unique group of Canadian citizens who are going to share with us in Kingston. Friends of Retarded Children are pleased to present the Sunshine Singers."

"We're on!" Nancy nudged me.

Stan led the way, pushing Annie's wheelchair across the stage. A map of Newfoundland was taped across her shins. The idea was to have the costumes from east to west in the right order to match the provinces, but at the last minute, Betsy, as Ontario, couldn't be persuaded to leave Annie's side on the east coast. Nancy, who had worked like a dog on the outfits, shrugged it off, "Don't worry about the geography; concentrate on the singing."

DIVISIONS

A group of teenage boys, William would have called them hoods, stood to the side of the stage, smoking and squinting into the sun. Bobby, arriving at the last minute with Edwin loping behind, had to squeeze past them to get to his spot in line. Bob was wearing the Alberta shirt with a sheaf of wheat embroidered over mountains. He was incapable of an elegant entrance. The notion that he simply had to get into line had taken hold, and he plundered through the gang, jostling the biggest out of his way. A smaller one caught up with Bobby, caught him by the arm, and tried to spin him around. Bobby shrugged him off, and the big guy cuffed his friend on the back of the head. The smaller one backed off but followed a few paces behind Bob, imitating his gait.

I saw all this from my place on the piano bench. A year ago, I would have been devastated and furious over the mean-spirited display. This year, I simply saw it as part of the world I'd chosen to live in. I scanned the area for Edwin, and he had seen it too and shot a look of disdain that was completely wasted on the tough guy, who was glancing around for approval.

The crowd became quiet, and I played the first few notes of "This Land is Your Land." The kids did their best, but it was hard to raise their voices above the wind and lake noises. The piano drowned them out, no matter how softly I tried to strike the keys. I could hear the people in the front rows shuffling and talking among themselves. The ending petered out, and only those closest to the stage could tell it was over. A smattering of civil applause signaled our finish. The kids looked lost; the big event had fizzled in spite of the rehearsals when they had belted out their lines. Bobby and British Columbia began to shuffle offstage, when William was back on the mike.

"Sunshine Singers, that was great, but I happen to know you can sing a lot louder than that. Would you be willing to try again?" He looked my way, and I liked what I saw.

"Let's do it!" I called up to him.

He held a hand up in a way that I knew meant, "Hold on a minute," so I paused with my fingers resting on the opening keys. "Ladies and gentlemen, we all know this song, so why don't you join in and together we'll make sure our voices are heard."

Nancy got the west coast to reverse and rejoin the country. William gave me a nod, and I hit the keys with gusto, ready to back off if I had to. Voices surged around me, and the song lifted above the wind and sailed over Kingston in a never-before-mixed potion. I glanced toward the tough guys, arms folded and cigarette packages tucked into sleeves. They weren't singing, but the big guy was nodding. The banty rooster held his sneer as if there was a prize for ugly.

The kids, delighted with this rousing effort, applauded as enthusiastically as the audience. Annie threw her head back in delight. My position at the piano was shrouded by a curtain, and William signaled me to come out to center stage.

"I want to introduce a talented lady and a driving force behind the Friends of Retarded Children..." I stepped forward. *How will he present me? As his wife?* "...Eleanor Cole-Buchanan."

The applause rippled through the crowd, and Bobby pulled out of Confederation to hug me. The kids began a disorderly descent from the stage, when a voice called out from the crowd, "Get a doctor! My wife's fainted."

The summer sun must have taken its toll, and a group of people formed a concerned circle around a lady lying in the grass. From the stage, I could see a bald head kneeling over her and May Wilson fanning her wide-brimmed hat over the woman.

Betsy, relishing her time on stage, pretended to help Stan with Annie's chair. She turned toward the stir in the audience. "Mommy!" she screamed. "That my mom—fall down."

DIVISIONS

Betsy darted to the edge of the stage and began an ungainly descent. She hooked one foot on the front of the stage, then lowered herself until her other foot touched grass. Her skirt, with an appliquéd Toronto skyline, hooked on a loose nail and tore. She didn't pause, but ran toward May and the prone body, hollering with every step. "Mom! Get up! What wrong, Mom? Mommy!"

The bald head lifted as she approached. He had the woman's hand in his own now and was chafing it. For a moment, I thought how much he looked like my dad.

"I'd better go help Betsy," I told Stan. "Is that really her mother?"

"I think so, yeah. May said they were coming up today."

Nancy and I took long steps across the grass toward Betsy and the skirt that now had a piece dragging behind her. Dr. Williams was inside the circle now, so everything would be fine. I stepped to Betsy's side. Her mouth was turned down, and she fumbled her fingers together in front of her.

I put my arm around Betsy's heaving shoulders. I looked at the woman on the ground, her dark hair fanned out in a pattern I'd seen every day of my life before coming to Kingston. "My wife's had a shock," the bald man told the doctor. It was a voice that was as familiar as my own. "Mommy," Betsy wailed.

"Mommy? Betsy, what are you talking about? That's my mother." My heart lunged. The bald man stepped over his wife and held his arms toward me, a vein bulging distinctly in his neck. "Dad." Betsy and I spoke the name at the identical moment. I swiveled to look at her. The man spoke.

"Eleanor, this is your sister—Elizabeth."

"Dad," I tried gently, "this is Betsy."

He wrapped an arm around Betsy's shoulder, and she snuggled in. "This my dad," she nodded. I looked to William for an explanation, but he seemed as bewildered as I was. May, her hat on her head now, stepped toward Betsy and my dad.

"Your mom'll be fine, honey. She just needs a little air."

"I know—" I started, but May was speaking to Betsy and brushing the hair from her face.

The only set of eyes that understood what was happening stayed focused on me, waiting.

"Dad? Dad, what's going on?"

"I said, 'This is your sister—Elizabeth,'" repeating what didn't make sense.

"Elizabeth? She's dead, Dad. She died a long time ago."

"No, she didn't die. That's a word we never used. We lost Elizabeth, that's what we told everybody. We lost her to an institution."

I looked to my mother, beginning to stir. Dr. Williams held her wrist and consulted his watch.

"So…" I shook my head. "How did you know I'd be here today?"

"Didn't." Dad bit down on his upper lip. "We heard from May that Eliz—Betsy would be singing, so we came to see her. We had no idea you were the accompanist. When you come out from behind that curtain, why-" he couldn't go on. Didn't need to.

Betsy was the only one who didn't look like she'd just been hit by a train. "Let's get this woman into the shade," Dr. Williams commanded, helping my mother to her feet.

"C'mon everybody," Nancy called out, arms held wide to include our thunderstruck group. We followed her to a canopied area behind the stage, where some folding chairs were scattered.

"Now everyone just find a chair; I've got some cookies and a thermos of Freshie here," Nancy announced. "We'll have a bite to eat and get this straightened out."

DIVISIONS

But I didn't need anything straightened out. I felt as if a missing part of me had just clicked into place. Betsy, with the same birthday as me, reached for my hand.

"We're sisters." My words came out in a whisper.

"Sisters," Betsy repeated, as if she had known all along.

"We're twins," I told her.

EPILOGUE
Labor Day

I walked more slowly than usual along the waterfront, because Betsy's plodding held me back. My parents had decided to move to Kingston to be close to "our girls," as my mother said. She was using that phrase a lot now, after spending a lifetime pretending Betsy was dead. They would be nearby—but close? I doubted it.

My parents hadn't given me the chance to try to cope with Betsy as a sister. Instead, they had raised me in a household built on the sandy foundation of lies and denials. To grow up with a gaping hole beside you, where you know your twin belongs, that's one kind of loss. But to find out she could have been there all the time, that was betrayal.

I told myself that I could have coped with her. But those times when she was odd, or inconvenient, or downright embarrassing—how would I have handled it? It was one thing to be slowed down temporarily while walking, but a lifetime of growing up with a twin who couldn't catch up: could I have done it?

As we rounded the corner onto Kensington Street, Inky bounded away from us to greet two visitors waiting for us on the front porch.

"Bobby!" Betsy shouted.

Bobby and Inky bounced up and down the steps while Edwin stood motionlessly. Sweat beaded his temples, but he wore his brown jacket stoically despite the heat.

"Mrs. Buchanan, I'll be brief. The Frontenac School Board has come to a decision, rather late, I'm afraid, to establish a school for the trainable mentally retarded. I am to be the principal, and to start, I have been given the budget to hire one staff member. I am here to offer you the position." Then, as if in afterthought, he added, "It starts tomorrow morning."

Job offer? He was stuck and needed me more than I needed him.

"You just want me because I'm available on short notice."

"That has nothing to do with it."

"You've changed your mind about me, then."

"Hardly. I think if you'd stayed in Faderton, George Knowles would be alive. Furthermore, Frank O'Donnell, no Einstein, but good enough I suppose, and your husband would be employed, reputations intact."

Still, he was here. Edwin Wallace, of all people, was offering what I'd always wanted. But I wanted him to say the words. I sat down on the top step so I could watch Betsy and Bobby. "So why the job offer?"

"Because I can see that you're good for Bobby and for your sister, and you'd be excellent with the children," Mr. Wallace said, and he looked as if he had just passed a kidney stone instead of a compliment.

There it was. Validation. The word came to me effortlessly.

DIVISIONS

He might not have liked me, but he liked my work. He saw in me what I thought I saw in myself.

"Too bad those two didn't have a school like that." I nodded toward our siblings playing like children on the front lawn.

"We can't rewrite history, Mrs. Buchanan. Do you want the job or not?"

But will I be good enough?

"*You have to find it for yourself, by yourself.*" It was Mrs. M's voice, so close that I turned to look for her.

Of course I didn't see Mrs. M What I did see was a sliver of hope, the first in a long while. It was there for children like my sister—and it was there for me too.

"How's the pay?" I asked.

"Lousy."

"And the hours?"

"Endless."

I hesitated. I wanted to make Mr. Wallace squirm, but I couldn't wait to give him my answer.

"Sounds perfect," I said. "I'll take it."

The End

ACKNOWLEDGEMENTS

To the many people who assisted with the writing of this book, thank-you for your generosity of time and information.

- Brian Henry, Tony Lanza and Carol Baricovich, writing coaches and editors who offered instruction and encouragement.

- Mike Schulz, who informed me about being a cop in Kingston, and Rae Gately, who toured me through the Kingston Penitentiary, your insights were invaluable.

- Sue Barnes and Audrey Dubé, who arranged for an insider's tour of the Canadian Parliament buildings, thank-you for going the extra mile.

- Lois Niblock, a teacher who explained the system in the heady days of teacher shortages, your information was a treasure.

Most of all, thank-you to the brave families who have worked and advocated for their disabled children. Your work is not forgotten; nor is it finished.

Made in the USA
Charleston, SC
23 January 2013